Amazonia

UNU Studies on Critical Environmental Regions
Edited by Jeanne X. Kasperson, Roger E. Kasperson, and B.L. Turner II

Note from the editors

This book is the third in a series from the United Nations University (UNU) research project, Critical Zones in Global Environmental Change, itself part of the UNU programme on the Human and Policy Dimensions of Global Change. Both endeavours explore the complex linkages between human activities and the environment.

The project views the human causes of and responses to major changes in biogeochemical systems – global environmental change broadly defined – as consequences of cumulative and synergistic actions (or inactions) of individuals, groups, and states, occurring in their local and regional settings. The study examines and compares nine regional cases in which large-scale, human-induced environmental changes portend to threaten the sustainability of an existing system. The aim is to define common lessons about regional trajectories and dynamics of change as well as the types of human actions that breed environmental criticality and endangerment, thereby contributing to global environmental change. The overall results of the comparative analysis are found in *Regions at Risk*, the initial volume in this series.

The subtitle of *Amazonia: Resiliency and Dynamism of the Land and Its People* hints at the main message of the book: environmental degradation and socio-economic obstacles to sustainability notwithstanding, many positive trends bode well for this diverse region. The authors arrive at this message from an in-depth analysis of five main categories of human driving forces – population, new technologies, socio-economic and institutional conditions, beliefs and attitudes, and income and wealth – that interact to alter the physical, social, and cultural environments of Amazonia. Taking a long view both backward and forward, they counter a popular propensity to relegate the whole of Amazonia to history's roll of environmental disasters by documenting the capacity of stressed environments to withstand and even rebound from ecologically damaging trends.

This long-term perspective revealed, well in advance of confirmatory satellite data, that deforestation in Amazonia has been and is likely to be less widespread than conventional wisdom would have it. The authors, while wary of generalizing on trends and opportunities for so vast and heterogeneous a region, recommend development strategies that will increase the productivity of already deforested areas in order to accommodate population growth without endangering the long-term viability of nature–society relationships.

Titles currently available:

- Regions at Risk: Comparisons of Threatened Environments
- In Place of the Forest: Environmental and Socio-economic Transformation in Borneo and the Eastern Malay Peninsula
- Amazonia: Resiliency and Dynamism of the Land and Its People

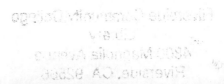

R

Amazonia: Resiliency and dynamism of the land and its people

Nigel J. H. Smith,
Emanuel Adilson S. Serrão,
Paulo T. Alvim,
and Italo C. Falesi

United Nations University Press

TOKYO · NEW YORK · PARIS

The views expressed in this publication are those of the authors
and do not necessarily reflect the views of the United Nations
University.

United Nations University Press
The United Nations University, 53–70, Jingumae 5-chome,
Shibuya-ku, Tokyo 150, Japan
Tel: (03) 3499-2811   Fax: (03) 3406-7345
Telex: J25442   Cable: UNATUNIV TOKYO

UNU Office in North America
2 United Nations Plaza, Room DC2-1462, New York, NY 10017
Tel: (212) 963-6387   Fax: (212) 371-9454
Telex: 422311 UN UI

United Nations University Press is the publishing division of the
United Nations University.

Typeset by Asco Trade Typesetting Limited, Hong Kong
Printed by Permanent Typesetting and Printing Co., Ltd.,
Hong Kong
Cover design by Joyce C. Weston

UNUP-906
ISBN 92-808-0906-7
03000 P

Contents

Preface

Development pressures are triggering rapid ecological, cultural, and economic changes in Amazonia, one of the world's largest remaining forest frontiers. Some of the environmental effects of development schemes and spontaneous settlement have local and potentially regional and global repercussions. The ecological issues surrounding deforestation include soil erosion, adverse changes in soil structure and fertility, shifts in rainfall patterns, and loss of biodiversity, particularly genetic resources. The driving forces behind land-use changes in Amazonia will be identified, the emerging awareness of economic, cultural, and ecological issues surrounding development will be discussed, and societal responses and management of natural resources will be analysed. A major focus of the study will be identifying resource management strategies for agriculture, particularly in agro-forestry systems, silviculture, and pastures. Such an approach should provide information useful for devising development plans for tropical forest ecosystems that are economically viable and environmentally sound.

In the first chapter, "Amazonia under siege," we explore some of the main themes threading through the book, particularly sustainability and one of its major components: resilience. Here we make the point that the ability of human-manipulated systems to rebound after major surprises is critical to the ultimate "success" of any land use. Criticality is defined and sorted into three main categories: *environmental criticality*, *environmental endangerment*, and *environmental impoverishment*. These broad categories represent varying degrees of "seriousness" of human impacts on the environment. These categories provide a convenient template when assessing the overall environmental condition of Amazonia, as well as when we spotlight micro-regions experiencing particularly rapid transformation.

Various real and imagined challenges to the health of the regional and global ecosystems are reviewed in chapter 2, "Environmental threats." Here we attempt to sort out what we consider to be the more ominous challenges to the integrity of Amazonian ecosystems, such as loss of biodiversity, from potential red herrings, such as the role of deforestation in purported global warming. The driving forces behind land transformation and overall societal responses to environmental change are explored in chapter 3, "Forces of change and societal responses."

Five chapters are dedicated to a more detailed examination of underlying causes of environmental change and human responses: "Forest conservation and management" (chap. 4), "Silviculture and plantation crops" (chap. 5), "Agro-forestry and perennial cropping systems" (chap. 6), "Ranching problems and potential on the uplands" (chap. 7), and "Land-use dynamics on the Amazon flood plain" (chap. 8). For each land use, whether forest extraction or ranching, cultural and socio-economic forces for change are highlighted and attempts at more rational use of resources are investigated. Emphasis is placed on what is actually transpiring on the landscape at the individual farm, ranch, and plantation level, rather than hypothetical models or results of experiment station trials.

In the final chapter, "Trends and opportunities," we return to an analysis of overall indicators of criticality, such as wealth and well-being and vulnerability. As more of the Amazon is transformed from wilderness to cultural landscapes, the risk of "surprises" is greater, and the need for resilience in human-managed systems increases.

Sizeable portions of Amazonia have already been cleared. If transformed areas were better managed, pressure on the remaining wilderness would be alleviated. A major challenge ahead is to boost the productivity of cleared areas so that population growth and more goods can be coaxed from altered areas without damaging the environment and its people.

A balance is needed between conservation for a variety of environmental services and economic development: success hinges on raising the productivity of all land uses. As productivity levels rise, so will the need to increase and sustain support for research on appropriate resource management strategies. Sustainable development in Amazonia will be possible only by applying modern science as well as tapping indigenous knowledge systems. Although efforts have been made to upgrade the research capacity of local institutions in Amazonia, much remains to be done. Adjustments to policy and fiscal incentives can certainly help improve the outcome of development and conservation projects in the region, but they will be ephemeral unless societies are equipped with the knowledge and skills to respond to challenges.

Acknowledgements

Many individuals kindly shared their thoughts and ideas on various aspects of Amazonian development and conservation with the authors during the preparation of this book. In particular, we would like to thank the following: Osmar Aguiar, Anthony Anderson, Emelecípio Botelho de Andrade, Ronaldo Baena, Edson Barcelos, Dale Bandy, Luis Coirolo, Peter Cooper, Erick Fernandes, Abe Goldman, Michael Goulding, Alfredo Homma, Socorro Kato, Dennis Mahar, Milton Motta, Olinto Gomes da Rocha Neto, Tatyana Sá, Jan Salick, Pedro Sanchez, Steve Sanderson, Robert Schneider, Rafael Seles, José Ferreira Teixeira Neto, Filemón Torres, Manoel Tourinho, Ann Thrupp, Steve Vosti, and Jonas Veiga. We do not wish to imply that any of the above individuals endorse our findings or views.

Roger Kasperson and William Turner II helped sharpen our thinking on conceptual and methodological issues related to criticality, the driving forces behind environmental change, and societal responses. We also benefited from interactions with other teams involved in case-studies in the series, particularly the opportunity to compare our findings and analytical approaches. An anonymous reviewer for the United Nations University Press made many useful comments on an earlier version of the book manuscript.

Two organizations provided financial support for the project. National Science Foundation grants in 1990 and 1991 launched the research effort and a grant from the United Nations University in 1992 helped complete the project. Funds from these sources permitted NJHS to travel to Brazil in January 1991 to initiate work on the project, provided resources for the co-authors to conduct field trips, and contributed to data analysis and writing.

Many institutions provided invaluable assistance and intellectual input. Several centres of the Brazilian Agricultural Research System (EMBRAPA) kindly provided logistical support and opportunities to interact with scientists working in the region, including CPATU in Pará, CPAF in Acre, CPAA in Amazonas, and CPAF in Rondônia. CPATU, in particular, offered vehicles and the valuable time of staff for numerous field trips in various parts of Pará. Discussions with scientists at the Federal University of Pará and the Museu Goeldi, both in Belém, enriched our thinking about environment and development in Amazonia.

Collaborative work with the above institutions as well as with CIAT (Centro Internacional de Agricultura Tropical) and the Latin America-Environment (LATEN) section of the World Bank enabled NJHS to make 10 field trips to the Brazilian Amazon between November 1991 and April 1993. During those trips, the senior author was able to gather field data and other information relevant to the book. The co-authors also made numerous field trips to the Brazilian Amazon in connection with other ongoing projects as well as this book.

The views and conclusions expressed in this book are those of the authors and do not necessarily reflect the opinions or positions of any institution.

1

Amazonia under siege

Considerable attention has focused in recent years on deforestation rates in Amazonia and on other ecological changes in the vast basin. Concern is mounting that deforestation in Amazonia is contributing to global warming, a reduction of the region's rainfall, ozone depletion, and more severe flooding along certain rivers (Denslow 1988; Myers 1984; Reis 1972). As forests are cut down to make way for new farms, ranches, and mining operations, biodiversity is lost and potential new crop plants and drugs may disappear. Also, people whose lives depend on the forest for sources of food and income can be adversely affected by the shrinking of forest habitats.

Heightened concern about resource management and the fate of forests in Amazonia has even stirred talk in some quarters that the region is global patrimony and should be conserved and developed more rationally. In 1988, President Mitterand of France suggested that countries might want to relinquish sovereignty over portions of their territory for the common good of humanity. To tackle the global warming issue, the United Nations Environment Programme (UNEP) helped forge an international climate treaty that calls for restrictions on burning tropical forests; the treaty was signed by many nations following the United Nations Conference on the Environment and Development in Rio de Janeiro in 1992 (Riebsame 1990). The Rainforest Preservation Foundation of Ft. Worth, Texas, has the status of a public utility in Brazil and solicits contributions of US$25 in magazines[1] to buy and preserve slightly under half a hectare of rainforest.

Such discussion by politicians and some environmentalists ignites

1

long-held fears in Brazil that foreign interests are intent on interfering or even expropriating Amazonia (ESG 1990; Reis 1960; Simons 1989; Sternberg 1987a). The international preoccupation with environmental issues is sometimes interpreted in Brazil as a smokescreen for the North's domination of the South (Benchimol 1992a,b; Mattos 1992). The notion that Amazonia is a major ecological "safety-valve" for the world and therefore should be under some form of control by the global community thus stirs concerns about sovereignty.

Repeated calls for some form of international intervention in Amazonia could create a nationalistic backlash and make governments intransigent about rectifying environmental problems. Although the Japanese government and multilateral development banks have backed away from supporting efforts to build a road from Acre to Pucallpa in the Peruvian Amazon, which would allow goods from the Brazilian Amazon to be exported via Pacific ports, the Brazilian government has vowed to proceed with this road-building plan in the future (Swinbanks and Anderson 1989). The President of Ecuador has flatly declared that external interference in Amazonian affairs will not be permitted.

Nevertheless, mounting pressure to address environmental and social concerns about development in Amazonia appears to be modifying government stances. Brazil has traditionally eschewed any discussion of debt-for-nature swaps in the Amazon because of concerns about foreign meddling with land-use decisions. Yet recent signs indicate that both the federal and state governments in Brazil are now more amenable to such deals.

Pressure for change is also coming from within countries with territories in Amazonia, although often with international connections. Some 2,000 non-governmental organizations (NGOs) have surfaced recently in Brazil, most of them concerned with policy aspects of social and environmental problems (Homma 1992a). Many of these groups readily capture the attention of the media, help mobilize public opinion, and thereby influence the political agenda. International donors, particularly foundations and NGOs based in major cities of North America and Western Europe, funnel increasing amounts of money and advice to the nascent NGOs with interests in Amazonia. The penetration of these NGOs on the political scene has been made possible by the wave of democracy sweeping Latin America.

Often impassioned debate about the future of the Amazon is thus under way in countries with direct stakes in the region, as well as in the industrialized countries. The media and many scientists and poli-

2

ticians in South America have expressed shock at the pace of destruction in Amazonia. Environmental changes in Amazonia have become the subject of some popular music in Brazil and abroad, such as Milton Nascimento's album *Yauaretê* (*Iauaretê* means jaguar in *lingua geral* and is the name of a small village in north-western Amazonas). The Grateful Dead, apparently revived by the growing international interest in the fate of rain forests, have written songs for a recently released album entitled *Deadicated*. Although the cover of the album features a red rose, rather than a tropical flower such as an orchid or heliconia, a proportion of the proceeds from the sales of *Deadicated* is supposed to help conserve rain forests (Killian 1991). Sting attended an encounter to "save the Amazon and her people" at Altamira, Pará, in February 1989, and has set up a foundation to help preserve tropical forests and defend indigenous peoples; the event was covered in other Latin American countries, such as Costa Rica (Alvarado 1990).

The exuberant flora and fauna of the region are depicted on T-shirts, dresses, swimwear, and even perfume, such as "Amazone" by Hermès. Fruits and nuts, purportedly collected "sustainably" from the Amazon forest, have found their way into exotic fruit juices, tempting ice-creams, environmentally friendly snacks, and politically correct breakfast cereals marketed in North America. The drama of the frontier in Amazonia with its environmental destruction and social tensions has even been captured in fiction (Mason 1991).

Signs are appearing that preoccupation with the fate of Amazonia is spurring action at the policy level. A number of policy changes over the past 15 years, such as withdrawal of fiscal incentives for creating cattle pastures in rain forests, have addressed some of the concerns about the environment in Amazonia. Article 225 of Brazil's new constitution emphasizes the need to live in harmony with the environment and to preserve nature and natural resources for future generations. Although lofty ideals sometimes remain ethereal, national consciousness is emerging in Brazil and neighbouring countries that Amazonia can be fragile and needs to be managed wisely. And Brazilians, Peruvians, Ecuadorians, Colombians, Bolivians, and Venezuelans will ultimately decide the fate of Amazonia.

Major objectives and regional coverage

The overall objective of this study is to analyse the main environmental threats to Amazonian ecosystems, including the societies that depend on them for a livelihood, to explore whether rural development efforts are "sustainable," and to assess whether the region has reached a critical stage in human-induced ecological change. The driving forces prompting environmental and social change will be identified and policy implications discussed.

All of the fieldwork for this volume was carried out in the Brazilian Amazon. We do not wish to imply that other portions of the Amazon basin are unimportant or that they are bereft of lessons for us to learn from. Indeed, biodiversity is often greater in the montane forests of western Amazonia, particularly in Peru and Ecuador. The choice of focusing on the Brazilian Amazon was dictated by the prior field experience of the authors and resource constraints. Most of Amazonia lies within Brazil's borders, and many of the development pressures are most intense there. When discussing environmental and socioeconomic change, however, relevant examples or cases from other parts of the basin are cited.

Collectively, the authors have travelled to all the states in the Brazilian Amazon within the past five years. Colonization zones and older settled areas on the uplands and Amazon flood plain were a high priority for data collection. Areas experiencing rapid transformation were targeted for closer scrutiny because sustainability and criticality are more likely to be significant issues in such places. Thus most of the upland farmers, ranchers, sawmills, and logging operations visited were in south-eastern Pará, Acre, and Rondônia, and along roads radiating from Santarém in the middle Amazon. Older, more established farming communities were canvassed for their experiences in the Bragantina zone east of Belém and on the Amazon flood plain near Santarém. In this manner, we were better able to appreciate such factors as distance to markets and age of settlement when assessing the sustainability of production systems.

The substance of sustainability

A number of definitions of sustainable development have emerged, reflecting different agendas and disciplinary perspectives. In spite of the plethora of interpretations of sustainability, a core concept is that technologies employed to raise productivity should not undercut the natural resource base and must benefit broad segments of the society (Brklacich, Bryant, and Smit 1991; FAO 1990, 1991a; NRC 1993; Serrão and Homma 1993; TAC 1988; Trenbath, Conway, and Craig 1990; York 1988). The welfare of generations to come is another important dimension to sustainability. Resources that are managed wisely provide intergenerational equity, a legacy for children that provides them with greater options in the future (Howarth and Norgaard 1990; Norgaard 1991).

Land-use systems for sustainable resource use must take into account biophysical aspects, such as nutrient cycling, soil erosion rates, resilience in the face of disease and pest pressure, the importance of microclimates, and soil moisture storage. Social dimensions to sustainable land-use systems include health and nutritional benefits, cultural viability, and political acceptability. Important economic facets of sustainable land use include the costs and benefits of external inputs, employment needs for given land uses, and income attributes (NRC 1993).

In our discussions of the economic development of Amazonia, environmental sustainability refers to situations in which nature–society relations support the continuation of land-use systems and can at least maintain current living standards. Further, options for the future are safeguarded by wise management of resources.

A major focus of our study will be agriculture and ranching since they are major factors in landscape change in Amazonia. Some definitions of sustainable agriculture underscore the importance of promoting equity and of eliminating purchased inputs. While improving the standards of living for as many people as possible is obviously a desirable goal for agricultural development, how this can be best achieved is not always clear, particularly if inputs are to be discouraged. Ideally, technologies deployed to boost yields should not promote inputs of environmentally damaging chemicals, trigger excessive soil erosion, or necessitate the clearing of natural vegetation. Further, crop varieties and management practices should be accessible to small- as well as middle- and large-scale enterprises (Smith 1990). Special emphasis will thus be placed on agricultural techniques that boost productivity on already cleared areas.

Technologies explored here will be as scale neutral as possible, capable of benefiting large as well as small operators. More progressive farmers often spearhead development in a region, and technologies should not be branded as unsustainable because they are not immediately adopted by the poorest farmers in a region.

Similarly, purchased inputs are often needed to sustain crop and livestock yields. Low-input agriculture does not necessarily mean sustainable agriculture. Purchased inputs that rely on fossil fuels should not be flagged automatically as unsustainable. Petroleum as a significant fuel will doubtless fade by the middle of the twenty-first century, but petroleum-based technologies are often sustainable in the short run. Sustainable agriculture hinges on the ability of farmers and the research and development system to adapt to change.

The capacity of farmers, ranchers, and extractivists to respond positively to shifts in the economic and ecological systems in which they operate is therefore a major focus of this study. All agricultural systems are in a state of flux, even "traditional" ones. How farmers tackle sudden environmental change and take advantage of new possibilities to market their goods is critical to understanding sustainability. No particular set of agricultural practices or crop varieties is likely to remain viable for long in the face of new disease and pest pressures as well as shifting market conditions.

Resilience is thus essential if ecological systems, including agro-ecosystems, are to overcome periodic disruptions (Holling 1986). Threshold effects, non-linear relationships, unexpected shifts in markets or environmental conditions, and constant readjustments are typical of society–environment relationships (Kasperson et al. 1995). Resilience of a particular ecosystem is the ability to maintain the basic structure and functions to support human uses during perturbations and to rebound quickly from such rapid, and often unpredictable, changes.

Another important dimension to our discussion of sustainable development in Amazonia is the beneficiary of social and economic change, and the losers in the case of environmental damage and farm failures. Agriculture, mining, and extraction of forest products, including timber, are thus the focus of much of our examination of economic activities in the region and their social and environmental impact. Small-, medium-, and large-scale producers are included in the analysis, since all are legitimate players and have a stake in Amazonia's future.

Although we examine strategies for conserving large blocks of Amazonia for future generations, we emphasize that better-managed farms, forests, ranches, and plantations will help reduce destruction of remaining wilderness. Also, we identify efforts to conserve resources and protect the environment by farmers, ranchers, plantation operators, and mining companies. Particular attention is paid to the integrity of nature reserves, strategies to reduce soil erosion and compaction, the importance of deploying diverse crops and varieties to help thwart pests and diseases, and the turnover of crops and varieties in response to environmental threats.

6

Sustainability is not a new issue in the region. Pre-Columbian cultures in the region grappled with the need to extract more food and other resources from the environment without undercutting the resource base. Some relatively complex cultures succeeded admirably, such as on Marajó Island, where well-fed and robust peoples built mounds and developed ornate polychrome pottery (Roosevelt 1989, 1991). Marajoara culture did not arrive as an advanced civilization at the mouth of the Amazon and then degenerate under the pervasive influence of the tropical forest (Meggers 1971); rather it developed *in situ* and flourished for nearly a thousand years (ca. A.D. 450–1300). Furthermore, Marajoarans were taller than the people living on the island today.

Other cultural groups succeeded in managing resources so that their numbers increased and prospered. The Tapajó, a much-feared chiefdom living at the confluence of the Amazon and the Tapajós, were actively expanding their territory when Europeans arrived in the early sixteenth century. In 1542, Carvajal reports that the numerous Tapajó repulsed attempts to land and trade with them for 150 miles along the Amazon (Hemming 1978: 194; Medina 1988: 103).

Even interfluvial forests, long thought to be inimical to dense human settlement in pre-contact times, now appear to have been greatly altered by sizeable indigenous groups. Various cultural forests in Amazonia have been identified, ranging from liana forests (*mata de cipó*) to Brazil nut groves (Balée 1989; Smith in press). Pioneer highways and accompanying settlement have exposed numerous black-earth sites with pottery, suggesting that sizeable and sedentary populations once occupied many upland forest sites (Smith 1980; Eden et al. 1984).

The agricultural underpinnings of such cultures were as varied as the peoples that developed them. Little is known from the archaeological record about which plants and animals were used, although new techniques, such as micro-sifting for plant remains and the search for phytoliths, promise to help unravel the mysteries of the subsistence base in the distant past. Some of the cropping patterns developed after millennia of farming experience persist and can provide useful clues for sustainable agriculture.

Strategies for sustainable agriculture employed by indigenous peoples in Amazonia include the deployment of several varieties of each crop, multiple-cropping, management of second growth, separation of fields by forest barriers, and soil enrichment. Many of these strategies help reduce pest and disease pressure and conserve

7

the topsoil. For example, over 100 manioc (*Manihot esculenta*) culti-vars have been found in a Jivaroan community in the Ecuadorian Amazon (Boster 1983).

The experience of indigenous cultures teaches us that both flood-plain and upland forest environments can be managed on a sustain-able basis to support dense populations. Such lessons should be taken to promote not the widespread destruction of wilderness but, rather, more rational utilization of already cleared areas. The history of pre-contact settlement in Amazonia implies not that all of Amazonia should be densely settled, only that environmental constraints to raising and sustaining agricultural yields can be overcome. The cur-rently sparse populations in interfluvial areas and along many rivers are not an indication of Amazonia's agricultural potential.

The question of criticality

Criticality as employed here denotes a state of both environmental degradation and associated socio-economic deterioration. Criticality can be divided roughly into three main states, each denoting various stages of environmental and socio-economic unravelling (Kasperson et al. 1995):

* *Environmental criticality* refers to situations in which the extent and/or rate of environmental degradation precludes the continua-tion of current human use systems or levels of human well-being, given feasible adaptations and societal capabilities to respond.
* *Environmental endangerment* refers to situations in which the tra-jectory of environmental degradation threatens to preclude the continuation of current human use systems or levels of human well-being, given feasible adaptations and societal capabilities to respond.
* *Environmental impoverishment* refers to situations in which the trajectory of environmental degradation threatens to preclude the continuation of current human use systems or levels of well-being in the medium to longer term, and to narrow significantly the range of possibilities for different uses in the future.

Indicators used to assess whether an area can be regarded as crit-ical, endangered, or impoverished include environmental degrada-tion, wealth, well-being, and economic and technological substitut-ability. Dimensions to environmental degradation include loss of soil fertility and structure, deteriorating air and water quality, and the draw-down of other natural resources.

Wealth is generally measured by gross national product and per capita income. Well-being includes a broad category of barometers, such as mortality rates, nutritional levels, and the incidence of disease. Economic and technological substitutability is the ability to mobilize technological and financial resources to confront challenges to current levels of productivity. Indicators will be addressed throughout the book, but are summarized in the final chapter.

Little evidence has emerged to suggest that Amazonia as a whole has entered the *environmental criticality* stage. Press and television coverage of Amazonia depicting a massive pall of smoke might give the impression that the region is being rapidly transformed into a bleak landscape, devoid of resources. But even in areas undergoing the most intensive environmental changes, such as along many parts of the Amazon flood plain and active colonization zones in south-eastern and south-western Amazonia, it would be difficult to argue that environmental degradation has reached the point that current land-use systems are collapsing. Some individual farms or ranches may have reached that point, but it is doubtful that areas on the scale of one or two square kilometres fall within that dire category.

Rather, areas occupied by people in Amazon fit better the *environmental endangerment* and especially the *environmental impoverishment* categories. Much of the Amazon still remains in forest, thus dampening many of the environmental effects of human interventions on a regional scale. Further, the majority of cleared areas or natural areas experiencing significant extractive activities are more representative of *environmental impoverishment*. Broad definitions and aggregate assessments do not mean that Amazonia is safe from irreversible ecological change or social marginalization. Environmental impoverishment of many settled areas means that options for future generations are being significantly narrowed by current management of land and aquatic resources (Turner et al. 1995). As will be emphasized in a later chapter, the flood-plain forests of the Amazon are among the most endangered ecosystems in Latin America.

Despite environmental impoverishment, however, many individuals are achieving higher living standards. Such overall improvement in economic well-being, in spite of a global recession, is heartening. Yet such an encouraging trend masks two worrisome realities. Some segments of society are benefiting little if at all from economic development. Second, substantial biodiversity is being lost. Whereas the plight of the poor is obvious, the disappearance of species and sub-species, many still unknown to science, is not currently a major rally

9

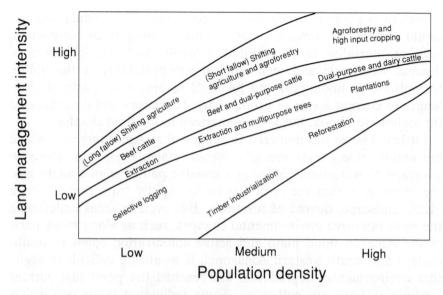

Fig. 1.1 **Trends in land management as a result of development and increasing population in the humid tropics (Source: adapted from Serrão and Toledo, 1992)**

cry for political action. In general, governments in tropical countries are much more concerned about urban environmental issues, such as air pollution and developing supplies of potable water for the ever-growing population of towns and cities. Politicians are more likely to gain votes by bringing a sewerage system to a city slum than by saving a remote tract of forest.

The haemorrhaging of species and variation within wild animal and plant species is conceivably the most serious environmental issue in Amazonia. And, unless land-use practices change in the future, more areas of the Amazon are likely to slip into the endangerment or even criticality categories.

The urgency of improved resource management

A central theme of this study is that Amazonia is indeed a rich realm of nature and culture and that some of the land-use changes under way in the basin could ultimately have regional or even global implications. In order to help avert any large-scale ecological catastrophe in the future, however, the productivity of farms, ranches, forests, and plantations will have to be raised and sustained. Some scientists have called for a doubling of crop yields over the next few decades to help slow deforestation rates (Pimentel et al. 1986).

As population increases in Amazonia, the need to intensify agricultural production becomes more urgent. Shifting agriculture based on annual crops will gradually be replaced by more permanent systems, such as agro-forestry, and, in some cases, by high-input cropping (fig. 1.1). Extractive activities, long an important source of livelihood for Amazonian people, are becoming less important. In later chapters we explore the trend lines for activities in farming and forestry.

By raising and sustaining agricultural and livestock yields, pressure to encroach on parks, Indian reserves, national forests, extractive reserves, and biological preserves will be mitigated. Some 30–40 million hectares in Amazonia have already been altered by human activities, mainly farming and ranching, which is equivalent to the farming area of France, England, and Italy (Homma 1990a; INPE 1990). Better utilization of already cleared areas should certainly enable farmers and ranchers to feed the region's roughly 10 million people;[2] even without adopting many of the intensive techniques of Western Europe, it should be possible to strive for increased productivity. Improving agriculture and raising rural incomes must go hand-in-hand with conservation efforts in Amazonia, as in other developing regions.

Notes

1. For US$25 the donor receives a "Preservation Deed"; apparently 740,000 ha of rain forest have been purchased in this manner, and the Rainforest Preservation Foundation has options on a further 2.2 million ha (*Earth*, January 1994, p. 65).
2. The population of Amazônia Legal is some 16 million. Amazônia Legal was created for administering fiscal incentives and is larger than the North region of Brazil since it includes the states of Mato Grosso, Tocantins, and western Maranhão.

2

Environmental threats

Amazonia has a long history of ecological change under human agency. Hunters and gatherers probably penetrated the region tens of thousands of years ago and artificially enriched their campsites with fruit and nut trees (Smith in press). Hunters undoubtedly fired woody savannas in Amazonia, such as in Roraima, to flush game long before farmers started to clear the forest.

Slash-and-burn farming in Amazonia probably began at least 10,000 years ago, based mostly on root crops, thereby creating a rich texture of forest interlaced with second-growth communities of various heights and ages. At first, such interventions were on a minor scale, but, as the population grew denser, more and more of the forest fell to the axe.

The myth of virginity

Contrary to the prevailing idea of a pristine Amazonian forest little disturbed by human activities until recently (Moran 1993a; Revkin 1990: 39; Richards 1977), much of the region has felt the influence of hunters and gatherers and farmers for a considerable time. Many of the forests of tropical America, including the Amazon, are anthropogenic (Denevan 1992; Turner and Butzer 1992). Assertions that the Amazon is being ravaged by development and floods of land-hungry colonists need to be put within the context of a region that has a long history of settlement and human modifications of the environment.

Archaeological research and unusual concentrations of certain economic plants in the forest suggest much higher human population densities in the past than has hitherto been accepted. Even with relatively inefficient stone axes, aborigines have cleared substantial tracts of Amazonian forests in the past (Huber 1910). Charcoal layers in soils of the upper Rio Negro have been dated to 6,000 years B.P. and some ceramic shards mixed with anthrosols are approximately 3,750 years old (Sponsel 1986). Along the Bragantina coast of Pará, charcoal and potsherds have been dated at 5,000 years B.P. (Simões 1981). The oldest recorded pottery in the New World is from the middle Amazon: ceramics from the Taperinha site near Santarém have been dated at 8,000 years B.P. (Roosevelt et al. 1991). Maize reached the Ecuadorian Amazon at least 6,000 years ago, providing farmers with another food option. Upland and flood-plain forests have thus been altered by farming activities for millennia (Bush, Piperno, and Colinvaux 1989).

Population densities reached high levels, particularly along silt-laden rivers, well before contact with Europeans (Moran 1990: 148, 1993b: 114). Estimates of human populations in Amazonia around 1500 range from 1 million to 6 million, or even higher (Smith 1980). Only recently has the region's population regained its former numbers, but with a distinct difference: a sizeable proportion of today's population lives in towns and cities. In pre-contact times, the population was much more rural than at present, and therefore more engaged in farming.

The indigenous population did not raise cattle, however, so cleared areas were devoted to crops and managed fallows. The higher population density in rural areas was thus possible with perhaps the same amount of cleared area as today. The overall cleared area in 1500 was probably close to that prevailing in 1990.

If pre-contact aboriginal populations of Amazonia reached in excess of 6 million people, forest fires in the region were probably as common as at present, but on a smaller scale. Indians would not have cleared fields the size of some ranches and plantations being opened up in the region, particularly in southern Pará, northern Mato Grosso, Rondônia, and Acre, but they likely lit many more smaller fires to prepare fields.

Instead of massive fires concentrated in active colonization zones, particularly in the south-eastern and south-western fringes of Amazonia (fig. 2.1), hundreds of thousands of smaller fires would have been scattered over the basin in pre-contact times. Agricultural activities in Amazonia before the arrival of Europeans were akin to

13

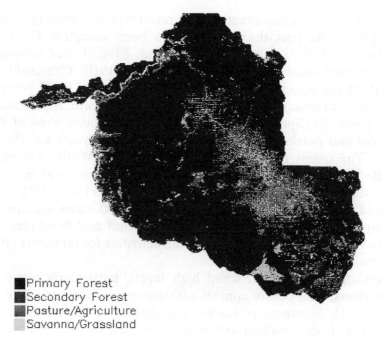

Fig. 2.1 **Cleared areas in Rondônia, Brazil, are concentrated mainly along pioneer highways opened in the 1970s and 1980s (Sources: adapted from Stone 1992; Stone and Schlesinger, 1992 – courtesy of P. A. Lefebvre, Jr., The Woods Hole Research Center)**

a buckshot event (Oldeman 1989); localized, small-scale clearings spread out over a large area. A Dante's inferno characterizes colonization zones today in the dry season, whereas the twinkling of innumerable small fires would have dotted the nocturnal landscape after the main rains in prehistoric Amazonia.

The shift to clearing larger sections of forest is ecologically more damaging than the scattered, insular fires of the past. When thousands of hectares are cleared for a single ranch or plantation, the ecological fabric of the area becomes simpler (Uhl, Buschbacher, and Serrão 1988). Instead of a patchwork quilt of various plant communities, more homogeneous landscapes emerge. Also, seed sources for forest regeneration became scarcer and soil nutrient recycling systems can be disrupted (Buschbacher, Uhl, and Serrão 1987; Nepstad, Uhl, and Serrão 1990, 1991; Serrão et al. 1979).

The implications of a dense, pre-contact human population in Amazonia are far-reaching. A salient lesson here is that Amazonia's diverse environments can support relatively large populations, even on nutrient-poor oxisols and ultisols, if resources are managed wisely. Although some have argued that nutrient deficiencies prevent continuous crop production on highly weathered ferrallitic soils of many parts of the lowland, humid tropics (Weischet and Caviedes 1993: 278), pre-contact indigenous populations probably deployed a wide variety of swidden systems that permitted relatively dense populations, even in inland areas.

People in Amazonia have greatly altered plant and animal communities and the distribution and population densities of certain plants and animals, and have probably triggered increased soil erosion and aggrading of smaller rivers and streams for millennia. The notion of a vast, undisturbed wilderness in Amazonia is an artefact of the indigenous population crash after contact with Europeans and the unleashing of introduced diseases such as smallpox and influenza.

Climatic change

The impact of deforestation on regional and global climate has received the most attention when environmental change is discussed in Amazonia (Bunyard 1987; Collins 1990; Dickinson 1987, 1989; Leopoldo, Franken, and Matsui 1985; Myers 1988; Prance 1986; Reis 1972; Wood 1990). Tropical deforestation is often pinpointed as a major culprit in the purported global warming trend[1] and, since Amazonia is the largest stretch of tropical forest, its fate is thought to have an important bearing on the future of the world's climate. Amazonia was probably also heavily cleared in pre-contact times, without triggering the greenhouse effect.

Global warming

Increased atmospheric levels of carbon dioxide and other gases, such as methane, nitrous oxide, and chlorofluorocarbons (CFCs), can potentially trigger a greenhouse effect (Raval and Ramanathan 1989). Many in the scientific community, and much of the reporting in the media, suggest that we are on a global warming course propelled by human activities such as burning forests and fossil fuels. But claims that a global warming has already begun may be premature (Byrne 1988; Flavin 1989; Schneider 1989). No firm evidence has yet emerged that the world is becoming significantly warmer (Abelson 1990a; Blinder 1992; Hansen and Lacis 1990; Ray 1993: 12;

15

Solow and Broadus 1989; Spencer and Christy 1990). Indeed, surface temperatures over the western Arctic Ocean have become significantly cooler during the 1950–1990 period (Kahl et al. 1993). Such inconsistent reporting on "global warming" points to major defects in current models of global climate and suggests a tenuous basis for drawing policy conclusions (Bryson 1989).

Although some data suggest a recent global warming trend, no valid correlation with greenhouse gases can be made, nor can we be sure how long this trend will last (Barnett 1990). Even if such changes will soon be confirmed, it will be difficult to separate natural climatic cycles from any greenhouse effect (Mitchell, Senior, and Ingram 1989). For example, the subsurface thickness of ice around the North Pole varies markedly from year to year, and no significant trend emerged during the 1977–1990 period (Langereis, Van Hoof, and Rochette 1992). Also, the effects of clouds, volcanic dust, and oceans on any possible greenhouse effect are imperfectly understood (Abelson 1990b; Jarvis 1989; Kerr 1989; Slingo 1989).

If evapotranspiration rates are substantially reduced in Amazonia as a result of landscape changes, less latent heat may be exported from the region in water vapour (Molion 1987). Whether reductions of the moisture level in warm air circulating from tropical regions to temperate areas in the Hadley cell would affect global climate is unclear. Reduced moisture levels could result in less latent heat being released during condensation, thereby cooling climates. Such a mechanism would help to counteract any greenhouse effect. Deforestation also tends to increase the albedo affect, further reducing energy for atmospheric heating.

In the event that the greenhouse effect takes hold, tropical deforestation will be only partly at fault (Radulovich 1990). Deforestation accounts for less than 20 per cent of greenhouse gas emissions (Flavin 1989: 13). The amount of carbon in initial, undisturbed ecosystems may have been overestimated, thus exaggerating the impact of deforestation on the release of carbon dioxide to the atmosphere (Post et al. 1990).

Carbon dioxide from the burning of fossil fuels, which occurs mostly in temperate countries, is the largest component of greenhouse gases. Just seven industrialized countries produce 40 per cent of carbon dioxide emissions worldwide (Turner et al. 1990a). The industrial countries are responsible for approximately 85 per cent of carbon dioxide build-up in the atmosphere (Parikh 1992).

The release of CFCs, used to make aerosols, refrigerants, and solvents, is responsible for a larger proportion of greenhouse gases entering the atmosphere than CO_2 emissions from burning forests. Industrial countries are responsible for most of the CFC emissions. The notion that developing countries must take a large share of the blame for any global warming has been ascribed to environmental colonialism (Agarwal and Narain 1991).

Deforestation in Amazonia may not be implicated in excessive emissions of nitrous oxide, a potent greenhouse gas, as previously thought. Although higher levels of nitrous oxide are released in pasture soils in the first 10 years after forest clearing, emissions of the gas subsequently decline to lower levels than those coming from tropical forest (Keller et al. 1993). This does not mean that cattle-raising is necessarily an appropriate land use for much of Amazonia from the policy standpoint; rather the ecological impacts of different land uses must be weighed according to a "basket" of criteria, and more long-term research is often needed to decipher the environmental effects of habitat change.

The idea that Amazonian countries should arrest forest clearing to save the world's climate while North Americans and Europeans continue to drive their increasingly more powerful cars and burn natural gas and coal does not rest well in Brasília, Bogotá, or Lima (Nisbet 1988). Developed countries will need to do more to reduce their own carbon dioxide emissions if they expect third world countries to tackle the issue (Caccia 1991). Some scientists have urged policy makers to separate "survival emissions," such as resource-poor farmers practising slash-and-burn agriculture, from "luxury emissions," particularly gas-guzzling cars plying the streets of major cities, particularly in the industrial countries (Agarwal and Narain 1991). Some industrial countries, such as Germany, the Netherlands, and Japan, have adopted carbon dioxide stabilization or reduction targets (Miller 1991), but many others are apparently waiting for a global consensus to emerge on appropriate action.

A cautious approach to formulating environmental and economic policy to address global warming has been adopted by several governments. Three main factors account for this wait-and-see attitude (Riebsame 1990). First, climate change predictions are too uncertain, particularly at the regional level. Second, current systems are thought to be capable of absorbing climate change without major disruption, at least for the next few decades. Third, technologies can be deployed to mitigate or compensate for some of the changes wrought by global climate change.

Sceptics about global warming can also point to the fact that C_3 crops, such as rice and wheat, would likely produce higher yields with a doubling of atmospheric carbon dioxide levels if sufficient water and nutrients were available. The C_4 crops, such as sugar cane and maize, are unlikely to be affected by increased carbon dioxide levels, at least for the foreseeable future. Also, some regions, such as the drier tropics, might benefit from a global warming since they could receive more rain.

The ability of countries to respond to global warming will depend in part on the strength of their agricultural research and extension systems to deliver new technologies. Areas with a shift to wetter climates will probably need crop varieties more resistant to fungal and bacterial diseases. Unfortunately, as the need for research institutions to be primed and ready to confront new challenges increases, their scientific capacity is at a low ebb.

In the 1970s and early 1980s, Brazil had one of the strongest agricultural research programmes among the developing countries, with an annual budget of close to US$200 million. Since the mid-1980s, however, high inflation and severe financial constraints have hampered EMBRAPA's (Empresa Brasileira de Pesquisa Agropecuária) ability to raise and sustain agricultural productivity (Ruttan 1991). The agricultural research systems of other countries with territories in Amazonia have also weakened over the past decade or so.

Another constraint on the deployment of technologies to meet the challenge of a possibly warmer world is the loss of biodiversity. As discussed in more detail later, the loss of habitats, particularly in the humid tropics, could have grave consequences for agriculture. The loss of genetic resources for crop improvement, and the disappearance of new crop candidates, could "tie the hands" of plant breeders trying to develop crops adapted to changing environments.

In spite of uncertainties about global warming trends and hazards, pressure is mounting for governments in both industrial and developing countries to take concrete steps to halt the build-up of greenhouse gases in the atmosphere. Tree planting is seen as one way to counteract the greenhouse effect, by providing a carbon sink (Myers and Goreau 1991). Although this popular notion empowers people to do something about a widely perceived problem, the impact of tree planting on the build-up of carbon dioxide in the atmosphere pales compared with what could be accomplished by the more efficient use of fossil fuels. At least 100 million ha would have to be planted to fast-growing trees to sequester a little over 10 per cent of the current annual build-up of carbon in the atmosphere (Myers and Goreau 1991). Once the trees reached maturity, they would no longer act as carbon sinks. That is an area equivalent to Britain, France, and Germany that would then cease to serve as a trap for carbon. The conversion of old-growth forests to fast-growing plantations would release carbon to the atmosphere, in spite of the greater net photosynthesis of younger trees (Harmon, Ferrell, and Franklin 1990).

Although rehabilitating degraded areas with trees would be desirable, simply filling the landscape with "greenhouse" trees without regard to cultural and economic needs could be counter-productive. Cultural landscapes could not easily accommodate hundreds of millions of hectares of tree planting without disrupting food production and other economic activities, even if the "greenhouse gas" trees formed integral parts of agro-forestry systems. Cleared lands are often fully occupied, and the logistical and managerial implications of massive tree planting would need careful study (Churchill and Saunders 1991).

Reduction of methane emissions, an often overlooked contributor to the greenhouse effect, could help mitigate any global warming. Methane is a far more potent greenhouse gas than carbon dioxide and landfills in the developed world are a major source of methane emissions (Hogan, Hoffman, and Thompson 1991). Recovery of methane from landfills not only would reduce the greenhouse effect, but could supply gas to generate electricity. Improved coal-mining and oil-production techniques would also reduce methane emissions. Ruminant livestock and rice cultivation are also significant sources of methane. Deforestation and burning also increase methane concentrations in the atmosphere, but, again, a large share of the onus for reducing this greenhouse gas rests with the industrial countries.

The spectre of parched deserts

In addition to temperature changes, deforestation has the potential of adversely affecting rainfall regimes. Half of the rain that falls in Amazonia is thought to come from evapotranspiration (Molion 1975: 101; Salati 1987; Salati and Vose 1984; Salati, Marques, and Molion 1978). Accordingly, it has been assumed that continued deforestation might lead to a drier regional climate (Hecht and Cockburn 1989: 43). A linkage between the loss of forests and reduced rainfall has been surmised for centuries, and was much discussed in India and parts of the Caribbean in the nineteenth century (Glacken 1967; Grove 1990).

19

Cattle-ranching and the destruction of Latin America's tropical forests have been blamed for reduced rainfall and increased droughts (Salati 1992; Shane 1986: 23). Some computer models predict a sharp drop in rainfall with continued, large-scale deforestation in Amazonia, thus raising the spectre of dust-bowls and desertification (Anderson 1972; Barros 1990: 20; FAO 1991b: 3; Goodland and Irwin 1975; Modenar 1972; Paula 1972; Roddick 1991: 206; Sioli 1987). Cattle-ranching is sometimes singled out as most likely to provoke desertification (Wesche 1974). But such rainfall models assume that Amazonia will be turned into a barren landscape (EMBRAPA 1989: 6).

It is highly unlikely that substantial areas of Amazonia will be converted to asphalt or a desert. Second growth soon begins the regeneration path to forest in all but the sandiest soils (Moran 1993a). The widespread struggle to keep pastures and crops free of weeds is a testament to the striking speed of secondary succession. Weeds, not deserts, are a major headache for farmers, ranchers, and plantation owners in Amazonia. How soon mature forest returns depends primarily on the texture and fertility of the soil and the proximity of seed sources. Also, more rainfall may be derived from the flux of water vapour from the Atlantic than has previously been supposed (Paegle 1987).

How much forest can be removed without affecting rainfall is not known. Realistic predictions of climatic change as a result of landscape changes in the humid tropics are fraught with difficulties (Henderson-Sellers 1987). Current models of forest and climate interactions in Amazonia are too imprecise to predict with any degree of certainty the impacts of deforestation on rainfall (Salati 1992). Evapotranspiration from groves of perennial crops and silvicultural plantations may be close to that of forest. Even pastures release substantial quantities of water to the atmosphere during the rainy season. During the dry season, though, pastures transpire less water than forest and experience significantly warmer mean surface temperatures (Nepstad, Uhl, and Serrão 1991; Nobre, Sellers, and Shukla 1991).

No evidence is available to prove that deforestation in Amazonia has led to reduced rainfall. The dry season around Manaus was accentuated in 1976, and again in 1979, when no rain fell for 73 days (Fearnside 1986: 50). The "summer" (*verão*) of 1992 was also severe, with many farmers experiencing reduced yields or the loss of seedlings of perennial crops. But it is hard to separate little-understood climatic cycles from long-term trends. To keep matters in perspective: after two particularly heavy burning seasons in Amazonia in 1987 and 1988, 1989 was a very wet year. So much rain fell in eastern Amazonia in 1989 that the dry season virtually disappeared.

Rainfall patterns are highly variable in Amazonia. In 1774, a drought assailed the Rio Negro watershed when deforestation rates were much lower than at present (Hemming 1987). River levels in Amazonia were unusually low in 1860 owing to poor rainfall (Chandless 1866). In 1958, 64 days passed without any rain in the Bragantina zone east of Belém (Penteado 1968: 138). The Amazon River was particularly low again in 1963. The big "push" to develop and open up the Amazon started only in the late 1960s.

Unusual weather patterns also prevailed in the southern United States in the 1980s. Record heat and drought seared the southern and eastern parts of the United States during 1987 and 1988, thereby provoking widespread concern about global warming. Summer 1989 and spring 1992 in the eastern United States, however, were wetter and cooler than usual, and talk of global warming in the media subsided. In Western Europe, several hurricane-force gales during the winters of 1988 and 1989 led to speculation among some politicians that global warming was under way (Maddox 1990). Some in the environmental movement may be concerned that a return to more "normal" weather will cool the ardour of politicians to tackle the issue of global warming.

Predictions about how dry the Amazon might become with continued deforestation are fraught with shaky assumptions. With satellite imagery, it should be possible to document the area of forest cleared each year. Through its remote sensing agency (INPE – Instituto Nacional de Pesquisas Espaciais), the Brazilian government monitors forest burning in Amazonia. But what happens to the land after it is cleared is crucial to the question of climatic drying. Landsat and Spot imagery can separate second growth, cropland, grassland, and forest, but it cannot readily differentiate between second-growth stages or types of crops. Aerial photography from aircraft would be too expensive on the scale needed to document annual vegetation changes in the region as a whole. More sophisticated satellites in the future may be able to help. Also, more information is needed about evapotranspiration rates in various vegetation communities, including croplands.

The environmental impact of smoke

Smoke from forest cut for agriculture and ranching may have global in addition to regional and local impacts. One component of biomass burning, methyl chloride, attacks ozone, and deforestation in Amazonia has been implicated as partly responsible for holes in the ozone layer over Antarctica (Cutrim 1990). Human-induced fires account for 5 per cent of the ozone-destroying chemicals in the atmosphere (C. Anderson 1990). Nevertheless, industrial countries release far more ozone-depleting aerosols into the atmosphere than do farmers and ranchers in the tropics.

Excessive smoke could lead to temporary climatic disruptions. Smoke reflects some incoming radiation back into the atmosphere, thereby helping to mitigate any greenhouse warming. A reduction in the solar energy reaching the earth's surface may reduce convectional activity and rainfall in some areas. The burning season in most of Amazonia extends from July to October; little smoke is generated during the rainy months.

Smoke from burning fires is thick enough temporarily to close some regional airports during the dry season, particularly in Rondônia and Acre. Temperature inversions can exacerbate the haze. In the dry season, cloudless skies facilitate radiative cooling of the land, thereby helping to create a layer of warmer air above that traps pollutants. Prior to 1970, the Brazilian Air Force had to close airports in parts of the Amazon because of the excessive haziness due to smoke. Although the shutting down of airports because of smoke is not new in Amazonia, the problem has become more acute for airfields in parts of Rondônia and Acre in the past two decades.

Smoke from cleared fields has been implicated in poor harvests of Brazil nut (*Bertholletia excelsa*) in Pará (Miller 1990). Smoke is believed to interfere with bee pollinators of Brazil nut trees, but such a linkage has not been demonstrated conclusively. Variable yields of Brazil nuts are more likely related to the severity of the dry season when flowers are formed. If the dry season is not pronounced, flowering is reduced and fruit production will be poor the following year. The dry season in 1989 was exceptionally wet in eastern Amazonia, and the 1991 harvest of Brazil nuts was correspondingly poor. At Tomé-Açu, for example, 220 mm of rain fell in October 1989, normally a dry month.[2]

Brazil nut harvests in the municipality of Marabá, the major centre for the Brazil nut trade, have varied from a low of 2,000 tons in 1985 to a high of 17,732 tons in 1970. Marabá was connected to the Belém–Brasília Highway along PA 332 (then PA 70) in 1970, so the peak of production in that year might be attributed in part to improved transportation. Traditionally, the Brazil nut harvest had been taken out by river and along a now defunct railroad from Jatobal to Tucurui on the Tocantins.

Brazil nut harvests have often been highly variable, ever since collecting in earnest began in the Tocantins watershed in the latter half of the nineteenth century. In 1895, for example, some 450 tons of Brazil nuts were collected along the Tocantins, whereas in 1896 the harvested amounted to only 250 tons. In 1987, however, 1,000 tons of nuts were gathered, and the harvest would have been closer to 2,500 tons if the Tocantins had not experienced a massive flood (Moura 1989: 153). Such oscillations in Brazil nut harvests could not be attributed to smoke since few people lived along the river at that time.

If smoke from fires was the principal cause of variation in Brazil nut harvests, one would expect a sharp decline during the 1970s and 1980s. Although harvests appear to have dropped during much of the 1980s, a shift of Brazil nut gatherers to more lucrative occupations, particularly gold mining, probably accounts for lower harvests (Smith et al. 1991a). Fluctuations in Brazil nut prices on world markets have also probably influenced collecting efforts.

Soil erosion and floods

Soil erosion is one of the most serious threats to the sustainability of agriculture, silviculture, and forestry in Amazonia. Although many of the region's soils are deep, extending down several thousand metres in some cases, fertility is usually concentrated in the first few centimetres of topsoil. The need to protect the soil is a major reason that perennial crops, silviculture, and properly managed pastures are among the more viable options for rural development. Soil erosion is a contributing factor in the decision of many farmers to abandon their fields and clear a fresh plot from the forest.

Soil erosion can lead to larger-scale environmental problems by aggrading river beds. Increased run-off from cleared land deposits silt and sand on river beds, thereby provoking more severe floods. A rising and lowering of water levels along streams and rivers in Amazonia is part of the normal seasonal pulse of wet and dry seasons (Sternberg 1975). Some unusually heavy floods along the Amazon in the mid-1970s raised the spectre that deforestation in the foothills of the Andes was having a tangible impact downstream (Fowler and Mooney 1990: 106; Gentry and Lopez-Parodi 1980; Smith 1981a: 122). But statistical analyses of flood peak levels do not reveal any trend to more intense flooding along the Amazon (Richey, Nobre, and Deser 1989; Sternberg 1987b). The greatest flood ever recorded along the Amazon was in 1953, well before major development projects were unleashed in Amazonia. The Amazon River reached unusually high levels again in 1993, although deforestation rates have abated since the 1980s.

Similar findings have been made along the Ganges, where flooding in Bangladesh is not a result of deforestation in the Himalayas, as is commonly thought (Ives and Messerli 1989). An important variable in runoff from deforested lands is the infiltration rate of the soil (Newson and Calder 1989). Some compaction of the soil is likely after the forest is cut, but how adversely infiltration is affected over the long term depends on land management and soil type.

Destruction of forests along streams and some river banks is surely affecting water quality and flow on a local scale. But the vast scale of Amazonia's forests appears to be masking the impact of deforestation on smaller watersheds. Landscape changes are not currently radical enough to affect Amazon hydrology on a large scale (Bayley 1989). Also, the variability of rainfall in different parts of the Amazon basin could lead to premature conclusions that floods are more pronounced along the Amazon.

Hydroelectric dams

Disruption of fisheries as a result of dam-building could be a serious threat to the livelihoods of many rural and urban folk in Amazonia (fig. 2.2). A number of fish important in commerce and subsistence, such as jaraqui (*Semaprochilodus* spp.) and catfish (*Brachyplatystoma flavicans*, *B. filamentosum*), migrate from the Amazon to spawn in tributaries (Barthem, Brito, and Petrere 1991; Goulding 1981, 1989). Changes in water quality and flood cycles are likely to interfere with the reproduction and feeding of many of the 2,000 or more species of fish inhabiting the myriad waters of Amazonia.

Little is known about the impact of dams built thus far on Amazonia's fisheries (Bayley and Petrere 1990). On 2 October 1992, a school of jaraqui (*Semaprochilodus* sp.) was observed swimming back and forth along the foot of the dam at Curuá-Una in a fruitless at-

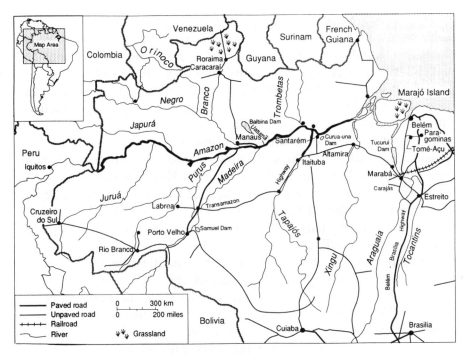

Fig. 2.2 **Major hydroelectric dams in Amazonia**

tempt to move upstream. The dam closed in 1976, so it is curious to see fish still trying to move upstream. Several other species have apparently disappeared above the dam, such as pirapitinga (*Colossoma bidens*) and jatuarana (*Brycon* sp.), but one interviewed farmer felt that fishing yields overall had not declined. Tucunaré (*Cichla ocellaris)* and charuto, in particular, are reportedly plentiful in the reservoir. The Curuá-Una reservoir spawned a population explosion of piranhas (*Serrasalmus* spp.) during the first two decades of operation (Ferreira 1984; Junk et al. 1981). For all their fame as dangerous fish, piranhas are eaten by locals and sell briskly in urban markets.

Some fish were killed by the lack of oxygen and hydrogen sulphide when the Tucurui dam closed in 1984 (Sioli 1986), but the reservoir has become a significant fishery for the highly prized tucunaré. Tucunaré from the Tucurui reservoir are marketed at least as far south as Carajás. The 2,100 km^2 Balbina reservoir on the Uatumã River, completed in 1987 to provide electricity for Manaus, has also become a significant fishery for this spirited predator.

Known as peacock bass to English-speaking sport fishermen, tucu-

25

naré may accumulate mercury released by gold miners. Also, tucunaré in the Curuá-Una reservoir near Santarém, Pará, became so heavily infested with parasitic nematodes that some locals declined to eat the highly prized fish (Junk and Nunes de Mello 1987).

Some fisheries downstream from the Tucurui appear to have suffered from the dam (Dwyer 1990: 44; Magee 1989). The productivity of fisheries appears to have declined mostly in the lower regions of the Tocantins in the vicinity of Cametá. One migratory species, *Anodus elongatus*, has virtually disappeared from the lower Tocantins (Merona, Carvalho, and Bittencourt 1987). Populations of *Curimata cyprinoides* have also diminished, at least temporarily. The Tucurui dam contributed to the collapse of the mapará fishery on the lower Tocantins by closing off a spawning route and reducing plankton biomass (Goulding, Smith, and Mahar in press).

Although the composition of fish communities has shifted below the Tucurui dam, the overall impact of this formidable barrier on fisheries has not proved especially serious from the perspective of local nutrition. A shrimp fishery based on *Macrobrachium amazonicum* was waning along the lower Tocantins well before the Tucurui dam closed; furthermore, this freshwater shrimp, which is used in a variety of regional dishes, thrives in the Tucurui reservoir (Odinetz-Collart 1987). The rapid turnover of water in the Tucurui reservoir, some six or seven times a year, helps avoid drastic changes in water chemistry and thermal stratification, thus reducing the danger of intoxicating fish (Barrow 1987).

Turtles, especially *Podocnemis expansa*, were abundant along the Tocantins in the seventeenth century and served as an important food for locals (Heriarte 1964: 30), but this resource had dwindled considerably long before construction of the Tucurui dam. The resulting reservoir, however, has covered many former nesting beaches and will probably preclude the chances of re-establishing sizeable populations of *P. expansa* along the Tocantins.

One concern about reservoirs in the Amazon is their potential role in favouring the population build-up of disease vectors. Soon after the Tucurui dam closed, some inhabitants and their livestock near the margin of the reservoir were plagued by swarms of mosquitoes (*Mansonia titillans*) and, to a lesser extent, horseflies (*Lapiselaga grassipes*). The former are known to carry two arboviruses, but no outbreaks of disease attributed to *M. titillans* have occurred near the Tucurui reservoir (Marques 1992). Populations of both flies appear to have dwindled, presumably as the new lacustrine ecosystem and surrounding areas have become more stable.

The Samuel dam on the Jamari River in Rondônia, which filled in 1989 to supply electricity to Porto Velho, has reportedly disrupted the upstream migration of some large catfish (João Paulo Viana, pers. comm.). Fisheries have also allegedly suffered downstream from the Balbina dam, but no quantitative data support such claims (Gribel 1990).

Some farmers have apparently benefited downstream from the Tucurui dam, whereas others have lost fertile planting ground. Regulation of water flow facilitates the irrigation of rice at the mouth of the Tocantins, but the reduced sediment load has resulted in a loss of flood plain for agriculture along the lower Tocantins (Barrow 1988).

No reservoirs created for hydroelectric dams in Amazonia are in imminent danger of losing electrical generating capacity because of siltation. The oldest dam, Curuá-Una, is nearly 20 years old and is still operational (fig. 2.3). All the other hydroelectric dams were built in the late 1970s and in the 1980s (table 2.1). Although the Tocantins

Fig. 2.3 **Drowned forest in the Curuá-Una reservoir. Near Santarém, Pará, 2 October 1992**

27

Table 2.1 **Major hydroelectric dams operating in Amazonia**

Dam[a]	River	Operational	Capacity (MW)	Reservoir area (km^2)
Tucurui	Tocantins	1984	2,000[b]	2,400
Balbina	Uatumã	1989	250	2,300
Samuel	Jamari	1989	216	560
Curuá-Una	Curuá-Una	1977	30	78
Paredão	Araguari	1975	40	23
TOTALS			2,536	5,361

Sources: Barrow (1988); Ledec and Goodland (1988); Serra (1992); Sioli (1986); field notes of NJHS at the Curuá-Una dam on 2 October 1992.
a. See fig. 2.1 for dam locations.
b. The Tucurui dam is expected eventually to generate 4,000 MW.

appears to be getting cloudier as a result of forest clearing, "storage pockets" abound in the reservoir bed and this dead space will take some time to fill with sediment.

The Tucurui reservoir has drowned tens of thousands of Brazil nut trees (fig. 2.4). The Tocantins valley has always been the most important centre for the Brazil nut trade, and the 2,000 km^2 reservoir has destroyed some valuable plant resources. It is difficult to measure the impact of such losses on yields, but some unique germplasm has surely been lost. As the Brazil nut's genepool shrinks, genes that could be useful for future improvement efforts also vanish.

Amazonia is relatively flat, so dam-building along major rivers leads to the drowning of substantial tracts of flood plain and upland forest. Iquitos on the Upper Amazon is 3,600 km from the Atlantic, yet only 80 metres above sealevel (Irion 1989). From Iquitos to the confluence with the Negro, the Amazon drops only 57 metres. Some dams are more "cost effective" in terms of kilowatts generated per flooded area (Ledec and Goodland 1988: 60). The Tucurui dam generates 30 kW/ha of reservoir, whereas Balbina delivers only 2 kW/ha of flooded area (table 2.1). Both dams are low in electricity generated per flooded area when compared with rivers with steeper valleys, such as the Itaipu dam on the Paraná (77 kW/ha) or the Grande Coulee on the Colorado (63 kW/ha).

The apparent and hidden ecological costs of building major dams in Amazonia must be weighed against the benefits hydroelectric dams bring to the region. Brazil's desire to tap the hydroelectric potential of waters in Amazonia is understandable in view of the burdensome bill for imported petroleum. Brazil produces less than one-third of its

Fig. 2.4 **Some Brazil nut (*Bertholletia excelsa*) trees drowned by the Tucurui reservoir. Tocantins River, Pará, August 1988. Brazil nut trees have massive, straight boles and twisting branches at the cauliflower-shaped crown**

petroleum needs, and most of the electricity generated in Amazonia has historically come from diesel-powered turbines. The Tucurui dam has benefited Belém and environs with reliable electricity and has created jobs, such as at the aluminium smelting plant at Bacarena.

Nevertheless, a series of smaller, more environmentally benign hydroelectric projects might prove more suitable over the long term. To supply power to the pulp mill at Jari, for example, a proposed hydroelectric plant at the Santo Antonio Falls will divert part of the river through a turbine and thus will not involve any flooding.

The environmental impacts of mining

Mining has become a major economic activity in Amazonia. The environmental impacts of mining operations by corporations are largely localized and of minimal significance, particularly since some earlier water pollution concerns have been addressed. At most, 4,500 km² of forest is likely to be cleared to gain access to all known exploitable mineral deposits in Amazonia (Hoppe 1992). Settlement and development activities associated with the poles of growth generated by mining concerns are likely to have more widespread impacts.

Corporate operations

Bauxite mining requires the removal of large quantities of overlying soil, and if precautions are not taken sediment can be washed into nearby watercourses. At one point, seven miles of Lake Batata near Mineração Rio Norte on the Trombetas had filled in with reddish-brown soil, thereby killing trees and destroying fish and wildlife habitats (Mee 1988: 279). Corrective measures have been taken by building a siltation pond, and Lake Batata is being restored.

Mineração Rio Norte, which operates the bauxite mine along the Trombetas, eventually replants areas scraped to gain access to the aluminium ore. Topsoil is stockpiled and then spread back once an area has been mined. Several native trees are planted to speed up restoration of the land (Gradwohl and Greenberg 1988: 173). Such recuperation efforts are costly, but Mineração Rio Norte is demonstrating leadership in environmental management, and technologies developed by the company are likely to prove useful at many other mining sites in the humid tropics.

The manganese field at Serra do Navio in Amapá has been mined by ICOMI since the early 1960s, and is nearing the end of its economic life. The ore is taken by rail to Porto Santana, a deep-water port on the northern bank of the Amazon. Sizeable oil-palm plantations and small-scale settlement have sprung up along the railroad. The manganese mines still operating in the vicinity of Serra do Navio are well managed and do not provoke any significant ecological damage. Oil-palm plantations along the railroad are well adapted to the climate and soils of the region and provide good ground cover.

At Carajás, forest-clearing around mines is minimized, and road and rail sidings are planted to *Brachiaria humidicola*, a perennial grass from Africa. Holding ponds to decant mining sediment have also been established by Companhia Vale do Rio Doce (CVRD) at Carajás. Outside the 400,000 ha concession granted to CVRD at Carajás, forest-clearing by farmers and ranchers is rampant, particularly along the 890 km railroad to Itaqui in Maranhão. The lesson learned here is that sound environmental management practices within a concession are no guarantee that natural resources will not be destroyed around the periphery. A broader, more integrated approach to regional development is thus called for that explores the linkages and interactions between land-use systems.

Itinerant gold miners and mercury pollution

In contrast to most corporate mining operations, small-scale gold-mining activities in Amazonia are causing widespread ecological damage. According to official figures, itinerant gold miners unearthed US$13 billion worth of gold in the Brazilian Amazon between 1980 and 1988 (Almeida 1992). The gold rush in Amazonia during the 1980s rivalled the California gold rush of the nineteenth century and is exceeded only by production from the mines of South Africa (Godfrey 1992). Clandestine gold trading probably increased that figure several fold. Little wonder that gold mining has attracted so much attention in the Amazon, even though few miners ever become wealthy.

Itinerant gold mining is causing one of the most serious environmental problems in Amazonia today: mercury pollution. Itinerant miners use the toxic element to precipitate gold when washing gravel. Between 5 and 30 per cent of the mercury is lost during this process, and much of the mercury finds its way back to water (Malm et al. 1990). A further 20 per cent vaporizes when the amalgamate is torched to obtain the gold, both in the field and in gold-buying stores. The high rainfall and humidity in the region facilitate reoxidation of vaporized mercury. Mercury pollution of the air is particularly acute in the districts of certain towns where gold stores tend to concentrate (Biller 1994: 8).

Approximately half a million gold miners (*garimpeiros*) were operating in Amazonia during the early to mid-1980s (Mallas and Benedicto 1986). In the 1990s, the gold fever has cooled somewhat, especially in Rondônia and southern Pará, but several hundred

31

thousand men and women are probably still engaged in gold mining in the Brazilian Amazon. By the late 1980s, about 100 metric tons of gold were being exported annually from the Brazilian Amazon. For every kilogram of gold produced, an estimated 1.32 kg of mercury is lost to the environment – 45 per cent into rivers and streams and 55 per cent into the atmosphere (Pfeiffer and Lacerda 1988). Some 100 tons of mercury were thus finding their way into the region's ecosystems at the close of the 1980s (Nriagu et al. 1992).

Mercury has been employed in gold and silver mining in Latin America since early colonial times, but the current scale of mercury use for mining is unmatched. A Mexican miner, Bartolomé de Medina, devised a process for extracting silver from its encasing ore with mercury in the mid-sixteenth century (McAlister 1984: 228). Mercury was used extensively as an amalgam in silver mining in Mexico and Peru during the sixteenth and seventeenth centuries. The Spanish employed quicksilver to refine a little gold in Hispaniola in the sixteenth century.

Brazil depends on imports for its mercury needs, and most of it is consumed by the informal gold-mining sector (Biller 1994: 6). Itinerant miners account for more than 70 per cent of Brazil's gold production, so the use of mercury is highly diffused in Amazonia and would be hard to control. Technologies exist for reducing mercury contamination, such as the use of retorts when torching amalgam, but thus far they have not been widely adopted.

During the colonial period in Colombia, placer miners separated gold from sediment rich in iron oxide by employing the glutinous sap of several plants, including crushed leaves of cordoncillo (*Piper* sp.), encinillo (*Weinmannia* sp.), and chica (*Jacquinia aurantiaca*). When mixed with water, the foamy sap captured the iron oxide flakes, allowing the gold particles to settle to the bottom of the pan (West 1952). Organic precipitates would be much more environmentally benign than mercury, although *Jacquinia aurantiaca* is a piscicide. Such ancient practices are worth investigating, particularly to compare gold recovery rates with mercury.

Gold mining in rain forests is not confined to Amazonia, although it is most prevalent there. Large numbers of itinerant miners are operating with mercury in other regions, such as southern Guyana, Venezuela, and parts of Central America (Parsons 1955). Gold miners had to be evicted from a park on the Osa Peninsula of Costa Rica where they were clogging rivers with sediment. The Costa Rican government relocated the miners at considerable expense. In southern Guyana, dredgers are sucking up river beds and discharging large quantities of sediment back into the water, thereby altering its turbidity.[3]

Although gold has been panned from alluvial deposits in the Tapajós valley since the 1950s, the Amazon gold rush started in earnest in 1980 when gold prices soared to US$850 per ounce. International investors had apparently grown anxious about the Iran–Iraq war and were buying substantial quantities of gold on the world market.

The most celebrated gold find in Amazon was at Serra Pelada, approximately 100 km south-west of Marabá in January 1980; within a few months, 20,000 *garimpeiros* had swarmed to the mountain once isolated in a sea of forest (Santos 1981: 161; Schmink 1985). In June 1980, Serra Pelada was producing about 6 kg of gold per day, and by 1986 the mountain had been reduced to a gaping pit, 110 metres deep (Mallas and Benedicto 1986). By 1990, most of the gold miners had moved on, but much of the forest around Serra Pelada had been cleared by settlers.

Every state in the Brazilian Amazon is currently experiencing a rapid influx of fortune-seekers. Regional airports, such as at Monte Dourado in Pará and Boa Vista in Roraima, are hives of activity, with small planes constantly ferrying miners and their supplies to and from remote airstrips. During the height of the gold rush in the 1980s, other regional airports, such as Santarém, Itaituba, and Marabá in Pará, Alta Floresta in Mato Grosso, and Porto Velho in Rondônia, also witnessed swarms of single- and twin-engined aircraft serving far-flung gold-mining camps.

The gravity of the mercury pollution problem has attracted the attention of the national press in Brazil. Few data are available, though, to assess the dimensions of mercury accumulation in fish. Mercury concentration in rivers and streams varies markedly by location, and mercury contamination in fish also varies according to species (Biller 1994: 8). Some Kayapó Indians have acquired dangerously high levels of mercury, presumably from eating fish and drinking water from polluted rivers and streams (Hecht and Cockburn 1989: 143). Of 106 individuals sampled in four communities in the Tapajós watershed, over 60 per cent had mercury levels in their urine high enough to warrant regular testing as recommended by the World Health Organization (Thornton et al. 1991). Around half of the 97 river sediment samples taken from the Tapajós and its affluents exceeded the 1 ppm mercury considered the limit for safety by the Brazilian environmental secretariat[4] (Thornton et al. 1991).

Predatory fish, such as tucunaré, pirarucu (*Arapaima gigas*), aruanã (*Osteoglossum bicirrhosum*), most species of piranha, and many species of catfish, are likely to accumulate mercury more rapidly than herbivorous species. In the Madeira river system, several species of predatory fish, such as dourado (*Brachyplatystoma flavicans*), filhote (*B. filamentosum*), and other catfish (*Pseudoplatystoma* spp.), have accumulated high levels of mercury, up to 3.81 μg mercury/g^{-1} (Malm et al. 1990; Pfeiffer et al. 1989). Levels of mercury in excess of 0.5 μg/g are generally considered a potential threat to human health. These large catfish are frozen and sent to markets in the United States and central and southern Brazil (Goulding 1981). Omnivorous fish, such as highly prized tambaqui (*Colossoma macropomum*), and eggs of detritus feeders, such as acarí catfish (Loricariidae), have also been found with high levels of mercury along the Madeira River (Martinelli et al. 1988). Preliminary analyses of fish and human hair along the margin of the Tucurui reservoir also reveal that mercury is entering the food chain along the Tocantins River (Braunschweiler 1991).

If mercury levels rise in fish, an important source of protein in the region, then the poor are especially likely to suffer. If the region's fish become unsafe to eat, wealthier inhabitants can more easily turn to beef, chicken, or imported fish. The long residence time of mercury in river sediments can contribute to health hazards long after the gold-mining frontier has moved on (Fuge et al. 1992), so damage from gold mining in Amazonia may be felt for decades to come. A trend towards gold mining from barges in rivers, such as the Madeira and the Negro, is particularly worrisome in this regard. In 1985, some 1,400 boats were pumping up sediment from the bottom of the Madeira in search of gold (Pfeiffer and Lacerda 1988).

The spectacular surge in gold mining is having other adverse environmental effects. Gold-mining camps are among the worst areas for malaria transmission in Amazonia. Gold miners may be introducing new strains of malaria (*Plasmodium falciparum* and *P. vivax*) to which local populations have no resistance. Thus Indians are likely to suffer more severe malaria symptoms if gold miners are operating nearby. In Roraima, for example, hundreds of Yanomami Indians have succumbed to malaria, owing in part to infections brought in by the nearly 20,000 gold miners who started arriving in 1987 (Robinson 1991). In a two-week period in 1992, 44 Yanomamo died from malaria in the Parafuri village alone.[5]

Gold miners are likely accelerating natural selection among malaria parasites for resistance to drugs used for prophylaxis and treatment. In some areas, miners are apparently employing drugs that are usually reserved for treating chloroquine-resistant strains of falciparum malaria. In the early 1970s, Fansidar was the drug of last resort for treating infections of falciparum malaria that would not respond to chloroquine treatment. Now Fansidar is largely ineffective in most areas of Amazonia, in part because miners have used the drug as a prophylaxis, thus increasing selection pressures for resistance.

The treatment and prophylactic strategies of gold miners warrant further study. A first impression was that gold miners often suffered so much from malaria because they were not taking adequate precautions, ranging from the use of mosquito nets to standard prophylaxis with chloroquine. If, on the other hand, significant numbers of miners are using last resort treatments for chloroquine-resistant falciparum malaria, such as mefloquine and doxycycline, as a prophylaxis then malaria is likely to become an even more widespread public health problem in the Amazon basin.

Although mercury contamination and invasion of indigenous lands remain serious issues in Amazonia, these threats have abated to some degree in the 1990s. Gold prices plunged to about US$340 an ounce in early 1993, and many *garimpeiros* have returned from mining camps to seek their fortunes elsewhere. The end of the Cold War has probably calmed investors' fears and the lustre of gold has diminished somewhat. The closing of many gold shops in Santarém and Porto Velho, as well as diminished small plane activity at such airports as Santarém and Itaituba, are symptoms of the decline in gold-mining activity. The extent to which gold mining has declined overall is hard to tell, and in some parts it is actually on the increase. If gold prices climb steeply once again, gold miners are likely to return in force to the backlands of Amazonia.

Petroleum extraction

Western Amazonia has witnessed some sizeable oil strikes within the past 30 years, and prospecting is under way in several parts of the basin. Most of Ecuador's oil production, some 300,000 barrels/day, comes from the Amazon region. Amazonia may yet become a major oil-producing area.

With current technologies and safeguards, oil drilling does not usually pose undue hazards to the environment. Some water pollution occurs around soil extraction sites, but overall such damage is usually localized. Major pipeline leaks cause much greater damage. Two significant leaks have occurred along the Trans-Ecuadorian Petroleum Pipeline: an earthquake ruptured a 30 km section of the pipeline in March 1987, while a massive landslide caused by heavy rains and deforestation sheared the pipeline in May 1989 (Hicks et al. 1990: 9). Civil unrest has occasionally led to sabotage of oil pipelines in Colombia and Peru; should more pipelines be built in Amazonia, such dangers could increase. On the whole, though, the oil industry is not causing any large-scale pollution of the air or waters in Amazonia. An even greater risk would ensue if large numbers of oil tankers began plying the Amazon. The dangers of running aground or colliding with other ships would increase and oil spills would be disastrous for fish production and many agricultural activities.

Roads created to facilitate petroleum extraction help settlers penetrate the rain forest. Roads built to oil fields operated by Texaco-Gulf in the Ecuadorian Amazon, for example, have opened up some 2 million ha of formerly undeveloped forest lands (Hiraoka and Yamamoto 1980). By the late 1970s, over 30,000 people had taken advantage of the oil company roads to eke out homesteads in the forest. Currently proven reserves of sweet crude in the Ecuadorian Amazon are expected to be depleted by the late 1990s, but substantial reserves of heavier grades of petroleum have been found in eastern Ecuador, which may be tapped in the twenty-first century.

A blizzard of cocaine

All the world's cocaine is produced from coca plantations on the eastern slopes of the Andes. The seemingly endless appetite for recreational drugs in industrial countries, and increasingly in developing nations, has spurred coca plantings in areas formerly in forest or planted to food crops. A crop once grown for local consumption has become so profitable that it is now much more widely grown than in the past. Traditionally, coca has been used in two forms: a mild stimulant by chewing the leaves or making tea; and as a snuff in rituals by certain indigenous groups of western Amazonia. Now large quantities of coca leaves are processed to concentrate cocaine. Coca cultivation is consequently spreading further into the Amazon lowlands, including Brazil.

Three latent environmental problems may surface because of the cocaine business: deforestation, coca eradication, and the dumping of chemicals used to process coca leaves into paste. Given the secrecy and peril involved in investigating the coca industry, information on such negative environmental impacts will be difficult to obtain. Presumably, they will have mainly local or regional impacts.

Reliable data on planting rates and the cultivated area in coca are understandably hard to gather. More than 700,000 ha of montane forest have apparently been cut in Peru to grow and process coca (Goodman 1993). More tropical forest in Amazonia has surely fallen at the hands of small farmers to grow coca than has been cleared by miners, both corporate and itinerant. The Andean portion of the Amazon basin is especially rich in biodiversity; it would be ironic if some individuals who partake of cocaine also buy albums and "rainforest" products that purportedly support "sustainable" use of tropical forests. Discussion about using defoliants, such as Spike, to eradicate coca plantations has elicited some concern, particularly from environmentalists and ecologists concerned about the impact of herbicides on non-target plants. Biocontrol efforts may prove more effective, provided they do not attack other plant species. On the other hand, coca bushes may do a better job of securing soil on steep Andean slopes than most food crops. While the international market for cocaine remains strong, farmers will find a way to continue planting a crop that produces a handsome profit.

Poppy fields are sprouting now in the Andes, in response to a resurgent demand for opium and a desire by drug cartels to diversify their product lines. Poppy fields cover at least 20,000 ha in the Colombian Andes (Goodman 1993), and cultivation may spread south into the Amazon basin. This introduced annual does not secure soils well on steep slopes. In discussions about the need for people in developed countries to reconcile their lifestyles with the planet and biodiversity, little attention has been paid to the hedonistic use of drugs. Efforts should be redoubled to educate people about the folly of taking recreational drugs in industrial countries, rather than try and blame coca growers in western Amazonia.

One of the most serious environmental issues associated with coca in Amazonia is the nature and quantity of chemicals used to process coca leaves. In 1986, Peru exported an estimated 6,400 tons of coca paste. Such big quantities would have involved the use of 32 million litres of sulphuric acid, 16,000 tons of quicklime, and 6.5 million tons of acetone.[6] In the Upper Huallaga valley alone, coca processors annually dump an estimated 56 million litres of kerosene, 8 million tons of sulphuric acid, and large quantities of acetone, toluene, and carbide (FAO 1990: 12). Coca is also processed in Colombia, Ecuador, and Bolivia. Most of these chemicals and compounds probably found their way into streams and the groundwater in various parts of western Amazonia. If these chemicals are not eliminating fish populations, they may render them unsafe to eat. Such compounds may also trigger mutations in at least some of the fish species important for subsistence and commerce.

The threat of coca-processing chemicals may be diminishing, at least in some areas. In Colombia, for example, coca refiners have recently begun recycling chemicals, rather than ditching them in streams.[7] Such measures do not reflect a concern for the environment; rather they are an effort to circumvent restrictions on the importation or production of precursor chemicals used in processing coca paste.

Habitat destruction and the loss of biodiversity

Of all the issues surrounding environmental change in Amazonia, threats to biodiversity are arguably the most serious in the long run. Species loss as a result of drastic habitat modification, such as logging, is an issue in many parts of the humid tropics, such as in Malaysia (Brookfield, Potter, and Byron 1995). Particularly worrisome is that such biodiversity losses are often not accompanied by any long-term economic benefits to the local people.

The effects of species loss may not be immediately obvious, and are thus not usually considered in economic development plans. Species loss can be hard to quantify in economic terms, and is considered an externality. The impoverishment of habitats is sure to reduce options for future development. Air and water pollution may be more tangible assaults on our living space, but the haemorrhaging of species will drain resources for future generations, quite apart from the ethical and moral questions posed by human-induced extinctions.

Some have argued that we do not really need nature's storehouse of genes because ingenious scientists can concoct novel genes in laboratories at will (Huber 1992). This notion is fallacious. The idea that we can safely dispense with tropical forests or other ecosystems because modern biotechnology has made them redundant is dangerous thinking. Genes need to be synthesized from models. Laboratories and computer memories cannot replicate dynamic evolutionary processes under way around the world.

Impressive advances in biotechnology only underscore the importance of conserving biodiversity since desirable genes can increasingly be switched from one organism to another. The glamour of genetic engineering should not blind the public and policy makers to the need to safeguard the integrity of natural ecosystems.

Loss of biodiversity as a result of development and environmental degradation has emerged as a global concern (Raven 1990; Wilson and Peter 1988). Concern over erosion of biodiversity was initially confined mostly to the scientific community, but is now spreading to the general public and politicians. Tropical deforestation is often at the forefront in debates on biodiversity loss; at least 27,000 species are thought to be lost from such widespread destruction every year (Myers 1993). Actual species loss may be much higher considering that many plant and animal groups are still imperfectly known (Wilson 1992). Amazonia has attracted particular attention in this regard because of its high degree of endemism and vast numbers of animal and plant species, many of them undocumented or poorly studied (Adis 1990). The region's diverse array of plant and animal communities contains many unique species and genes.

Amazonia contains the largest stretch of tropical forest, spanning 5,000 km from the Andes to the Atlantic, and some 4,000 km from the Guianas and the Upper Orinoco to the scrub cerrado of the Brazilian shield and the seasonally flooded grasslands of the Pantanal. This vast mosaic of forest communities, second growth, natural and man-induced grasslands and swamps contains the richest assortment of plant and animal species in the world, as well as a rich storehouse of genes for crop improvement.

Deforestation can adversely affect biodiversity on two accounts: outright habitat destruction, and ecological changes along the contact zone of remaining forest stands. Whereas deforestation rates in Amazonia appear to have been less dramatic over the past decade than has previously been thought, perhaps in the order of 15,000 km^2 per year during the 1978–1988 period, some 38,000 km^2 of forest may have been degraded (Skole and Tucker 1993). The edge effect of disturbance, ranging from microclimatic changes to the encroachment of swidden and pasture fires, can allegedly alter plant and animal communities as much as 1 km into the forest. Although some may dispute how deeply human influences penetrate the forest in terms of significant ecological disturbance, it is clear that outright deforestation alone is an insufficient measure of biodiversity change. In drier areas of the Amazon, such as around Marabá in southern Pará and in southern fringes of the rain forest in Mato Grosso, the border of isolated patches of forest can easily catch fire when fields or grazing areas are torched in preparation for planting or to destroy weeds and promote new growth of pasture grasses.

Endangered gene pools

Rampant deforestation fuelled by development schemes and pioneer farmers now threatens to destroy the genetic resources of many economic plants and potential crops before they can be tapped for the benefit of people throughout the world (NRC 1991; Smith et al. 1991b, 1992). Also, loss of tribal cultures is resulting in the disappearance of unique varieties of many annual and perennial crops.

Wild populations of crops, and in some cases their near relatives, are increasingly sought by plant breeders for desirable traits, such as pest and disease resistance and tolerance to problem soils. To help make farming more sustainable, researchers, development organizations, and farmers are increasingly seeking genetic solutions to agricultural constraints rather than costly, and sometimes environmentally damaging, chemical applications.

Ironically, forest-clearing to establish farms and plantations can eliminate the very genes that could be used to improve the crops being planted. The shrinking of wild populations of over 47 perennial crop species is currently under way in Amazonia (Smith and Schultes 1990). Perennial crops are important to the livelihoods of most small farmers in the tropics as well as operators of large plantations. Perennial crops that originated in Amazonia provide food, beverages, shelter, medicines, oils, resins, cosmetics, food colourants, and latex for citizens on every continent.

The Amazon contains wild gene pools of such commercially important crops as rubber (*Hevea brasiliensis*) and cacao (*Theobroma cacao*), as well as regionally important food and beverage crops such as peach palm (*Bactris gasipaes*) and guaraná (*Paullinia cupana*), a popular soda in Brazil and now exported to developed countries such as Canada. As the heart-of-palm trade destroys many wild stands, particularly species of *Euterpe*, entrepreneurs in several Latin American countries are planting peach palm for palmito. Plantations of peach palm for the heart-of-palm trade are especially well developed in Costa Rica and Mexico. The ability of developing countries in the Amazon region as well as in other parts of Latin America, Africa, and South-East Asia to raise and sustain yields of several important cash and food crops will hinge to a large extent on their ability to marshal genetic resources to overcome constraints to production.

The Amazon forest also contains wild populations of hitherto minor crops such as annatto (*Bixa orellana*) and cupuaçu (*Theobroma grandiflorum*). Annatto is used by some Indians for body paint and is commonly used as a food colourant in Latin America. Known as achiote in Spanish and urucú in Brazil, annatto occurs spontaneously in various parts of Amazonia and probably originated in Acre. Traditionally, annatto has been grown as a backyard plant but it is now being cultivated on a commercial scale in several Latin American countries, particularly Brazil. After artificial Red Dye No. 3 was banned in the United States because it is a carcinogen, interest in annatto rebounded. Natural red bixin from annatto is increasingly used to colour foodstuffs and cosmetics in both industrial nations and developing countries. Annatto is used to enhance the colour of some peach-flavoured yogurts in the eastern United States, although few consumers probably make any connection with Amazonia when they relish that healthy treat.

Football-sized cupuaçu, a relative of cacao, grows in the forests of eastern Amazonia and is cultivated in backyards and fields for its refreshing pulp, which is used to make drinks, ice-cream, cakes, and puddings (fig. 2.5). Cupuaçu sells briskly in Amazonia and is penetrating markets in southern Brazil, and more recently in the United States and Japan. Cupuaçu has made the transition from an extractive product, to an occasional plant in home gardens, to a full-fledged crop, often grown in agro-forestry systems. How many other "cupuaçus" linger in the forest that could one day delight the palate of people in the region and abroad?

Amazonia's lush and diverse forests also contain many plants that could be incorporated into our menu of cultivated species, or are currently on the threshold of domestication. The nuts of patauá (*Jessenia bataua*) palm, for example, contain an oil similar to the quality of olive oil. The fruits are collected in the wild to make refreshing drinks. Brazil nut is now being grown on a small scale on several private landholdings in the Brazilian Amazon as well as in Malaysia. Domestication of Brazil nut is an important step considering that wild stands of the giant forest tree are falling for ranches, farms, and reservoirs.

Forests also contain pollinators and dispersal agents of wild populations of many crop plants as well as their near relatives (fig. 2.6). Intricate and often fine-tuned relationships between plants and animals need to be maintained if the integrity of many wild populations of our crop plants is to be ensured. For example, Brazil nut is dispersed by

Fig. 2.5 **Cupuaçu (*Theobroma grandiflorum*), in the window, and peach-palm (*Bactris gasipaes*) hanging on post of a small farmer's home along the Castanhal–Marudá road. Pará, May 1982**

agoutis (*Dasyprocta* spp.), which bury many of the nuts after gnawing open the hard capsules that encase the protein- and oil-rich nuts (Huber 1910). Some bats pollinate forest trees while others disperse their seeds, and many birds, such as toucans, guans, and curassows (Cracidae), also disseminate many forest fruits. Conservation of forest environments, as well as field gene banks, is thus essential for the long-term viability of many crops important for subsistence and commerce.

Conservation of genetic resources and regional development in Amazonia are intertwined. More studies are needed, however, to document genetic variation in wild populations and domesticated gene pools of Amazonian crops. Also, hard economic data are needed to convince policy makers of the value of preserving forest habitats as resources for development.

Another dimension to the loss of botanical resources in Amazonia is that an invaluable medicine chest is literally being depleted before we can assess even a fraction of the potentially useful drugs. The rapid decline of many indigenous societies represents a loss not only of crop plants and unique varieties, but of ethno-botanical knowledge

Fig. 2.6 **An eighteenth-century artist's rendition of a dusky parrot (*Pionus fuscus*) feeding on a guava fruit (*Psidium* sp.) in the Brazilian Amazon (Source: Alexandre Rodrigues Ferreira, *Viagem Filósofica*, vol. 2, Plate 101, Conselho Federal de Cultura, Rio de Janeiro, 1971)**

about which trees, shrubs, and herbs in the forest might offer cures for a wide variety of health complaints (Plotkin 1993). Many drugs are eventually synthesized in laboratories but, as in the case of genes for crop improvement, they have to be discovered first.

The indigenous knowledge base

A salient lesson from global efforts to conserve crop genetic resources is the need to maintain the cultural integrity of indigenous groups. People with a long history of interaction with the forest have much to teach us about sustainable agricultural practices and plant resources. Rural folk are particularly knowledgeable about the location and natural history of wild populations of crops and their near relatives. Tribal peoples are also knowledgeable about the medicinal value of plants in the forest and in their home gardens, a priceless heritage that is increasingly threatened by encroaching civilization (Schultes 1988; Schultes and Raffauf 1990, 1992). Biodiversity and cultural heterogeneity are vital to sustainable development.

Although rural peoples often have affinity with the surrounding plant and animal world, their practices do not always result in conservation of resources. Peasants and ranchers alike frequently clear fields and home gardens up to the margins of streams or rivers. If water courses were left in forest, natural corridors would remain for animal and plant dispersal in cleared areas.

Farmers in the Brazilian Amazon report three main reasons why they fell riparian forests, even if they contain economically important species such as açaí palm (*Euterpe oleracea*). First, several crops important for domestic consumption and commerce grow well in the moist, organic-rich soils flanking streams and small rivers in contrast to the generally highly acidic, nutrient-poor upland soils. The common bean (*Phaseolus vulgaris*), maize (*Zea mays*), and vegetables reportedly yield better when grown in humid, valley bottoms. It is also easier to irrigate vegetables when they are close to a perennial water source. Second, farmers want to eliminate habitat for predators on their small livestock, particularly ocelot (*Felis pardalis*), margay (*Felis wiedii*), and various hawks. Third, newcomers to the region do not yet appreciate the value of some riparian trees and wish to create open, more "productive" landscapes.

Faunal resources

The forests and rivers of Amazonia also contain an abundant array of wildlife important for hunting (Ayres and Ayres 1979; Ayres et al. 1991; Bodmer, Fang, and Ibanez 1988, 1991; Dourojeanni 1974; Rios, Dourojeanni, and Trovar 1973; Smith 1976). Some game animals, such as various species of turtle (*Podocnemis* spp.), could be domesticated or reared in captivity and the young released to the wild. Of the many species of mammals, birds, and reptiles of lowland South America, only one species has been domesticated, the muscovy duck (*Cairina moschata*). Muscovy ducks still grace the extensive lakes and lagoons of the Amazon flood plain, and some of these wild populations could be helpful to further breeding efforts.

Several wild animals are kept around homes for eventual consumption and some of them are in the process of being domesticated. Most are captured while still young, particularly when their mothers are killed during hunts. Capybara (*Hydrochaeris hydrochaeris*) and black-bellied tree ducks (*Dendrocygna autumnalis*) are kept around homes by some farmers along the Amazon flood plain, and they sometimes breed in captivity. Options for animal domestication will be foreclosed if wild populations of such species are drastically reduced.

Habitat destruction is the principal threat to wildlife in the region. The issue of dams and fisheries has already been highlighted, but the clearing of flood-plain forests by farmers and ranchers also eliminates breeding and feeding grounds for fish. At least three-quarters of the fish species important in commerce and subsistence derive their nutrition directly or indirectly from flooded forests (Goulding 1980, 1993). A better understanding of land-use systems is thus essential for improved development and conservation efforts.

Policy implications

Although Amazonia is rich in plant and animal species, particularly in forests cloaking the eastern slopes of the Andes, policies that might deflect settlement and development to relatively empty areas, such as cerrados and thorn scrub, need to be considered carefully. Some of the drier areas of South America have higher levels of mammal endemism than the rain forests (Mares 1992). The campos, cerrados, and thorn scrub woodlands (caatinga, Chaco) of South America are much richer in animal and plant species than is generally appreciated (Pimm and Gittleman 1992). Wholesale destruction of low rainfall environments would also greatly reduce biodiversity – and future options for sustainable development in those areas.

The expansive flood plain of the sinuous Amazon River is another perceived venue for increased development efforts. The Amazon flood plain has always been regarded as an underutilized environment in Amazonia with enormous potential for raising food crops, livestock, and fish. Yet the idea that the flood plains can help absorb development pressures from the "fragile" upland forests warrants careful scrutiny. Flood-plain forests along the Amazon have already been largely logged out and extensively cleared. Endemism is especially high in the seasonally flooded forests of the Amazon River. Efforts to boost the productivity of flood-plain areas should focus on already cleared areas, rather than promote the wholesale destruction of the remaining forest and aquatic habitats with their rich assortment of wildlife.

To help preserve the remaining biodiversity in Amazonia and to reduce pressures to develop contiguous regions, the productivity of agriculture, managed forests, plantations, and ranches must be raised within the well-watered basin. Whenever feasible, such land-use systems should be ecologically diverse. Agro-forestry systems, highlighted later as one of the more viable options for agricultural development in the region, could help maintain some level of biodiversity. Compared with simple monocultures, agro-forestry permits the survival of more animals and plants (Holloway 1991). Also, monocultures of perennial crops, such as oil-palm, create micro-environments for such plants as lichens and mosses that cannot survive in fields of rice or maize.

Notes

1. McDonalds has highlighted the contribution of tropical deforestation on one of its place-mats distributed in May in parts of Florida and possibly other areas. The place-mat was entitled "Ten City Blocks of Rainforest Lost Per Minute" and had a sub-heading with the title "Things are heating up."
2. Meteorological records at the INATAM station of EMBRAPA (Empresa Brasileira de Pesquisa Agropecuária), Tomé-Açu, Pará. The rainy season in eastern Amazonia generally begins in November or December.
3. "Poor man's gold rush," *The Economist*, 12 May 1990, pp. 42–46.
4. SEMA (Secretaria do Meio Ambiente), now merged with IBAMA (Instituto Brasileiro do Meio Ambiente e dos Recursos Naturais Renováveis).
5. *Correio Braziliense*, Brasília, 3 September 1992, p. 14.
6. "The general and the cocaleros," *The Economist*, 9 December 1989, pp. 40–41.
7. "High in the Andes," *The Economist*, 13 February 1993, pp. 45–46.

3

Forces of change and societal responses

A major preoccupation with Amazonia hinges on loss of forest cover and biodiversity, and much attention focuses on how to arrest this destruction. But deforestation does not necessarily mean environmental degradation. What happens to the land after forest-clearing is crucial to the long-term productivity of the environment and to the impact on flora and fauna. Some deforestation in Amazonia for development is inevitable; the more sustainable the development on land already cleared, the better the chances of saving substantial tracts of the region's ecosystems until they can be permanently removed from economic activities, or at least better managed. A more comprehensive understanding of the dynamics of land use and the driving forces behind change can thus help development and conservation efforts.

A confluence of forces is implicated in forest destruction in Amazonia and other tropical lands. The preponderance of forces responsible for the retreat of forest varies according to such factors as access to markets, road infrastructure, and fiscal incentives. Loggers, cattle ranchers, dam builders, small-scale farmers, plantation operators, and miners are all involved in deforestation. Throughout the tropics, small-scale farmers account for more deforestation (some 60 per cent) than the next two agents of destruction, commercial loggers and ranchers, combined (Myers 1991). Small-scale farmers probably account for more than half of the mature and second-growth forest cleared each year in Amazonia.

A variety of driving forces propels these actors in transforming the region. Proximate agents of environmental change are not necessarily

47

to blame for adverse ecological impacts. An analysis of the driving forces behind these agents of forest removal will help clarify policy issues for future development.

Although many forces propel environmental change, they may be conveniently grouped into five main categories: changes in population; new technologies; socio-economic/institutional conditions; the influence of beliefs/attitudes; and levels of income/wealth. The interplay of these factors varies considerably from one part of Amazonia to another, but they are all involved in altering the region's expansive landscapes and intricate cultures.

Population change

Population pressure is often portrayed as a root cause of environmental degradation in many developing countries, particularly with regard to deforestation (Westoby 1989: 45). Although rapid population growth undercuts the natural resource base in some developing regions, it is hard to conceive of Amazonia as having a population problem. The pre-contact population of Amazonia was denser in many rural parts of the basin than it is today, but little long-term damage was exacted on the environment. Even in regions perceived as suffering from overpopulation, overtaxing of the land may be due to inappropriate technologies or highly skewed land-ownership patterns, among other socio-economic factors.

Except in a few restricted areas, such as south-western and south-eastern Amazonia, population growth is a relatively minor force behind environmental change in the region. The population of Rondônia, for example, grew from about 110,000 in 1970 to approximately 1 million by 1990 (Southworth, Dale, and O'Neill 1991). Even then, migrants, rather than natural population growth, mostly account for the swelling ranks of farmers, itinerant miners, and ranchers in Amazonia (Schmink 1988a).

Population growth in parts of north-eastern, central, and southern Brazil is propelling migrants into the Amazon basin (fig. 3.1). When coupled with natural hazards or overcrowding in environmentally sensitive areas, such as the Andean altiplano, migrants can arrive in waves. Periodic rain failures in the North-east region of Brazil, for example, have uprooted farmers into Amazonia for over a century. A substantial proportion of the inhabitants of the Brazilian Amazon trace their ancestry to the arid backlands of the North-east. Skewed land-distribution patterns exacerbate droughts in the North-east.

Fig. 3.1 **The regions and states of Brazil**

Most of the people in the North-east are poor and till marginal land in the rain shadow of the coastal range, areas particularly vulnerable to rain failure.

Two main migration currents are discernible in countries embracing Amazonia: a substantial rural exodus to towns and cities, and settlers penetrating the Amazon basin along pioneer roads. For every migrant heading for Amazonia, many more have opted for towns and cities. During the 1970s, some 766,000 people migrated to the Brazilian Amazon, accounting for only 5 per cent of the flow of people moving from the countryside to urban areas (Wood and Carvalho 1988: 234). Amazonia is clearly not serving as a convenient safety-valve for population growth and socio-economic problems in other regions.

In Latin America, urban population growth is generally much faster

Fig. 3.2 **Paragominas, one of a string of "boom towns" along the Belém–Brasília Highway. Pará, 3 April 1991**

than in rural areas, and this holds for countries with territories in Amazonia (fig. 3.2). Throngs of sharecroppers, unsuccessful or dispossessed farmers, and grown children of rural families have caught buses or trucks in search of new lives in Latin America's swelling cities. Rural–urban migration has severely stretched the ability of governments to provide services for newcomers, and many settle in slums without potable water or sewerage hookups. Some shanty settlements around cities eventually improve, or people eventually move into better neighbourhoods. But urban migrants rarely return to live or even work in their source areas.

Cities are a magnet to prospective migrants. Urban areas, in spite of their higher living costs, crime, and pollution, offer better opportunities for jobs, schooling, and health care. In contrast, pioneer areas of Amazonia have fewer health and educational facilities, and roads that become impassable in the rainy season can isolate farmers from markets, hospitals and clinics, schools, and needed supplies. This impressive sponge effect of cities has undoubtedly saved the Amazon from even more extensive deforestation.

More jobs are needed in cities and towns to better absorb the endless stream of rural–urban migrants. A diversified agricultural economy would help stem the tide of people leaving rural areas so that cities could adequately accommodate arrivals. In addition, viable farms could help foster agro-industries in urban areas to generate more employment opportunities. Sustainable agriculture could thus help alleviate both rural and urban poverty.

The Andes and southern Brazil are currently the main source regions for Amazonian migrants. The crowded Andean valleys of Peru, Bolivia, Ecuador, and Colombia have sent aspiring landowners down into western and south-western Amazonia for several decades (Crist 1963, 1967; Eidt 1962, 1966; Hicks et al. 1990: 2; Hiraoka 1980a; Rudel 1983; Stearman 1978). In Brazil, the North-east region has long served as an important source of migrants for much of the Amazon basin, but the numbers of *Nordestinos* fleeing poverty and failed rains have been eclipsed by the growing throngs of settlers from southern Brazil.

The greatest influx of settlers into the Brazilian Amazon since the 1970s has come from such states as Paraná, Rio Grande do Sul, São Paulo, Minas Gerais, and Espírito Santo (fig. 3.3). Population growth is partly responsible for the flow of migrants to Amazonia, particularly in Paraná and Rio Grande do Sul, where small farms are divided up among sons and in some cases have become too small to be economically viable. In north-western Rio Grande do Sul, areas pioneered in the 1940s were already becoming "full" by the early 1970s.

Other factors also account for out-migration from rural parts of southern Brazil to Amazonia and cities, however. Unequal distribution of land in some areas propels the landless in search of new lives and homesteads. Also, changes in farming methods, to be discussed shortly, can lead to redundancy for some farm labour.

In spite of over two decades of intensive efforts to accelerate settlement and development, Amazonia remains relatively sparsely settled. The 3.8 million km² Brazilian Amazon contains only 10 million inhabitants, less than the megalopolis of São Paulo (table 3.1). The Brazilian Amazon accounts for 45 per cent of Brazilian territory, but less than 7 per cent of its population. If one considers the Legal Amazon (Amazônia Legal), a larger administrative unit set up by Brazil's federal government to distribute development funds and fiscal incentives, population density is still low. The Legal Amazon comprises 5.1 million km² and contains some 16 million inhabitants, thus embracing some 60 per cent of the national territory but only 10 per cent of its population.

Overall, population pressure has clearly not reached any serious

Fig. 3.3   **Settlers from Espírito Santo at Sitio Biazate. Linha 601, near Theobroma, Rondônia, 18 February 1992**

proportions in Amazonia. Environmental degradation in the region is thus only tenuously linked with population growth. Some rural areas of Amazonia have actually lost people to cities in the past two decades. A little over half of the population in Amazonia resides in urban areas, and Belém alone has over 1 million inhabitants. Population growth rates in Amazonian towns and cities far exceed those in rural areas (Godfrey 1990).

Technological change

Technological changes in agriculture, the logging industry, and mining, among other activities, sometimes adversely affect the environ-

Table 3.1 **Area and population of the Brazilian Amazon, 1989**

State	Area (km²)	Population[a] 1989	Population[a] 1992
Rondônia	238,379	1,021,229	1,130,400
Acre	153,697	411,984	423,918
Amazonas	1,567,954	2,141,323	2,082,720
Roraima	225,017	130,070	206,000
Pará	1,246,833	4,996,596	5,046,314
Amapá	142,358	258,395	285,811
Tocantins[b]	277,321	965,704	919,918
TOTALS	3,851,559	9,925,301	10,095,081

Sources: IBGE (1989); *Veja*, 22 January 1992, pp. 58–63.
a. Brazil's population in mid-1991 was estimated at 146 million.
b. The state of Tocantins was created in 1988 by splitting the old state of Goiás in half; northern Goiás then became Tocantins. Tocantins contains a mixture of forest and woody savanna.

ment. Few would deny that humankind's ability to alter the face of the earth and the atmosphere has increased dramatically with ever more potent technologies. The literature is replete with examples of technological changes that have wrought ecological destruction and social disruption (Bennett et al. 1974; Nelson 1973; Norman 1981; Turner et al. 1990b). But technologies can also be employed to help manage resources more wisely, as is occurring in various parts of Amazonia.

Technological changes in agricultural areas of southern Brazil have been accused of forcing people off the land. Some of those no longer able to farm or find work in rural areas have moved to Amazonia. A switch to machine-intensive soybean production from more labour-intensive coffee production in parts of Paraná, for example, has contributed to the rural exodus (Wood and Carvalho 1988: 207). The widespread use of tractors on soybean farms has allegedly displaced labour, thereby contributing to migrants streaming into Amazonia (Muller 1988a). But most of the displaced small farmers have migrated to cities, not to the Amazon (Romeiro 1987).

The agricultural landscape of southern Brazil started shifting dramatically in the early 1970s from mixed cropping based on maize, field beans, and wheat, to monocropping, particularly with soybean. This kaleidoscopic change was triggered by a 1973 drought in the United States and a temporary ban on soybean exports. Japan scrambled for alternative sources of the pulse and turned to southern Brazil. Brazilian farmers responded eagerly to new market opportunities and traditional food crops, such as maize, field beans, and wheat, were often neglected in the rush to plant soybean.

Mechanization may have reduced on-farm labour needs, but it is not clear whether or not the increased use of tractors in southern Brazil has spurred migration to Amazonia or other parts of the country. The manufacture and servicing of agricultural machinery, combined with the impressive volume of soybean transportation and processing in Brazil, have undoubtedly created many new jobs. Some farm labourers are likely to have moved to the service sector in urban areas, rather than try their hand at farming in Amazonia.

Mechanization does not necessarily push small farmers off the land. In areas of Paraná settled by private land companies, or where farmers are members of efficient cooperatives, smallholders remain viable in the face of mechanization and soybean cultivation (Muller 1988b). Rapid soil erosion and consolidation of landholdings by ranchers in Paraná, rather than technological change, have been mainly responsible for the demise of some small farms and an exodus of people from rural areas (Muller 1988b).

Sophisticated technologies are not necessarily a major cause of destruction in Amazonia. Small-scale farmers employing axes, machetes, and in some cases power saws are probably clearing more primary and secondary forest in Amazonia than any other actors. Even large landholders generally employ work gangs armed with power saws or axes to clear land. Indians formerly employed stone axes to fell forest, and, as has been argued previously, were quite capable of radically altering the plant geography of Amazonia. In pre-contact times, many of the larger trees were simply ringed rather than cut down in fields. Stone axes were used to farm large areas of the Amazon basin effectively.

A theme we wish to develop in later chapters is that a combination of new and traditional technologies is vital for sustainable development in the region. We place major emphasis on technologies for agriculture and silviculture that are being deployed to overcome soil and other constraints to raising and upholding yields. New technologies, developed by public research institutions and the private sector, could be a powerful means to reduce environmental degradation in Amazonia and create more options for farmers.

Socio-economic and institutional change

The fiscal and agrarian policies of the Brazilian government have significantly shaped land use in Amazonia since the late 1960s. Beginning in 1967, companies could invest up to half of their taxes in approved development projects in Amazonia. Administered by the Superintendency for Amazonian Development (SUDAM – Superintendência do Desenvolvimento da Amazônia), projects supported by tax incentives were responsible for clearing over 10 million ha of forest, mostly for cattle pasture (Hecht and Cockburn 1989). Fiscal incentive pastures were planted on an area equivalent to two Costa Ricas.

The large-scale conversion of forest to cattle pasture has proved to be the single most controversial aspect of fiscal policies in Amazonia during the 1960s and 1970s. As concern mounted over the ecological implications of such a rapid land transformation, and the often disappointing productivity of many new ranches, the government suspended fiscal incentives for cattle pasture development in "dense" tropical forest in 1979. Nevertheless, many projects approved before 1979 were still being implemented in the 1980s. Furthermore, transitional forest skirting the basin was eligible for fiscal incentives to create pasture. Fiscal incentives accelerated pasture development in Amazonia, particularly in southern Pará and northern Mato Grosso, but overall they have not proved to be the main forces behind deforestation in the region (Mahar 1989: 15). On 25 June 1991, President Collor signed a decree removing fiscal incentives for cattle-ranching in any forested portion of the Amazon, including transitional forest.

Even without fiscal incentives, cattle-ranching remains one of the most common land uses in recently cleared areas of Amazonia (fig. 3.4). Cattle-ranching is a favoured occupation of small-, medium-, and large-scale operators in the region because labour is scarce and a ready market exists for beef, particularly in the rapidly growing urban centres (Hicks et al. 1990: 14). If roads are impassable, cattle can still reach market. Cultural factors stemming from the tradition of cattle-raising in Iberia have sustained the conversion of formerly forested land to pasture in many parts of the region (Hiraoka and Yamamoto 1980).

Government-directed colonization schemes have opened up vast stretches of hinterland to settlers. In 1970, the Brazilian government

Fig. 3.4 **A ranch house on a 50 ha property. Near Parauapebas, Pará, February 1990. The surrounding guinea grass pasture is less than a decade old and has been largely taken over by weeds**

announced the national integration plan (PIN – Programa de Integração Nacional), which called for a system of pioneer highways to crisscross Amazonia, with the 3,000 km Transamazon Highway serving as the main east–west axis for the new highway system. PIN highways were initially designed to provide homesteads for drought victims from the North-east region and the landless and small farmers with large families from other parts of Brazil. They were further designed to create access to resources, such as minerals. The road network in the Brazilian Amazon has grown spectacularly, from a total of 6,350 km in 1960 to 43,672 km by 1985 (Homma, Teixeira Filho and Magalhães, 1991). Tens of thousands of settlers have followed quickly in the wake of bulldozers to take up lots in government-sponsored settlement schemes, to squat on unoccupied land, or to invade reserves and private holdings. By the mid to late 1970s, several private land companies were opening up substantial tracts of land in southern Pará and northern Mato Grosso to small- and medium-scale farmers.

Planned settlements, however, account for a relatively small proportion of the settlers who have streamed into Amazonia over the past two decades. Government-operated settlement schemes were soon overwhelmed by the flood of migrants seeking land. Many settled on public land, and in some cases private property, particularly at the end of side-roads.

Occupation of Amazonia would occur even without government incentives. A case can be made that certain government policies have accelerated rates of settlement and forest conversion, but they can hardly be blamed for widespread ecological change in Amazonia. Government policies have influenced the locations of such change, but many land-hungry settlers and investors are already motivated to try their luck in Amazonia. A desire to tap natural resources and seek new fortunes is a powerful enough incentive, and, as frontiers close in other parts of Brazil, eyes would naturally turn to Amazonia, one of Brazil's last remaining frontiers.

Migration to and within Amazonia is sometimes attributed to a skewed distribution of land. Unequal access to land both within Amazonia and in other parts of Brazil, it is argued, uproots people and obliges them to seek a new life in frontier zones. Debate on whether drought, population growth, or latifundia are responsible for the long history of out-migration from north-eastern Brazil has continued for a long time (Hall 1978). All three factors are responsible in varying degrees, depending on the area in question. Without stepping too far into this complex question, suffice it to say that land-ownership patterns have undoubtedly caused social conflicts in some parts of Brazil, particularly southern Pará, and are partly responsible for migration to and within Amazonia (Becker and Egler 1991: 154; Schmink and Wood 1992).

The need for some degree of land reform and the expediting of secure land titles has been recognized for a long time in parts of Brazil and other areas of Latin America. Confusion over land titling has fuelled deforestation, since one of the most visible ways to place a stamp of ownership on the land is to clear it, even if the opened space is not used productively (Schmink and Wood 1987).

Historically, the politically more expedient solution to the greatly skewed land-ownership pattern in Latin America has been to open up "unoccupied" land for the needy, rather than tackle powerful land-owning interests or invest in technologies to boost productivity (Wood and Schmink 1978). But even if significant land reform were carried out in Brazil, it is debatable whether breaking up large estates would greatly alleviate the flow of people to Amazonia. Land reform could exacerbate social problems by reducing agricultural production and dismantling managerial expertise for certain agricultural enterprises.

Subdividing land is thus not necessarily a cure-all for sustainable development and for saving vast tracts of Amazonia. In southern Brazil, minifundia rather than large landholdings are a significant cause of out-migration to Amazonia. Further subdivision of lots for future generations is not feasible in many areas of southern Brazil, such as around Tenente Portela in Rio Grande do Sul. In Peru, land reform has been carried out for several decades, but thousands of migrants still pour out of the packed altiplano in search of jobs in cities, such as Lima, or to eke out a living in the forests carpeting the eastern flanks of the Andes.

An interesting change in the institutional and political landscape of Amazonia is the move to subdivide municipalities. Traditionally, some municipalities in the Brazilian Amazon have rivalled the size of smaller European nations. In an attempt to gain more control of their own affairs, to tap resources from Brasília, and to ensure better social services, people in many areas of the Brazilian Amazon have lobbied successfully to create new municipalities. Along the Altamira–Itaituba stretch of the Transamazon Highway, for example, several new municipalities have formed recently, including Medicilândia, Uruará, Rurópolis, and Pacajá (Homma et al. 1992a). Competition for seats in these municipal legislatures is keen, with a hundred or more candidates disputing a handful of positions at election time. The chance to be on a government payroll, even at the modest salaries paid to *vereadores*, no doubt draws some prospective council members. Roving cars and trucks with powerful loudspeakers blaring the virtues of candidates have become a common feature of rural and urban life in the Brazilian Amazon.

Such new, more decentralized structures create fresh opportunities for communities to seek local solutions to their problems. Decentralization of political power is not a panacea, however. Municipal governments can be corrupt and ineffectual. The power of Brasília has certainly waned over the past decade; it remains to be seen whether the resulting vacuum will be filled effectively by local initiatives. Non-government structures such as growers' associations, community organizations, and the private sector are currently taking a more active role in the development and diffusion of technologies. The track record of such organizations is highly variable, but one thing is clear: private enterprise is sure to play an ever-more important role in shaping the development of Amazonia.

Beliefs and attitudes towards development

Amazonia has long been considered a cultural and economic back-water. Although still considered exotic and steeped in mystery, at least in the public's mind, Amazonia is rapidly being incorporated into the heartlands of countries with a stake in the sprawling region. Brazil has been the pace-setter in implementing projects to integrate the region better into national society.

In the 1960s and 1970s, the Amazon was thought to have great potential that warranted massive investments, from both national governments and international agencies (Hurrell 1990). Enormous investments were made to upgrade transportation, communication, and electrical power networks. New roads would carve avenues to El Dorados long entombed under the mantle of forest.

Although heavy government investments in Amazonia continued in the 1980s, the prevailing attitude of national governments shifted to the idea that the region should start "paying" for itself. The downturn in the global economy during the 1980s and the mounting budget deficits of governments prompted governments to perceive the region more as a fountain of revenue, rather than as a sinkhole for public investments. Attempts were also made to shift more of the burden for development to the private sector, in part because some of the public sector investments, such as in planned settlements, were expensive and sometimes produced disappointing results.

The authoritarian governments that ruled Brazil from 1964 to 1985 laid down bold development strategies for the Brazilian Amazon. The intellectual girders of these development plans were laid by several military strategists associated with the military academy (Escola Superior da Guerra), particularly the now-deceased General Golbery Couto e Silva. Civilian scholars and scientists were also involved in rationalizing development plans, such as the economists Delfim Neto and Mário Henrique Simonsen. Gifted civilian technocrats were thus a critical part of the "revolutionary" governments and often occupied key administrative posts.

The "revolutionary" military governments that steered Brazil for 21 years have been blamed for much of the rampant destruction in Amazonia (Bunker 1985; Hecht and Cockburn 1989). The World Bank has also been criticized for funding portions of the Polonoroeste project, which included asphalting the Cuiabá–Porto Velho Highway through Rondônia.

The process of incorporating Amazonia into the respective national orbits would have occurred without SUDAM-approved projects, government settlement schemes, or loans from multilateral development banks. The building of roads into Amazonia was inevitable. Before the road to Brasília was opened in 1960, Belém could be reached only by air or by sea. Even asphalting highways does not necessarily speed up settlement; rather, all-weather roads increase land values and farmers may be more inclined to invest in more intensive farming methods.

No single political ideology or belief system can be "blamed" for the environmental changes under way in Amazonia. Indeed, democracy in Brazil is bringing its own threats to the environment, with increasing pressure to open up the forest to settlement and development (Foresta 1991: 257). Several governments with different organizational structures and ideologies have been involved in the region over the past few decades. All have sponsored development and settlement schemes in the region. Only Venezuela and Colombia have been relatively cautious about opening up their Amazonian territories, but then they occupy comparatively small segments of the region. Trends towards cattle-ranching, increased gold mining, petroleum exploration, and deforestation are common to all countries with stakes in Amazonia (Barbira-Scazzocchio 1980; Hemming 1985a,b; Hiraoka and Yamamoto 1980; Moran 1981; Schmink and Wood 1984).

The notion that authoritarian governments are more damaging to Amazonia than democratic regimes does not hold water. In Peru, the democratically elected government under Alan García, who held office until 1990, did not stem widespread deforestation in western Amazonia. Brazil has had democratic governments since the late 1980s and development pressures on Amazonia continue.

A development ethic, suffusing particularly authoritarian governments and financial institutions, is sometimes thought to be responsible for the ravages of Amazonia. If only governments in Amazonia would turn away from economic growth models, it is sometimes argued, the environmental balance would be restored and prosperity would ensue. Although there is room for debate about the merits of different development strategies, natural resources in the region will continue to be tapped.

The idea that forest-clearing in the region must be halted at all costs is unrealistic. To many Brazilians, at least, the connection between halting deforestation and national well-being is unclear. Most of Haiti is deforested and it is one of the poorest countries in the hemisphere, but over 90 per cent of Western Europe's forests have been cleared, yet inhabitants of that region enjoy some of the highest standards of living in the world. A similar situation prevails in Japan, an economic superpower. Developing countries with the fastest economic growth rates are along the Pacific Rim, and much of their forests have been or are being destroyed. We will make the case for conserving forests and other environments in Amazonia, but it is tied to economic development and improved standards of living.

Many government organizations involved in development now recognize the importance of the environmental impacts of projects they promote. Recent publications of the regional development agency for the Brazilian Amazon, SUDAM, underscore the importance of conserving the environment and the ecological sustainability of economic activities (SUDAM 1990). At a May 1989 meeting of the Amazon Pact countries in Manaus, the heads of state of Bolivia, Brazil, Colombia, Ecuador, Guyana, Peru, Suriname, and Venezuela endorsed the need to use and protect natural and cultural resources, and highlighted the value of maintaining biodiversity.

Although some might argue that utterances from political leaders and development agencies may amount to little more than lip-service, there is a genuine concern about the ecological and social dimensions to Amazonian development among a broad range of government and development agencies. How much of this concern is likely to be translated into concrete action is debatable, but a change in values and attitudes is always a precursor to policy shifts.

Some indicators that the "green" positions adopted by politicians and development agencies are more than mere window-dressing include evidence of changes in priorities for research and development in the region. Several regional research institutions, such as those belonging to the Brazilian agricultural research system (EMBRAPA), the Museu Goeldi and the Federal University of Pará in Belém, and the National Institute for Amazonian Research (INPA – Instituto Nacional de Pesquisas da Amazônia) in Manaus all have mission statements or strategic plans that focus explicitly on sustainable development and a better understanding of natural resources. Various international organizations, such as the Food and Agriculture Organization (FAO) in Rome and CIAT (Centro Internacional de Agricultura Tropical), based in Cali, Colombia, have been approached by regional research and development bodies for guidance and technical assistance in sustainable agriculture (FAO 1990).

61

Income and wealth issues

The mounting foreign debt of developing nations is sometimes depicted as one of the "root causes" of tropical deforestation (Bramble 1987; Gradwohl and Greenberg 1988: 45; OTA 1992: 6; Serrão and Homma 1993; Spitler 1987). Many developing countries, it is suggested, have plundered natural resources to help pay off bank loans. Recent governments in Brazil have been accused of exploiting the Amazon rain forest to solve foreign exchange problems (Moran 1988a). Some political leaders complain that debt repayment obligations force countries to overexploit natural resources in order to generate foreign exchange (Wood 1990). But the linkage between foreign debt and accelerated environmental degradation has not been clearly established, particularly for the Amazon region (Rudel 1989; Sanderson 1992: 93; Shilling 1992). Amazonia accounts for only 5 per cent of Brazil's GNP, and Brazilian exports are increasingly dominated by manufactured goods (Hurrell 1990).

Although banks in developed countries and multinational corporations are sometimes cast as the "villains" with regard to Amazonia, investments from southern Brazil are much more significant than international capital. The dominant drive to develop the Brazilian Amazon is internal (Hurrell 1990). It is true that some Amazonian resources are directly linked to the export trade, such as iron ore from Serra dos Carajás and pulp from the Jari plantations, but domestic investment from the industrial heartland of Brazil is a major factor in many development schemes. Companies headquartered in São Paulo have much greater investment exposure in Amazonia than the World Bank or private banks in the United States, Europe, or Japan.

Investments in Amazonia from São Paulo can be envisaged as a means to redistribute some of the wealth accumulated in the nerve-centre of Brazilian business. To others, the great disparity of wealth between São Paulo, with its diverse agricultural and industrial base, and relatively undeveloped Amazonia contributes to the latter's demise. São Paulo is seen as exporting pollution to Amazonia and exploiting its resources with little long-term benefit to the region.

Given that forces of change in Amazonia, ranging from population growth, institutional and socio-economic factors, to questions of attitudes and distribution of wealth, are likely to remain essentially the same for the foreseeable future, we concentrate on ways to promote the sustainable use of forests, plantations, and agricultural lands. This is not to deny the validity of efforts to change the driving forces, but rather an attempt to display options for development that can be used by societies guided by a variety of principles and forms of government. Attempts to address driving forces should go hand-in-hand with efforts to harness natural resources in a rational manner.

A central theme is the need to uncover and promote sustainable systems that generate a cash surplus to provide rural peoples and companies with more options and greater flexibility to grasp opportunities and adapt to change. Also, viable farms, ranches, plantations, and carefully managed forests are likely to relieve pressure on the remaining wilderness.

Our approach recognizes that there are many models for agricultural development in Amazonia, ranging from small-scale farms, to communally operated forest reserves, to ranches and large plantations. The role of managed forests in regional development is also discussed. The importance of developing and sustaining linkages to markets is underscored, whether we are dealing with individual farmers, cooperatives, or giant corporations. A mosaic of land uses is called for involving small- to large-scale operators.

Societal responses

Strategies for sustainable agricultural development and forest management are discussed in more detail in later chapters. An attempt will be made to identify responses by decision-makers in Amazonia, ranging from small to large holders, to raise and sustain yields. In the next chapter, we discuss efforts to set aside parks and reserves in Amazonia. Here we focus on the growing awareness of environmental issues in Amazonia, particularly at the regional and national levels. Although increased awareness alone will not solve the environmental and social problems facing the region, the open debate about the causes of change and appropriate responses is healthy and will help clarify issues and goad concrete responses.

The role of the media in increasing awareness of environmental issues

In Brazil, media coverage of environmental and social problems in Amazonia began well before the transition to democracy in the mid-1980s, but increased markedly after 1985. Coverage of environmental issues reached almost blitz proportions up to and during the UNCED meetings in Rio in June 1992. A parallel increase in reporting on environmental and political issues related to Amazonian development also occurred in the influential *New York Times* (Cohen 1990). Although press censorship has operated to varying degrees in several of the governments with territory in Amazonia, a surprising amount of reporting on environmental and social issues has surfaced. Today, the press is essentially free in all governments operating in the region.

The military governments of Brazil supported the penetration of television into the far corners of the country as a strategy of national integration. Most inhabitants in the region have had access to radios for many decades, but many small towns in the Brazilian Amazon now receive at least one television station. Television and radio coverage of environmental issues is critical in stirring public consciousness about such issues as pollution and loss of biodiversity.

Although impressive strides have been made to improve literacy rates in Brazil, approximately one-third of the population over five years old still cannot read (IBGE 1989: 197). Television and radio are thus important media for disseminating information. Discussion of Amazonian development and conservation issues, ranging from the climatic impacts of deforestation to social conflicts over land use, is frequent on Brazilian television and radio. The airwaves have thus opened the eyes of many rural peoples in the region.

The growing influence of NGOs

Another response to the perceived need to tackle environmental and social problems in Amazonia is the striking growth in the number of non-governmental organizations (NGOs) operating in the region. At least 1,000 NGOs are currently operating in Brazil, and many of them focus on environmental concerns (Homma 1992a; Landim 1988).[1] This blossoming of NGOs seems to be a global trend; tens of thousands of grass-roots environmental groups have sprung up to raise public awareness of ecological problems and to press for policy changes (Brown 1991).

About three-quarters of the NGOs in Brazil arose in the 1980s in response to increasing awareness at various levels of society about contentious development and environmental issues. A sense emerged in many quarters that prevailing models of economic development were not adequately addressing social equity or sustainability issues, and that more "extra-official" channels were needed for development assistance (Montecinos and Altieri 1991).

Many NGOs have targeted international media and organizations, as well as state, local, and federal governments. The primary mission of many NGOs is to promote the cause of disenfranchised groups, such as Indians, rubber tappers, and women, but they have skilfully "piggybacked" their agendas on the global preoccupation with the environment. Some groups advocating the rights of rubber tappers and Indians have seized the growing concern about the environmental impacts of development in Amazonia as an opportunity to strengthen their hands and obtain greater media coverage and leverage with government and donor agencies.

Indigenous rights groups, such as UNI (União das Nações Indígenas), and organizations attempting to galvanize rubber tappers, such as the National Council of Rubber Tappers (Conselho Nacional dos Seringueiros), have lobbied aggressively for land rights and for the defence of nature in Amazonia. The Institute for Amazon Studies (Instituto de Estudos Amazonicos), headquartered in Curitiba in southern Brazil, has coordinated efforts to pressure authorities in Brazil to safeguard rubber groves against outside developers. Many other organizations have sprung up in Amazonia to promote the cause of disenfranchised groups and to promote "sustainable development" and conservation. Some of these groups have received support from foreign donors, such as bilateral aid agencies and foundations and international NGOs based in the United States and Europe (Revkin 1990).

Although some NGOs are jockeying for position as saviours of the forest, particularly in the eyes of the media, this confluence of environmental and social concerns might turn out to be an ephemeral marriage of convenience. NGOs promoting the cause of disenfranchised groups have mixed agendas, and environmental concerns may well be peripheral in some instances.

An often-overlooked aspect of NGOs promoting the cause of indigenous groups and peasants is that they may misrepresent the needs and aspirations of their "clients." With little experience in dealing with the varied cultures of Amazonia, NGOs may insert their own agendas, rather than attend to the real needs of the people they are supposed to help. Insertion of key words such as "grass roots" in their work does not ensure that NGOs have correctly diagnosed problems, let alone drawn up appropriate plans of action.

Recent experiences with indigenous groups in contact with national society illustrate some of the disparities between expected behaviour and reality. Some of the Kayapó have profited from illegal timber sales on their land. The Surui and Cinta Larga of south-western Amazonia are avid sellers of timber from their reserves (Brooke 1991). Gold miners have invaded the Yanomamo reserve in Roraima. In view of the cultural and ecological damage that ensued, the Brazilian government has taken steps to expel miners and relocate them to other parts of Roraima. But at least some Yanomamo Indians have opposed the forced removal of miners from their lands, claiming they want to learn from the miners and extract some gold themselves.

The market for NGOs in Brazil and many other developing regions is getting crowded. Attrition is sure to trim the number of NGOs operating in the future. Major donors and development banks are likely to look more closely at the effectiveness of NGOs with which they may have been collaborating. To some degree, NGOs are catering to the agendas of donors, which may shift. Some development agencies may eventually bypass NGOs and attempt to work directly with community leaders or growers' associations. Although some NGOs have solid track records and will continue to play valuable roles in promoting equitable development and conservation, others will succumb to dwindling support.

Efforts to tackle mercury contamination

Mercury pollution from gold mining is probably one of the hardest ecological problems to tackle in the region. With hundreds of thousands of fortune-seekers operating over such a vast territory, any effort to minimize the use of mercury would be extremely difficult. The larger operators working from barges are more visible, and thus easier to control. In the early 1990s, the government of Rondônia prohibited the approximately 300 gold-mining barges from operating along a 200 km stretch of the Madeira River near Porto Velho (Brooke 1991). Mercury is imported to Brazil for the dental trade; even if restrictions were imposed on the amounts of mercury allowed in, Brazil's porous borders with neighbouring countries would soon ensure a clandestine trade.

Efforts are under way to improve the recovery rate of mercury using simple field techniques. For the time being, though, the price of gold will largely determine how much mercury finds its way into Amazonian food chains.

Debt-for-nature swaps

Until recently, the Brazilian government rejected the notion of debt-for-nature swaps on the grounds that such deals would compromise its sovereignty. In 1991, however, the federal government decided to authorize the conversion of US$100 million of the US$123 billion external debt for environmental projects. These debt-for-nature dollars will be used mainly to demarcate national parks and reserves and to compensate landowners or settlers in protected areas for leaving their claims. Although effective protection and management of reserves and parks in Brazil will cost an estimated US$2 billion, the relinquished funds will certainly help.

Resources liberated by this debt-for-nature swap will be administered as a "patrimonial fund" under the federal government's control. This adroit move allows the Brazilian government to avoid relinquishing any of its sovereignty while reducing, albeit slightly, its debt burden. At the same time, sizeable grants will be available for certain worthwhile environmental causes, and the government achieves a public relations coup at virtually no cost.

Deforestation rates

Many of the environmental issues related to development in Amazonia hinge on the scale and rates of deforestation. A spurt in forest removal occurred from the late 1960s to the mid-1980s, associated in part with the opening of pioneer highways and investments in cattle-raising (Malingreau and Tucker 1988). A surge in deforestation in 1987 in the Brazilian Amazon has been linked to the formulation of Brazil's new constitution, passed in 1988, which called for expropriation of unproductive land (Nepstad, Uhl, and Serrão 1991). Landowners' fears that unoccupied land might be confiscated are thought to have triggered a clearing frenzy (Revkin 1990: 180). This widespread effort to "tame" Amazonia's wilderness and to integrate the region into the national economy, which was particularly noticeable in Brazil, stirred concern about the future of the forest and raised the spectre of deleterious regional and global environmental change.

Considerable controversy has characterized the debate about deforestation rates in Amazonia (Bonalume 1989a). Different definitions of forest, the difficulty of separating advanced second growth from forest, and whether one considers temporary or permanent forest removal in the equation have contributed to different scenarios and conclusions about the dangers of deforestation. Some groups may have exaggerated deforestation rates to further conservation aims, while others may have downplayed figures in order to encourage further development of the region. The claim that 8 million ha of forest were cleared in the Brazilian Amazon in 1987 alone is now being challenged (Monastersky 1993).

No attempt will be made here to sort out all the claims and counterclaims as to how much of the Amazonian forest has been truly "lost." Three main points are worth emphasizing here: the notion of virgin Amazonian forests is a myth anyway; considerable areas of Amazonia are still in mature forest, particularly in western and northern parts of the basin; and deforestation rates appear to be declining.

The decline in deforestation appears to be real, rather than an artefact of manipulating remote sensing data, or of changes in the definition of forest (Bonalume 1989b, 1991). Deforestation slowed in Rondônia, an acknowledged "hot spot" for forest destruction, after 1985 (Fearnside 1989a). Satellite imagery reveals an approximate 27 per cent drop in deforestation rates in the Brazilian Amazon from 1989 to 1990 alone. In 1989, an estimated 2.1 million ha of forest were cleared in the Brazilian Amazon, dropping to 1.4 million ha in 1990 (Alcantara 1991). According to Brazil's remote sensing institute (INPE – Instituto Nacional de Pesquisas Espaciais), deforestation in the Amazon dipped further to 1.4 million ha in 1991, and unofficially to 0.9 million ha in 1992.

The precise causes of this slowdown are unclear, but several factors were probably involved, including the severe recession that gripped Brazil in the late 1980s and early 1990s; the blocking of substantial portions of savings accounts by President Collor in 1990; and the desire of farmers and ranchers to put second growth back into production or to upgrade weed-choked pastures.

Forests have waxed and waned in the face of economic cycles in other regions, such as the Mediterranean (Westoby 1989: 64). Farmers and ranchers in the Altamira area of the Transamazon Highway, for example, are cutting more second growth than forest; a similar pattern prevails among middle-scale ranchers in the Paragominas area. The burning season in Rondônia also focuses more on scrub that has grown up in pasture and on the second growth that soon envelops abandoned fields, rather than on mature forest (Brooke 1991). Second growth is increasingly cut because, as a colonization zone matures, regrowth becomes more common and accessible than mature forest.

Increased pressure to protect parks and reserves and to enforce environmental regulations in Amazonia has probably had negligible impact. The notion that the removal of fiscal incentives for cattle-ranching in the Brazilian Amazon has slowed deforestation is implausible.

The implications of the recession being a major factor in the slow-down in forest destruction, if correct, are worrisome. When the economy resumes growth on any significant scale, deforestation rates could pick up again. Only by adequately addressing the need for a broad-based raising of economic living standards in the region, coupled with a more systematic approach to environmental protection, will ecological problems in the region be alleviated.

Unless alternatives to deforestation are offered, any widespread effort to halt forest-clearing could lead to lowered food production and more unemployment. Because of the depletion of soil nutrients, weed invasion, and the build-up of pests and diseases, many farmers periodically clear new fields from forest. Farming methods that minimize forest-clearing, such as agro-forestry, thus need to be developed and promoted for various soil and other environmental conditions.

Note

1. *Grassroots Development* 14/1 (1990), p. 56; *Jornal do Brasil*, Rio de Janeiro, 5 May 1991, p. 19.

4

Forest conservation and management

Parks and preserves

A large number of parks, national forests, biological preserves, and Indian reserves have been created in Amazonia. In the Brazilian Amazon alone, 37 million ha are embraced in parks, reserves, and national forests (table 4.1). In addition, Rondônia has 5.5 million ha in various categories of state and municipal conservation units, including state forest reserves. Acre has set aside the 66,000 ha Antimari state forest reserve, among other conservation areas.

Over 16 million ha have been designated as national parks or biological reserves in the Amazonian portions of Bolivia, Colombia, Ecuador, Peru, and Venezuela (table 4.2). Of the 38 million ha in the Colombian Amazon, 22.5 million ha are designated as parks or Indian reserves (Bunyard 1989). The 70,000 Indians living in the Colombian Amazon have been decreed 18 million ha. Colombia is thus highly unusual in that 41 per cent of its Amazonian region is set aside from conventional development. More parks and reserves are planned for various parts of the Amazon basin.

Indian reserves

Indigenous reserves are extensive, and more are likely to be created. In July 1991, the Venezuelan government decreed an 8 million ha reserve for the Yanomamo, and the Brazilian government followed suit in November by creating a 9 million ha reserve for the widely scattered group in Roraima. Because people already live in them,

Table 4.1 **National parks, national forests, biological reserves, and ecological stations in the Brazilian Amazon with at least 10,000 ha**

Park/reserve	Category	State	Year created	Area (ha)
Roraima	National forest	Roraima	1989	2,664,685
Jaú	National park	Amazonas	1980	2,272,000
Pico da Neblina	National park	Amazonas	1979	2,200,000
Gorotire	Forest/resource reserve	Pará	1961	1,843,000
Serra do Araça	State park	Amazonas	1990	1,818,700
Tucumaque	Forest/resource reserve	Pará	1961	1,793,000
Parima	Forest/resource reserve	Roraima	1961	1,756,000
Amazonas	National forest	Amazonas	1989	1,573,100
Mundurucania	Forest/resource reserve	Pará	1961	1,377,000
Mamirauá	Ecological station	Amazonas	1990	1,124,000
Tefé	National forest	Amazonas	1989	1,020,000
Amazônia	National park	Amazonas/Pará	1974	993,500
Pacaás Novos	National park	Rondônia	1979	764,801
Taracua I	National forest	Amazonas	1990	674,400
Pari Cachoeira II	National forest	Amazonas	1989	654,000
Cabo Orange	National park	Amapá	1980	619,000
Piraiauara	National forest	Amazonas	1990	615,000
Serra do Divisor	National park	Acre	1989	605,000
Guaporé	Biological reserve	Rondônia	1982	600,000
Tapajós	National forest	Pará	1974	600,000
Rio Corumbiara	State park	Rondônia	1992	586,031
Araguaia	National park	Tocantins	1959	562,312
Uatumã	Biological reserve	Amazonas	1990	560,000
Taracua II	National forest	Amazonas	1990	559,504
Tarauacu II	National forest	Amazonas	1990	551,504
Içana-aiari	National forest	Amazonas	1990	491,300
Saracataquera	National forest	Pará	1989	429,600
Cubate	National forest	Amazonas	1990	416,532
Amapá	National forest	Amapá	1989	412,000
Xie	National forest	Amazonas	1990	400,000
Lago Piratuba	Biological reserve	Amapá	1980	395,000
Caracaraí	Ecological station	Roraima	1982	394,560
Trombetas	Biological reserve	Pará	1979	385,000
Anavilhanas	Ecological station	Amazonas	1981	350,000
Gurupi	Biological reserve	Maranhão/Pará	1988	341,650
Mapia	National forest	Acre	1989	311,000
Jutaí-Solimões	Ecological/biological reserve	Amazonas	1983	288,187
Abufari	Biological reserve	Amazonas	1982	288,000
Niquia	Ecological station	Roraima	1985	286,600
Inauini-Teuini	National forest	Amazonas	1988	285,000
Bom Futuro	National forest	Rondônia	1988	280,000
Jarú	Biological reserve	Rondônia	1979	268,150

Table 4.1   (cont.)

Park/reserve	Category	State	Year created	Area (ha)
Guajará-Mirim	State park	Rondônia	1992	258,813
Purus	National forest	Amazonas	1988	256,000
Jari	Ecological station	Amapá/Pará	1982	227,126
Jamari	National forest	Rondônia	1984	215,000
Iquê	Ecological station	Mato Grosso	1981	200,000
Caxiuanã	National forest	Pará	1961	200,000
Içana	National forest	Amazonas	1990	195,000
Tapirapé/Aquiri	National forest	Pará	1989	190,000
Macauã	National forest	Acre	1988	173,475
Juami-Japurá	Ecological/biological reserve	Amazonas	1983	173,200
Monte Roraima	National park	Roraima	1989	116,000
Cuiari	National forest	Amazonas	1990	109,000
Sauim Castanheiras	Ecological/biological reserve	Amazonas	1982	109,000
Cuniã	Ecological station	Rondônia	1986	104,000
Tapirapé	Biological reserve	Pará	1989	103,000
Maracá	Ecological station	Roraima	1981	101,312
Serra dos Tres Irmãos	Ecological station	Rondônia		98,813
Urucu	National forest	Amazonas	1990	96,000
Rio Acre	Ecological station	Acre	1981	77,500
Maracá-Jipioca	Ecological station	Amapá	1981	72,000
Rio Ouro Preto	Ecological/biological reserve	Rondônia	1992	46,438
Serra dos Araras	Ecological station	Mato Grosso	1982	28,700
Nhamundá	State park	Amazonas	1989	28,370
Tracadal	Ecological/biological reserve	Rondônia	1992	22,540
Samuel	Ecological station	Rondônia	1989	20,865
Pari Cachoeira I	National forest	Amazonas	1989	18,000
Taiamã	Ecological station	Mato Grosso	1981	14,325
Reserva Ducke	Biological reserve	Amazonas	1963	10,072
TOTAL				37,673,665

Sources: Anderson (1987); Álvares-Afonso (1992); Aline da Rin P. Azevedo (pers. comm., 14 August 1992); Companhia Vale do Rio Doce, Carajás; Eden (1990: 200); Gradwohl and Greenberg (1988); IBDF (1982); Secretaria do Meio-Ambiente (SEMA; now merged with IBDF to form IBAMA), Brasília; Instituto Brasileiro do Meio Ambiente e dos Recursos Naturais Renováveis (IBAMA), Brasília; Map of *Áreas de Proteção Ambiental Acre, 1991*, Governo do Estado, Secretaria de Meio Ambiente.

Table 4.2 **National parks and biological reserves in the Amazon region of Colombia, Ecuador, and Peru**

Park/reserve	Category	Location	Area (ha)
Cahuinari	National park	Colombia	575,000
El Tuparro	Biological reserve	Colombia	290,000
Amacayacu	National park	Colombia	170,000
Yasuní	National park	Ecuador	678,000
Cuyabeno	Biological reserve	Ecuador	254,760
Limoncocha	Biological reserve	Ecuador	5,261
Manu	National park	Peru	1,532,806
Pacaya-Samiria	Biological reserve	Peru	1,388,000
Tingo Maria	National park	Peru	18,000
Canaima	National park	Venezuela	3,000,000
Serranía la Neblina	National park	Venezuela	1,360,000
Yapacana	National park	Venezuela	320,000
Duida-Marahuaca	National park	Venezuela	210,000
Jaua-Sarisarinama	National park	Venezuela	330,000
Manuripi	Biological reserve	Bolivia	1,844,375
Bella Vista	National park	Bolivia	90,000
Isoboro Secure	National park	Bolivia	1,100,000
Ulla Ulla	Biological reserve	Bolivia	240,000
Huanchaca	National park	Bolivia	541,000
Beni/Chimane	Biosphere reserve	Bolivia	1,633,000
Isiboro-Sécure	National park	Bolivia	1,233,000
TOTAL			16,813,202

Sources: Aline da Rin P. Azevedo (pers. comm., 14 August 1992); Eden (1990: 200); Foresta (1991: 25); Gradwohl and Greenberg (1988); Renner, Balslev, and Holm-Nielsen (1990).

Indian reserves are less prone to illegal incursions than are nominally protected parks and biological reserves. Still, they are not immune to invasions by gold seekers, farmers, and loggers. By the mid-1980s, most of Brazil's indigenous reserves had been invaded (Foresta 1991: 184).

Indigenous peoples cannot always be expected to treat the forest in ways that can be considered harmonious with its long-term survival. As native people become increasingly integrated with national societies, some of them will forge new economic relationships, with potentially drastic consequences for the forest. Some Kaiapó leaders, for example, are profiting handsomely from the lumber trade in their 3.2 million ha reserve, and now own brick homes, cars, and aircraft.[1] Between 1989 and 1991, the Kaiapó sold at least US$43 million worth of timber. Logging on Kaiapó land is mostly conducted by outside crews, and no credible claims to its sustainability are being made. Some indigenous communities are also raising cattle and participating in the gold rush. To argue that indigenous peoples should not be free to emulate economic activities around them would deny them the right to control their futures.

The private sector and conservation

In spite of the growing momentum to set aside parks and reserves in Amazonia, such efforts alone are unlikely to save much of the remaining forest. Only the military or private landholders are currently capable of effectively policing large tracts of forest in the region. Respect for military muscle in conservation matters in developing countries is tacitly recognized in Guatemala, where some army conscripts spend the first few months of their service as armed guards in national parks.

Legislation alone is unlikely to safeguard Amazonian forests. First, most reserves and parks in Amazonia have been invaded by loggers, miners, cattle ranchers, or squatters. This holds true for most parks and reserves in developing regions, such as in South-East Asia (Brookfield, Potter, and Byron 1995). Enforcement of park and reserve boundaries is difficult given the vast areas and limited manpower. Colombia's Indian reserves appear to be less affected by such illegal incursions, but development pressures are less pronounced in the Colombian Amazon.

Second, no agreement has emerged among biologists about priority areas for conservation. Earlier efforts to use the refugia theory to pinpoint areas of high biological diversity are increasingly disputed (Sternberg 1982). Some of the proposed refugia may have been too cold to support rain forest during Pleistocene glacial periods (Colinvaux 1987, 1989; Liu and Colinvaux 1985). Also the locations of at least some of the proposed Pleistocene refugia may be artefacts of collecting efforts (Nelson et al. 1990). Some progress towards a consensus on high-priority areas for conservation has been made, but more information is needed about patterns of diversity and palaeoecology in Amazonia (Prance 1990). Compromises will have to be made between a desire to conserve unique ecosystems and the need to develop resources.

Third, although the total area of existing parks and reserves is impressive, it represents only a minute portion of the Amazon basin. What happens outside such preserved areas will be critical to their survival. The more productive and sustainable the farms, ranches, and plantations are outside parks and reserves, the greater their chances for survival.

In the short term at least, the private sector will do a better job of saving substantial tracts of Amazonia's forests from the axe and power saw. The Jari operation has been accused of promoting massive deforestation (Nigh and Nations 1980), but 90 per cent of Jari's 1.6 million ha is slated to remain in forest. The consortium of companies that operates Jari allows miners to use the airport at Monte Dourado, but does not permit mining, hunting, or logging on its property. Regular jaguar sightings at Jari are one indication that the forest is left relatively intact.

At Carajás, Companhia Vale do Rio Doce (CVRD) has a 411,000 ha concession to exploit minerals. Adjacent to CVRD's area, the Xikrin Indian reserve occupies 439,000 ha (fig. 4.1). The 190,000 ha Tapirapé/Aquiri national forest straddles part of the northern borders of CVRD's area and the Xikrin reserve. Adjacent to this national forest, which has been set up for sustainable forestry, is the 103,000 ha Tapirapé biological reserve. Finally, a buffer zone of forest has been designated along the northern margin of CVRD's area. This

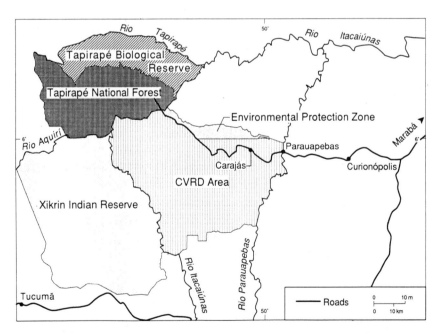

Fig. 4.1 **Protected areas in the vicinity of Carajás, Pará**

buffer zone, known as an environmental protection area, encompasses 21,600 ha and is rich in Brazil nut trees, among other valuable forest resources.

The Xikrin reserve is under the aegis of the Indian service (FUNAI – Fundação Nacional do Indio), and the border with CVRD's area will afford it some protection. The environmental protection area, the Tapirapé biological reserve, and the Tapirapé/Aquiri national reserve are under the jurisdiction of the Brazilian agency for the environment and renewable natural resources (IBAMA – Instituto Brasileiro do Meio Ambiente e dos Recursos Naturais Renováveis). IBAMA lacks the manpower to oversee these reserves, so CVRD has been given the authority by the federal government (decrees 97.718, 97.719, and 97.720) to administer the properties jointly. CVRD's armed guards, backed by helicopters, speedboats, and vehicles, readily detect and expel intruders. The total area thus protected is 1,164,600 ha.

In the long term, the task of properly administering parks and reserves rests with competent government agencies. But even in developed countries, such as the United States, only a small fraction of the national territory is in parks and other protected areas. Also, safeguarding such areas is a daunting task even for countries with relatively abundant resources. National parks in the United States pose a wide range of management problems, including control of poaching. How long it will take for governments with territories in Amazonia to install sufficient park guards in the region is difficult to tell. Unless a substantial infusion of funds arrives from international donors specifically for protecting reserves and parks, other pressing demands on scarce budgetary resources are likely to preclude efficient parks services in the region for some time to come.

What, then, are the options for conserving substantial areas of Amazonia? First, scientists and administrators need to be honest about the benefits of conserving forests versus more immediate needs to provide access to land and other resources. One can point to a wide range of environmental services provided by forests and suggest potential uses, but such arguments often crumble in the face of development pressures. Efforts can be made to try and make forests "pay" for themselves, such as by creating extractive reserves, but such models are often fraught with shaky economic assumptions, or fail to take into account social and cultural needs.

The best hope for conservation in the long run is to raise living conditions in the region, in both rural and urban areas. More employment opportunities need to be created in towns and cities to absorb the rural exodus that is likely to continue even with land reform. If farms, ranches, plantations, and extractive reserves can be made more productive while minimizing damage to the environment, then people living in Amazonia are more likely set aside and safeguard large areas of the world's largest remaining forest wilderness for future generations.

Extractive reserves

The main idea behind extractive reserves is that local communities own and control the harvesting of forest products. An attractive feature of this form of land use is that, in theory at least, much of the forest cover remains while people live in the area. Rather than fence people away from the forest, extractive reserves are supposed to permit people to manage the forest without destroying it.

The push to set up extractive reserves in Amazonia began in Acre, Brazil, in the mid-1980s under the leadership of Chico Mendes, a rubber tapper and community organizer. Mendes was attempting to galvanize rubber tappers to defend the forest against encroaching development, particularly cattle ranches, until he was shot in his backyard in December 1988. The murder of Chico Mendes catapulted the issue of extractive reserves to the forefront of the discussion of development policies for Amazonia, both within Brazil and abroad.[2]

Environmental and labour groups coalesced around the charismatic figure of Chico Mendes. As a result of domestic and international pressure, the Brazilian government has created 12 extractive reserves covering over 3 million ha (table 4.3). The Chico Mendes Reserve, located at Xapuri, Acre, is the largest created thus far, with close to 1 million ha. The extractive reserves created in 1989 (Decreto Lei 7.804) fall under the jurisdiction of the federal land reform agency INCRA (Instituto Nacional de Colonização e Reforma Agraria). On 14 March 1990, more extractive reserves were created by order of President Sarney during his last day in office, this time under the auspices of IBAMA. Two government agencies with sometimes conflicting agendas are thus charged with overseeing extractive reserves: one traditionally engaged in opening up forest for settlement, the other preoccupied with trying to protect forests and their biological resources. So much external pressure has been applied on the Brazilian government to set up extractive reserves that the rubber

Table 4.3 **Extractive reserves in the Brazilian Amazon**

Extractive reserve	Location	Year created	Area (ha)	No. of families
Chico Mendes	Acre	1990	976,570	7,500
Alto Juruá	Acre	1990	506,186	500
Rio Cajari	Amapá	1990	481,560	5,000
Antimari	Amazonas	1989	260,227	867
Maracá III	Amapá	1989	226,500	760
Rio Ouro Preto	Rondônia	1990	204,583	3,410
Terruã	Amazonas	1989	139,295	426
Maracá I	Amapá	1989	75,000	214
Santa Quitéria	Acre	1988	43,247	150
São Luis do Remanso	Acre	1989	39,752	130
Riozinho	Acre	1989	35,896	32
Figueira	Acre	1987	25,973	380
Cachoeira	Acre	1989	24,973	80
Maracá II	Amapá	1989	22,500	94
Porto Dias	Acre	1989	22,145	83
TOTALS			3,084,407	19,626

Source: Rodrigues (1991); Map of *Áreas de Proteção Ambiental Acre, 1991*, Governo do Estado, Secretaria de Meio Ambiente.

tappers' movement has been accused of trying to "internationalize" the Amazon region (Souza 1990: 21).

The rubber tappers' movement was envisaged as a dual-purpose cause to improve regional living conditions for some 55,000 tappers and to preserve the forest (Allegretti 1989). Although Mendes has been referred to as an ecologist and portrayed as a saviour of Amazonian nature in the press (Bendix and Liebler 1991; Podesta 1993), it should be remembered that his struggle was primarily for the social rights of a poor and relatively disenfranchised group of people. The "green" aspect to his crusade is largely an artefact of diverse international and national groups who have skilfully exploited the drama of Chico Mendes' life and martyrdom as a way to further their goals.

Although the notion of extractive reserves has some appealing aspects, claims that extractive reserves can compete with other land-use options in Amazonia may be premature (Gradwohl and Greenberg 1988: 150; Revkin 1990: 219). The claim that 1 ha of forest near the village of Mishana on the Nanay River in the Peruvian Amazon has a net present value of US$6,330 for non-timber forest products has generated considerable discussion in the environmental and development communities (Peters, Gentry, and Mendelsohn 1989). Fruits and nuts alone can purportedly generate almost US$650/ha each year from the Mishana site. Such provocative findings should not be taken as indicative of the current economic value of forest throughout the basin. The Mishana study suggests that sustainable exploitation of non-timber products from rain forests could produce three times the income derived from converting the forest to other uses, such as agriculture.

The ecological heterogeneity of Amazonia makes it difficult to extrapolate findings from one area to another. In some forested areas, unusual concentrations of economic species, such as the buriti palm (*Mauritia flexuosa*) near Iquitos (Padoch 1988), or the açaí palm (*Euterpe oleracea*) in the Amazon estuary, provide substantial food and income for riverside dwellers. In the Marabá area, cupuaçu (*Theobroma grandiflorum*) and Brazil nut are relatively common in the forest and are frequently collected by locals, whereas in the vicinity of Paragominas, some 250 km to the north-east, neither species occurs; instead, bacuri (*Platonia insignis*), uxi (*Endopleura uchi*), bacaba (*Oenocarpus distichus*), inajá (*Maximiliana maripa*), piquiá (*Caryocar villosum*), and cupuí (*Theobroma speciosum*) are the main species collected from the forest, but only for home consumption. It is doubtful that most patches of Amazon rain forest could generate three times as much income from harvesting of wild products as from alternative uses; if that were so, then forests would surely be less threatened.

The economics of extractive reserves needs further work. The notion that the traditional barter system in rural Amazonia (*aviamento*) is a principal stumbling block to making extractivism more profitable (Allegretti 1992) is simplistic. In the *aviamento* system no money changes hands; rather manufactured goods and foodstuffs are advanced against the future delivery of natural products. Under this arrangement, many individuals remain permanently indebted to their traders. The assumption that the *aviamento* system is the major hindrance to advancing the interest of peasants has led to efforts to help organize inhabitants of extractive reserves so that they process and market their products, thus bypassing existing trading networks.

Although such efforts are a worthy experiment, they will not necessarily ensure prosperity for extractivists, particularly if market prices for their products are low, and significant management problems arise. For all its faults, the *aviamento* system has long provided credit and goods to people who would otherwise be cut off from such

79

assistance. Furthermore, *aviadores* have high operating costs in remote areas (Cleary 1990).

Economic analyses of alternative uses of land must reflect the array of options available to rural people (Pinedo-Vasquez, Zarin, and Jipp 1990). The ability of extractive reserves to wrest rubber tappers from poverty and to safeguard the forest from wanton destruction is by no means assured (Homma 1989a,b; Ryan 1992: 27). Dependence on gathering jungle products alone is unlikely to raise and sustain living conditions for forest inhabitants (Lavelle 1987).

Extractive reserves might be better regarded as supplements to the diet and income of people living in them (Homma 1992b). To raise living standards, communities would have to undertake other activities, such as farming (Benchimol 1992a: 108). In several parts of Amazonia, farmers manage fallows so that they remain productive long after they have been "abandoned." Swidden plots are not always farmed for a few years and then left to second growth. Sometimes they are deliberately planted with various perennials to form polycultural orchards. In other cases, certain spontaneous plants may be encouraged or a few species deliberately planted in among the rapidly encroaching weeds. Whether farmers are managing fallows, planting orchards, or simply leaving fields to regrowth, extractivism is a supplement, rather than a mainstay, to income and subsistence.

The cultivation of crops would mean clearing parts of extractive reserves. For political reasons, the need to raise crops and even cattle in extractive reserves has been resisted (Sawyer 1990). Nevertheless, the inhabitants of some extractive reserves in Acre and Rondônia are clearing land for crops and cattle, even if such practices are not condoned by government agencies, NGOs, and the international donor community.

If the inhabitants of extractive reserves were encouraged to engage in farming practices that minimize damage to the environment, such as agro-forestry, then the reserves might become more economically viable (Anderson 1989). Under current restrictions, a family can clear up to 5 ha for subsistence crops, but no more than 2 per cent of an extractive reserve is supposed to be felled (Fearnside 1989b). With existing limitations on clearing and the raising of cash crops, extractive reserves could condemn their inhabitants to poverty, at least for the foreseeable future.

Signs are already appearing that people living in extractive reserves will not adhere strictly to limitations on clearing. Ironically, some rubber tappers have cleared forest for pasture in extractive reserves within Acre, and there is a growing recognition of the need to raise crops for subsistence and commerce (Homma 1990b). Most rubber tappers would probably prefer to try their hand at a range of income-generating activities rather than spend the rest of their lives making daily rounds of the forest in the pre-dawn darkness to tap rubber trees or gather Brazil nuts. The young are especially eager to seek out other opportunities, particularly in towns and cities. Improving access to education is one of the laudable social goals of extractive reserves, and such opportunities will inevitably help individuals find outside employment and contribute to the evolution of extractive reserves into multiple-use systems.

In the case of extractive reserves in Acre, rubber and Brazil nuts appear to be the main economic products, unlikely candidates to extricate communities to new levels of prosperity. Three-quarters of Brazil's consumption of natural rubber is met by imports from South-East Asia. Rubber tapped from forests cannot compete in the marketplace with rubber derived from plantations in South-East Asia. In 1950, rubber from the forests of Amazonia accounted for virtually all of Brazil's need for the product, but by 1990 latex tapped from wild trees in the North region had dwindled to less than 10 per cent of Brazil's need for the commodity (Alvim 1991).

Until recently, natural rubber produced in Brazil was subsidized at a rate three times the world price for over two decades (Homma 1989a). To prop up domestic production of natural rubber, the Brazilian government exacted a tax on imported rubber. Known as TORMB (Taxa de Organização e Regulamentação do Mercado de Borracha), this tax amounted to a subsidy of close to a US$1 billion over 22 years (Goodyear 1989: 26). But, in March 1990, President Collor started implementing a policy of reducing import tariffs for certain products, including natural rubber. Prices for natural rubber tumbled in Brazil, thereby imperilling the economic viability of extractive reserves in Acre (OTA 1992: 10).

Political pressure is mounting in Brazil to re-impose stiff import fees for natural rubber. Both the private sector involved in plantation rubber in Brazil and organizations promoting rubber tappers have lobbied state and federal governments in Brazil to erect trade barriers for natural rubber coming into the country. A former Minister of the Environment, Fernando Coutinho Jorge, even organized an inter-ministerial commission to coordinate efforts to shore up the price of natural rubber in Brazil.[3] Such measures may bring temporary relief to rubber tappers and some plantation owners in Brazil,

Table 4.4 **Area planted to rubber (*Hevea brasiliensis*) in Brazil, by state, April 1990**

State	Area (ha)
Mato Grosso	52,965
Rondônia	39,967
São Paulo[a]	23,820
Bahia[a]	23,200
Pará	17,687
Amazonas	15,039
Espírito Santo[a]	10,954
Acre	8,996
Maranhão	5,450
Pernambuco[a]	5,220
Paraná[a]	4,670
Minas Gerais[a]	3,608
Mato Grosso do Sul[a]	1,950
Goiás[a]	955
Tocantins	535
Rio de Janeiro[a]	478
Amapá	291
Roraima	25
TOTAL	215,810

Source: Gerência de Heveicultura/Divisão de Silvicultura, Instituto Brasileira do Meio Ambiente e dos Recursos Naturais Renováveis (IBAMA).
a. States where *Microcyclus ulei*, the causal agent of South American leaf blight, has not been recorded.

but the likelihood that natural rubber collected from forests will become a rewarding enterprise seems remote.

Latex tapped from wild trees is losing ground to plantations. Production of rubber from plantations in Brazil surpassed that from the forests of Amazonia in the late 1980s (Alvim 1991; Parfit 1989). The contribution from plantations, particularly in São Paulo and Espírito Santo, is increasing because South American leaf blight, caused by a fungus (*Microcyclus ulei*), is absent in the colder parts of Brazil, and high-yielding, cold-tolerant rubber clones have been selected (table 4.4). Rubber tapping in the forests of Amazonia is on a long, steady decline (Souza 1990: 26).

The virtual collapse of rubber prices in Brazil has propelled Brazil nuts to the forefront of extractive products in reserves in Acre. Just as rubber tappers have come to rely increasingly on Brazil nuts as a source of income and employment, Bolivia has emerged as a major supplier of the product. Historically, Brazil has dominated exports of the nuts, mainly through powerful merchants in Belém and Manaus. Bolivia has emerged as a player in the market because factories in the vicinity of Riberalta are able to sell the product for about a third less than Brazilian suppliers (Holt 1992). Although Bolivian producers do not always undercut Brazilian prices, they nevertheless pose a threat to the economic viability of extractive reserves since increased competition could drive prices down. Also, the European market generally demands a high-quality product, since many of the nuts are covered with chocolate. Quality control problems with Brazil nuts have surfaced in at least some of the extractive reserves in Acre as the rubber tappers attempt to master the art of operating small factories. The cooperative at Xapuri has on occasion been forced to buy Brazil nuts from dealers in Belém to fulfil orders from the United States.

Extractive reserves may not live up to their promise as safe havens for nature, either. Extractive products in the Amazon are generally exploited without regard to their sustainability (Browder 1992). Simply recommending the development of markets for forest products will not guarantee the sustainability of extractive reserves. Many forest plants and animals are highly susceptible to human disturbance and the inhabitants of extractive reserves may well respond to market opportunities by overexploiting forest resources (Bodmer and Ayres 1991; Mori 1992; Redford and Sanderson 1992).

Given hard economic choices, communities living in extractive reserves may opt to cut down substantial tracts of forest for pasture, plantations, or field crops, in spite of restrictions on deforestation. Without proper management, some forest species may be overexploited; boom and bust cycles typify the exploitation of wild plant and animal resources in Amazonia. Also, hunting for meat could reduce seed dispersal agents, such as monkeys, leading to local reduction or even extinction for some tree species (Janzen 1970; Redford 1992). Agoutis (*Dasyprocta* spp.) abscond with Brazil nut seeds and bury many of them. Some popular game birds, such as pheasant-like guans and turkey-sized curassows (Cracidae), also disperse seed for some forest trees. Tapir (*Tapirus terrestris*) pass intact seeds of numerous forest plants, including buriti, whose vitamin C-rich fruit is used to make pulp for juices and ice-cream throughout Amazonia (Bodmer 1990, 1991).

The relative contribution of forest products to the regional economy peaked in 1910 during the rubber boom, but has since declined.

By the 1950s, the value of agricultural production had surpassed that of forest products in Amazonia (Homma 1990c: 7; Pinedo-Vasquez, Zarin, and Jipp 1990). Rubber from the forest is unlikely to return as a mainstay to the regional economy.

One way to strengthen the contribution of extractive reserves to the income of local people as well as regional development is to develop new markets for existing forest products, as well as to discover new economic species. Cultural Survival, a non-profit human rights organization based in Cambridge, Massachusetts, has established a non-profit trading company to help find markets for Amazonian forest products that have been collected in a "sustainable" manner. Through the efforts of Cultural Survival, one ice-cream manufacturer in the United States, Community Products, is selling "Rainforest Crunch," a blend of Brazil and cashew nuts. The Community Products company has agreed to repatriate 40 per cent of its profits from "Rainforest Crunch" to Brazil nut gatherers. Commercial cashew production takes place on plantations, usually outside of rain forests in the drier tropics.

Rainforest Products buys Brazil nuts from Cultural Survival and markets them in two cereals: "Rainforest Crisp" and "Rainforest Granola."[4] Seven per cent of Rainforest Products' profits are distributed to environmental groups. Brazil nuts from extractive reserves in Brazil have also recently turned up in "Rainforest" cookies in some markets in the United States. Body Shop, a British cosmetics firm, is testing oils and essences from Amazonian forests for its impressive line of creams and lotions now sold in boutiques around the world (Pearce 1990).

Although such efforts and developments are commendable, the dollar volume of this business is miniscule. In 1989, for example, the production capacity of "Rainforest Crunch" was only 680 kg a day (CGBD 1989). To make a larger impact, rain-forest products need to conquer shelf-space in major supermarkets, restaurants, and fast-food chains in both domestic and international markets.

One way to increase the perceived economic value of forests is to introduce new foods and fruit juices based on wild and semi-domesticated trees, particularly in industrial countries. If a market is developed for such products, the tree or shrub would warrant domestication. The worth of wild populations of the new crop would then increase, rather than diminish, as a source of novel traits.

Increasingly sophisticated consumers are receptive to interesting new foods. But gaining a niche for novel products requires sustained efforts and a large advertising budget. The development costs for new products in complex and highly competitive markets, such as North America and Europe, can be exorbitant. In general, only a few food products dominate baked goods, cereals, fruit juices, and ice-creams in North America and Europe. Many variants of this limited stock of basic foodstuffs occupy much of the space in supermarkets. Furthermore, few companies are likely to be as generous as Community Products in sending back such a large share of their profits to Amazonia.

Continued efforts to find expanded or new markets for rain-forest products are warranted, but reliance on extractive activities alone to provide for the material needs of rain-forest dwellers and to safe-guard the forest is a shaky proposition. Any plant product that be-comes important is usually domesticated or its relevant constituents are synthesized in a laboratory (Pendelton 1992). Rosewood (*Aniba rosaeodora*) harvesting in the Brazilian Amazon has essentially ceased now that linalool, used extensively in the perfume industry, is manufactured in laboratories. Wild stands of rosewood were being destroyed by overzealous collecting anyway.

Plants are domesticated to improve yields and other qualities, and forest would have to be cleared, or substantially altered, to cultivate them. Rubber is such an example, and Brazil nut is also being do-mesticated. One ranch near Itacoatiara, Amazonas, has established Brazil nut trees on 4,000 ha of degraded pasture (Smith et al. 1992: 400; fig. 4.2). Brazil nuts provide approximately half of the cash in-come in some extractive reserves (Schwartzman 1989), but eventually much of the production of Brazil nuts is likely to come from planta-tions. If extractive reserves are successful, their value may be more in saving forest resources for further study and for later domestication and synthesis of some of the useful chemical compounds.

Shifts in the market-place can undercut some extractive products from forests. At one time, for example, inhabitants in the vicinity of Belém valued forest-shrouded streams as a source of *Heliconia* leaves to wrap foodstuffs. An advantage of this banana relative is that the leaves rapidly disintegrated after use. Now ubiquitous and cheap plastic bags have virtually put a stop to the harvest of *Heliconia* leaves. Discarded plastic bags are a blight in urban areas and another source of water pollution, particularly at ports.

Each extractive reserve will have a different mix and concentration of economic plant species. Ideally, the potential economic value of forest products should be considered before selecting areas for ex-

Fig. 4.2 **Six-year-old grafted Brazil nut (*Bertholletia excelsa*) on a former pasture. Strips of forest or second growth are left every 50 metres, a practice that may help sustain pollinators and improve the micro-climate for young Brazil nut trees. Fazenda Aruanã, km 215 Manaus–Itacoatiara Highway, Amazonas, 15 November 1991**

tractive reserves (Prance 1989). Yet careful inventories and economic analyses are not preceding the selection of sites for extractive reserves. Extractive reserves may be only marginally feasible in a few favoured locations with the current tight restrictions on forest-clearing (FAO 1990: 3).

Another concern about extractive reserves is that they might be oversold as a model for regional development. Extractive reserves can support relatively few people on a sustainable basis, at least for the foreseeable future (Anderson 1989; Mori 1992; Sawyer 1990). The 3 million ha of currently established extractive reserves contain only 20,000 families (table 4.3). If rubber is the principal product, then at least 500 ha is needed per family (Allegretti 1989). Extractive reserves would have difficulty absorbing the waves of migrants entering Amazonia (Fearnside 1989b). If the inhabitants of Amazonia were to live by extractive activities alone, only about 1.5 million people could be supported in the region, compared with the approximately 10 million people currently residing there (Benchimol 1991). Extractive reserves are in effect helping to close Amazonia's frontier;

they are best viewed as part of the mosaic of land-use systems in the region, rather than as a social and ecological panacea.

Medicinal plants, potential new crop plants, and genes from wild populations of existing crops may ultimately prove more valuable than current major uses of forests. But it will take time to discover such uses and to test products before they reach the market. In the case of new pharmaceuticals, for example, testing alone can take up to three years and tens of millions of dollars before the new product is deemed safe enough for public consumption.[5] Market prices for forest products will fluctuate, as in the case of farming, silviculture, and ranching. Sustained harvesting of forest products will need more botanical and faunal inventories coupled with natural history studies. Such studies should combine scientific expertise and folk knowledge and involve locals in the research effort.

Extractive reserves will probably evolve to include a wide range of extractive and farming activities. One possible model for this is the Arara community some 35 km east of Marabá. In 1987, a group of 93 families, mostly from Maranhão, were transferred from lands of the Gavião Indians to a former *castanhal* (grove of Brazil nut trees) between the Transamazon Highway and the Tocantins River. In 1992, a further 30 families arrived in the area hoping to obtain plots for farming and forest extraction. With assistance from CEPASP (Centro de Educação, Pesquisa e Assessoria Sindical e Popular), settlers derive appreciable income and subsistence from the forest as well as from their fields. Farmers collect Brazil nuts and cupuaçu from the forest on their 60 ha lots, while CEPASP helps market the nuts and frozen cupuaçu pulp. One farmer harvested 1,000 cupuaçu fruits and 600 kg of Brazil nuts from the 30 ha of forest on his land. Farmers belonging to the Arara community also obtain other fruits from the forest for domestic consumption, such as cajá (*Spondias mombim*), bacaba, bacuri, tucumã (*Astrocaryum vulgare*), and açaí (*Euterpe oleracea*).

With financial assistance from the World Wildlife Fund, CEPASP has purchased four freezers with 600 litres capacity each to store cupuaçu pulp while prices are low. The freezers are kept in Marabá where electricity is available and transportation to markets in Belém, Castanhal, São Luis, and Brasília can be arranged more easily.

The Arara community relies heavily on agriculture for food and income. Farmers are planting a variety of perennial crops, including cupuaçu and Brazil nut, for future income. In the meantime, food crops such as rice, beans, manioc, and bananas provide nourishment.

87

Some Arara settlers raise a few head of cattle. Nevertheless, outside subsidies are critical to the success of this mixed venture of forest extraction and farming, at least in the short term. Resource-poor farmers are unlikely to be able to afford to buy freezers on their own, and electricity is not available in the community. The Arara experience may not be easily replicated throughout Amazonia since forests in the Marabá area are well known for their rich concentration of Brazil nuts and cupuaçu. Only 300 km further north around Paragominas and Tomé-Açu, neither of these economically important trees is found in the forest. The combination of agriculture and forest extraction is the pertinent lesson from the Arara experience.

The extraction of non-timber forest products by settlers

Rural peoples of Amazonia have always collected an assortment of products from forests and continue to do so outside of formally established "extractive reserves." The lifestyles of people living inside extractive reserves are likely increasingly to mirror those on the outside who farm, raise livestock, and extract forest products, including timber.

Settlers and long-time residents of Amazonia obtain a large array of foods, medicines, and building materials from forest on their property or from land they farm (table 4.5). For example, cipó titica (*Heteropsis* sp.) is gathered along the Transamazon and sold in Santarém to make wicker furniture; the forest vine is also sold in Acará, Pará, for the same purpose. A farmer along Ramal Andirobalzinho near Alter do Chão, Pará, complained that deforestation along streams has drastically reduced populations of guarumã (*Ischnosiphon obliquus*), a marantaceous shrub used to make a traditional sleeve (*tipití*) for squeezing cassava dough. The broad leaves of other moisture-loving marantaceous plants are used to wrap meat, tapioca, and other foodstuffs. A shift to mechanical presses in the process of making cassava flour and the widespread adoption of non-degradable plastic bags have substituted in part for several traditional forest-based products or technologies.

The number and amount of plant species harvested varies considerably within a community and between different areas of the Amazon basin. The ecological heterogeneity of the region is evident in the variation in species harvested at the different sites (table 4.6). Natives of Pará (*Paraenses*), for example, are generally more aware of forest resources and harvest them consistently. More recent arrivals, on the

Table 4.5 **A small sample of non-timber forest products collected by peasants in the Brazilian Amazon. Several thousand wild plants in Amazonia are put to a wide variety of uses, in food, beverages, construction, crafts, and medicines**

Plant	Scientific name	Uses	Location
Abacate bravo	?	Large trunks are hollowed out to make bins, about 1.5 m high, for storing beans	São João Batista, municipality of Itupiranga, Pará
Açaí	*Euterpe oleracea*	Fruit used to make drink	Amazonia
		Inflorescence used for broom	Nenas Souza, km 46 Santarém–Rurópolis, Pará
Açaí da terra firme	*Euterpe precatoria*	Fruit used to make drink	São João Batista, municipality of Itupiranga, Pará
Andiroba	*Carapa guianensis*	Oil from seeds spread on wounds to promote healing	Juliano Pereira, Comunidade Boa Esperança, km 70 Santarém–Rurópolis, Pará
Babaçu palm	*Attalea speciosa*	Ground nuts used as bait for siri crabs	Mosqueiro, Pará
		Fronds laid across wooden bridges as a base for dirt fill	Marabá–Araguaia stretch of Transamazon, Pará
		Fronds used to thatch huts	Brazilian Amazon municipalities of Marabá and Itupiranga, Pará
		Oil extracted from nuts for cooking	Municipalities of Marabá and Itupiranga, Pará
		Heart-of-palm eaten and sold locally	Mato Grosso
Bacaba palm	*Oenocarpus distichus*	Fruit for making drink	Pará
Brazil nut	*Bertholletia excelsa*	"Navel (*umbigo*)" of the capsule is burned to make tea for treating haemorrhage	São João Batista, municipality of Itupiranga, Pará
		Nuts	Amazonia
		Empty capsules used as burning containers to create smoke for dispelling black flies	Agrovila Coco Chato, km 42 Marabá–Altamira, Transmazon

89

Table 4.5 (cont.)

Plant	Scientific name	Uses	Location
Carapanaúba	*Aspidosperma* sp.	Bark used in treating fever, esp. malaria	Juliano Pereira, Comunidade Boa Esperança, km 70 Santarém–Rurópolis, Pará
Cipó imbé	*Philodendron imbe*	Vine used to make baskets	Nenas Souza, km 46 Santarém–Rurópolis, Pará
Cipó timbó	*Derris* sp.?	Vine segments tied together to make broom	Ramal de Curupira, side-road from km 39 of Santarém–Curuá Una, Pará
Copaíba	*Copaifera multijuga*	Resin used for treating cuts and abrasions	São João Batista, municipality of Itupiranga, Pará; Juliano Pereira, Comunidade Boa Esperança, km 70 Santarém–Rurópolis, Pará
Cupiúba	*Goupia glabra*	Trough made from trunk to hold cassava dough	Ramal de Curupira, side-road from km 39 of Santarém–Curuá Una, Pará
Cupuaçu	*Theobroma grandiflorum*	Fruit for making drink; pulp sometimes sold	Municipalities of Marabá and Itupiranga, Pará
Quina	*Geissospermum* sp.	Bitter bark used for treating malaria	São João Batista, municipality of Itupiranga, Pará
Inajá palm	*Maximiliana maripa*	Leaf base ("*capema*") used for carrying rice	São João Batista, municipality of Itupiranga, Pará
Jatobá	*Hymenaea courbaril*	Resin melted, stirred in water, then 3 drops put into each eye to "clear" them	São João Batista, municipality of Itupiranga, Pará
Toboca bamboo	?	Baskets, mortar	Lastancia, municipality of Itupiranga, Pará
Taboqui	?	Baskets	Lastancia, municipality of Itupiranga, Pará
Taboquinha	*Olyra micrantha*?	Baskets	Lastancia, municipality of Itupiranga, Pará
Ubim palm	*Geonoma* sp.	Fronds used to thatch huts	Lastancia, municipality of Itupiranga, Pará

Source: Field notes of NJHS, 1990–1993.

Table 4.6 **Some non-timber products collected from upland forest in the vicinity of Paragominas, Marabá, and Santarém**

Product	Marabá	Paragominas	Santarém
Brazil nut	+ + +		+
Cupuaçu	+ + +		
Bacaba	+		+
Babaçu	+ + +		+
Guarumã[a]			+
Cacauí[b]	+ +	+ +	+
Cacao[c]	Absent	Absent	+
Curua			+
Taboca[d]	+ +		
Taboquinha[d]	+ +		
Taboqui[d]	+		
Ubim palm[e]	+		
Macaúba[f]	+		+
Quina[g]	+		
Conduru[g]	+		
Copaíba[g]	+		+
Jatobá[g]	+		+
Açaí (*Euterpe oleracea*)			+
Açaí da terra firme[h]			+
Piquiá	+	+	+
Andiroba[g]			+
Cajá	+		
Bacuri	+		
Tucumã palm[i]	+		+
Inajá palm	+	+	+
Uxi		+	+

a. *Ischnosiphon obliquus* (Marantaceae); a moisture-loving plant used to make tipitís for squeezing cassava dough.
b. *Theobroma speciosum*; a relative of cacao with edible fruit.
c. Apparently wild populations in forest.
d. Several species of bamboo are used to make baskets and for light construction.
e. Unidentified palm used to thatch houses.
f. *Acrocomia* palm; oily fruit eaten by people and fed to livestock.
g. Medicinal plant.
h. *Euterpe precatoria*; fruit eaten.
i. *Astrocaryum vulgare*; fruit eaten and fibre used for hammocks and cord.

other hand, tend to use the forest less, at least initially. Some widespread species, such as babaçu, are used throughout much of Amazonia, although the custom of cracking open the hard endocarp to obtain the oil-rich nuts appears to be confined to eastern Pará where dense stands of the massive palm have arisen after repeated cycles of swidden farming (Anderson, May, and Balick 1991).

In addition to plant products, forests and second-growth communities provide game and fish. Game is an important source of meat to farmers in much of the Amazon Basin (Ayres and Ayres 1979; Ayres et al. 1991; Dourojeanni 1974; Smith 1976). White-lipped peccary (*Tayassu pecari*), white-collared peccary (*Tayassu tajacu*), tapir (*Tapirus terrestris*), and brocket deer (*Mazama americana*) provide appreciable quantities of protein and fats for rural folk, particularly during the early years of settlement. Some species, such as brocket deer and agouti, thrive in second-growth areas but, overall, game yields decline the more forest is cleared (Smith 1976).

The contribution to rural diets of fish from rain-forest streams is virtually undocumented. In part this may stem from a focus of fisheries research on major rivers or reservoirs. Fish from streams are thought to be too small and few in number to be of much consequence from the nutritional or economic standpoint. Nevertheless, the sight of boys and their fathers returning from a fishing expedition in the forest is not uncommon. As colonists and ranchers frequently clear right up to the margin of streams, and cattle often pollute waterways, fish populations undoubtedly suffer as the landscape is cleared.

How much forest settlers leave on their land depends on a host of factors, including how many children they have and where they choose to live, the productivity of fields, and the availability of other options to generate revenue. Although many settlers attest to the usefulness of forest, in reality not much forest is likely to remain on many lots given current technologies and land-use practices. As game and fish become scarce, settlers rely more on chickens, ducks, pigs, and in some cases cattle for meat. It is likely, however, that the intake of high-quality protein declines as game and fish populations are depleted or their habitats destroyed. Livestock need to be fed and cared for, and few colonists can afford to purchase meat, fish, or eggs in markets and stores on a regular basis. Finding ways to boost the productivity of fields and pasture, discussed in more detail in chapters 6 and 7, in order to reduce pressure on the remaining forest is thus imperative.

One could formulate arguments to the effect that forests provide a multitude of products and environmental services to local communities. More work is certainly warranted in this regard. The difficulty of quantifying in meaningful economic terms the value of such products and the role of the forest in supplying good-quality drinking water, for example, has hindered policy formulation with regard to land use in tropical forest areas. But reliance solely on a strategy of proving the worth of forests is unlikely to stem the tide of destruction. Forest extraction must be analysed within the framework of the larger land-use mosaic if fruitful policy recommendations are to ensue.

Forest management for timber and charcoal

As in the case of extractive reserves, attempts to manage forests in Amazonia for timber or charcoal production are in their infancy (FAO 1990: 11; Fearnside 1989c; Kirmse, Constantino, and Guess 1993; Silva and Uhl 1992; Whitmore 1990: 126). Current wood-harvesting practices for timber in the region often damage the recuperative capacity of the forest.

Traditionally, most of the lumbering in Amazonia has been concentrated along rivers where access to timber is easier. Ucuúba (*Virola surinamensis*), however, has been logged out of much of the flood-plain forests. As pioneer highways started slicing across the uplands in the 1960s, loggers penetrated deeper into the forest, such as around Itacoatiara near Manaus, and along feeder roads off BR 364 in Rondônia (Browder 1989a; Wesche and Bruneau 1990: 59).

The tempo of timber extraction in Amazonia continues to increase as the regional network of roads expands. The number of licensed sawmills in the Brazilian Amazon increased seventeen-fold between 1952 and 1982 (Browder 1989a). Between 1985 and 1987 alone, the number of sawmills operating in the municipality of Rio Branco in Acre almost doubled, from 23 to 44 (FUNTAC 1990a: 50). In 1973, 287 sawmills and 5 plywood and veneer plants were registered in the Brazilian Amazon; by 1986, the number of sawmills and plywood plants had grown to 2,231 and 70, respectively (Yared and Brienza 1989). Between 1975 and 1984, log production nearly quadrupled in the Brazilian Amazon to 17.4 million m³, reaching 24.6 million m³ by 1988 (Anderson 1987; Browder 1989a; Silva and Uhl 1992). The North region is now Brazil's foremost source of industrial sawlogs, and Pará is the leading producer of timber in the Brazilian Amazon (Homma 1989b).

The advent of larger trucks in the Brazilian market has increased the effective logging radius of sawmills. Longer and more powerful trucks, made by such companies as Mercedes Benz and Volvo, have payloads of 28 tons, in comparison with the 13-ton capacity typical of

Fig. 4.3   **Sawmills on the outskirts of Paragominas, Pará, April 1991. Note the igloo-like earthen kilns in the left foreground, used for making charcoal from scrap wood**

yesteryear. Larger trucks can profitably pick up logs as far away as 200 km, and, by making two trips a day, can bring back 80 m^3 of wood. The smaller trucks are essentially confined to a 100 km radius from sawmills.

Paragominas, a cattle town founded in the mid-1960s along the Belém–Brasília highway, has emerged as the most important logging centre in the Brazilian Amazon (fig. 4.3). In 1992, 140 sawmills were operating within the urban fringe of Paragominas (D. Callegario, pers. comm.). Other major concentrations of sawmills in Pará are found in the vicinity of Tailândia along the PA 150 highway, Tucuruí and Goianeza, and around Tomé-Açu. The municipality of Tailândia alone has 73 registered sawmills (W. Kronbauer, pers. comm.).

The quickened pace of the timber trade has raised questions about the sustainability of logging practices. In a study of a logging operation near Paragominas, Pará, one-quarter of the trees with a diameter at breast height of at least 10 cm were killed or severely damaged by logging activities (Uhl and Vieira 1989). The canopy cover was reduced by half. The amount of damage from logging appears to vary widely, however. In parts of Indonesia, loggers sometimes damage as much as 70 per cent of the remaining trees (Whitten et al. 1987: 480).

Logging does not always damage most of the trees or destroy half the canopy. If only a few desirable species are removed, as is typically the case in the Brazilian Amazon, perhaps only a quarter of the canopy is usually affected. During a 40 minute overflight of forest patches on heavily logged ranches near Paragominas in April 1991, only 10–30 per cent of the canopy had been torn open. Light gaps are important for generating many commercially important timber trees, such as mahogany (Kirmse, Constantino, and Guess 1993).

Loggers largely ignore regulations designed to conserve timber resources and protect valuable fruit and nut trees. Brazil nut trees are avidly sought by sawmills because of their durable and lustrous red-brown wood. Although it is illegal to cut down Brazil nut trees, landowners frequently allow loggers to remove the trees, particularly if they need cash. A Brazil nut tree can be legally cut down if it is dead or dying or in the way of urban expansion. In the early 1970s, some Transamazon colonists deliberately lit fires at the base of Brazil nut trees to obtain a cash windfall from loggers. In the late 1980s, some loggers in parts of northern Mato Grosso obtained permits to fell Brazil nut trees deemed in the way of urban expansion, even though some of the trees were several kilometres from the nearest house (Rubens Lima, pers. comm.).

Piquiá, another canopy-emergent in the Amazonian forest, is also persecuted by loggers even though it provides a widely appreciated fruit. The light yellow pulp of piquiá fruits is cooked and relished in April and May, particularly by poorer people. Piquiá also produces an excellent hardwood, and many trees are converted to handsome yellow-brown tables, chairs, doors, and dugout canoes.

As the more desirable species become scarce in heavily logged areas, sawmills shift to second- and third-tier species. The Rosa Madeireira sawmill in Paragominas, for example, was working with 58 named timber trees in the early 1990s. Some common names of timber trees encompass several species: faveira, a widely used leguminous timber, includes species in several genera, such as *Enterolobium, Macrolobium, Parkia, Piptadenia, Stryphnodendron, Vataireopsis*, and *Vatairea*. Rosa Madeireira actually processed over 100 species of timber trees in 1990, some of which are used for veneer production. In July 1992 alone, Dalsam Madeiras of Paragominas processed logs from 47 timber species (table 4.7).

Where road conditions are less favourable, such as in the Marabá

Table 4.7 **Timber species and volume processed into sawlogs at Dalsam Madeiras, Paragominas, Pará, July 1992**

Common name	Scientific name	No. of logs	Volume (m³)
Maçaranduba	*Manilkara huberi*	667	866
Faveira	*Vataireopsis* spp. and various other Legume genera	125	282
Guajara	*Neoxithese* sp.	146	217
Angelim pedra	*Hymenolobium petraeum*	64	161
Piquiá	*Caryocar villosum*	52	136
Mandioqueira	*Qualea* spp.	62	130
Quarubatinga	*Vochysia guianensis*	71	129
Ipê	*Tabebuia* spp.	49	117
Estopeiro	*Couratari* sp.	61	117
Jatobá	*Hymenaea courbaril*	64	103
Uxi	*Endopleura uchi*	54	79
Louro vermelho	*Nectadra rubra*	32	73
Cupiúba	*Goupia glabra*	36	72
Taxi	Species of *Tachigalia* and *Sclerolobium*	40	66
Quaruba cedro	*Vochysia* sp.	34	66
Tatajuba	*Bagassa guianensis*	25	62
Tanibuca	*Terminalia* sp.	28	51
Louro canela	*Ocotea dissimilis*	26	48
Amesclão	*Trattinickia buserifolia*	18	47
Pau roxo	*Peltogyne lecointe*	21	45
Corrúpixá	*Rauwalfia paraensis*	27	44
Piquiarana	*Caryocar glabrum*	19	44
Caju	*Anacardium* sp.	19	41
Murure	*Trymotococus paraensis*	15	40
Amapá	*Parahancornia amapa*	28	40
Timborana	*Pseudopiptadenia* sp.	25	37
Angelim vermelho	*Dinizia excelsa*	11	36
Burangi	?	13	26
Tamaquaré	*Caraipa densifolia*	17	26
Sapucaia	*Lecythis* sp.	15	24
Copaíba	*Copaifera multijuga*	16	23
Sucupira pele de sapo	*Diplotropis* sp.	20	23
Orelha de macaco	*Enterolobium schomburgkii*	10	17
Muiracatiara	*Astronium gracile*	13	16
Jarana	*Holopyxidium jarana*	9	15
Goiabão	*Planchonella pachycarpa*	12	11
Ciringarana	?	6	9
Cumaru	*Dipteryx odorata*	6	9
Imbirucu	?	5	8
Morototo	*Didymopanax morototoni*	4	7

Table 4.7   (cont.)

Common name	Scientific name	No. of logs	Volume (m³)
Ingá	*Didymopanax morototoni*	4	6
Araracanga	*Inga* sp.	2	3
Marupa	*Aspidosperma* sp.	1	2
Iare	*Simarupa amara*	1	2
Angelim fava	*Helicostylis*?	1	2
Tuere	*Hymenolobium* sp.	1	1
TOTAL	?		3,379

Source: Dalsam Madeiras, Paragominas, Pará, August 1992.

area, sawmills tend to work with fewer, more valuable species. Ma-decil Serraria, the largest sawmill in Marabá, accepts only about 20 species, whereas the smaller Madeireira Marabá buys or harvests only 10 species (table 4.8). Ipê, particularly *Tabebuia serratifolia*, appears to be the most important timber tree in the Marabá area in terms of volume, whereas mahogany, known locally as mogno, is the most valuable species.

One of the common perceptions about logging in Amazonia is that it is geared primarily to the export trade, particularly to industrial countries. In fact, most tropical timber is harvested for domestic consumption; less than one-third of tropical roundwood and processed wood is typically exported (Atkin 1993; Vincent 1992). International trade accounts for a diminishing share of consumption of tropical timber (Vincent 1992).

Although it is true that some of the premier woods, such as mahogany, are largely sent abroad, much of the timber production in Amazonia is for the domestic market (fig. 4.4). In the Paragominas area, sawmills send about 80 per cent of their production to markets in central and southern Brazil, such as Rio, Espírito Santo, Belo Horizonte, and in the North-east region. Dalsam Madeiras, a medium-sized sawmill in Paragominas, sends 80 per cent of its production to markets within Brazil. An estimated 90 per cent of the timber sawn at Tailândia is sent to national markets (W. Kronbauer, pers. comm.). Further south along the PA 150 highway in Marabá, Madeireira Marabá, one of about 20 sawmills in the rapidly growing town as of 1992, also dispatches 90 per cent of its planks to the Brazilian market, divided roughly equally between the North-east region and the South region (Sinisvaldo Mota, pers. comm.). In spite of the recession, de-

Table 4.8 **Some timber species processed by sawmills in Marabá, Pará, 1992**

Local name	Scientific name	Madecil	Madeireira Marabá
Angelim pedra	*Hymenolobium petraeum*		+
Cedro	*Cedrela odorata*	+	+
Cedroarana	*Cedrelinga cateniformis* and/or *Scleronema micranthum*		+
Cumaru	*Dipteryx odorata*	+	
Inhare	*Helicostylis* sp.	+	
Ipê	*Tabebuia* spp.	+	+
Jatobá	*Hymenaea courbaril*	+	+
Maçaranduba	*Manilkara huberi*		+
Maracatiara	*Astronium lecointei?*		+
Melanceiro	?		+
Mogno	*Swietenia macrophylla*		+
Pitiuba	?	+	
Sucupira	*Bowdichia nitida*		+
Tatajuba	*Bagassa guianensis*	+	+

mand is growing for lower-quality timber for general construction purposes, such as moulds for concrete.

The increased logging activity may ironically help save some forest stands. In the vicinity of Paragominas, for example, several ranchers have halted deforestation on their properties because of rising income derived from periodically selling logging rights to sawmills. The owner of Fazenda São João, which has 600 ha of pasture, "sold" his 400 ha of forest to sawmill operators in 1982, 1986, and 1988. Although the forest on the São João ranch was unlikely to yield sufficiently valuable timber to justify logging three more times in the 1990s, the shift to less desirable species means that cutting cycles of around a decade could generate reasonably high levels of supplemental income. In some cases, income derived from logging has been reinvested to upgrade pastures.

Another notable trend is for sawmills to acquire and manage land. In part, this shift to forest management is in response to the requirements of IBAMA for sawmills to have a "management plan" in order to operate, or to contribute to a fund for purchasing national forests. IBAMA has few inspectors to verify if such plans are being carried out, and one sawmill operator was curious why the national government had not done more to acquire forests for lease to timber companies. Demand for expertise in forest management is particularly

Fig. 4.4 **Sawn hardwoods for local construction. Itacoatiara, Amazonas, 15 November 1991**

strong in the vicinity of Paragominas, since many of the sawmills also own ranches with sizeable portions of their land still in forest. Offices have sprung up in various towns in the Brazilian Amazon, such as Marabá, offering services in devising "forest management plans."

How well forests are being managed is unclear. In theory at least, blocks of forest are harvested on a rotational basis and care is taken to avoid damaging seedlings. At least some of the sawmills concerned with their long-term survival are apparently taking seriously the need to harvest trees in a rational manner. The larger sawmills, in contrast to the small, mobile ones, are more likely to practise some form of forest management because they often own land and have a greater fixed investment.

In the case of Paragominas, many of the sawmills own ranch or farm land with stands of forest. Dalsam Madeiras, for example, owns two ranches with total area of 11,500 ha, 10,000 ha of which are in forest. Blocks of forest are logged on a rotational basis and most trees are cut only if they are larger than 1.2 metres in circumference. The more valuable species, such as ipê, sucupira (*Bowdichia nitida*), and freijó (*Cordia goeldiana*), are felled even if they are smaller than 1.2 metres in circumference. Near Tailândia, the W.K. Brasil sawmill owns 2,778 ha of forest, of which 1,000 ha are currently managed. Half of the sawmills in Tailândia now own forest (W. Kronbauer, pers. comm.).

The Madeireira Marabá sawmill processes some 12,000 m³ of logs a year and has a project to manage 3,500 ha. With a yield of some 40 m³/ha in the forests within 200 km, this medium-sized sawmill harvests timber from some 300 ha annually. The 3,500 ha management area is unlikely to sustain a cutting cycle of about 12 years for long. Tropical foresters generally recommend longer cycles, such as 70 years in the case of the dipterocarp forests of Indonesia (Whitten et al. 1987: 481). One problem that sawmills are encountering with acquiring land for forest management is that definitive title to large holdings must be approved by Congress, a time-consuming, expensive, and unpredictable process.

At km 101 of the Santarém–Cuiabá Highway, CEMEX (Comercial Madeiras Exportação, S.A.) owns 6,900 ha, mostly in forest, of which 2,930 ha are managed on a 12–30-year cutting cycle (fig. 4.5). On the first cutting cycle, 70 m³ are removed; it is not known whether this relatively high extraction rate is sustainable, since CEMEX has been managing forest for only six years. The minimum size at which trees are harvested varies by species: jatobá (*Hymenaea courbaril*), for example, is allegedly cut only when its diameter at breast height

Fig. 4.5 **Truck removing logs from the CEMEX property along a side-road at km 101 of the Santarém–Rurópolis Highway. Pará, 1 October 1992. Most logging is conducted in the dry season to avoid equipment becoming stuck in mud**

(dbh) reaches 60 cm, whereas ipê and virola (*Virola* sp.) are felled when they reach a dbh of 45 cm and 25 cm, respectively (José Baranek, pers. comm.). Trees with obvious defects, such as twisted trunks, are left as seed sources, while a few undesirable species, such as taxi preto (*Tachigalia paniculata*) and abiurana (various species of *Chrysophyllum, Pouteria, Radlkoferela, Ecclinusa,* and *Micropholis*), are ringed.

If the prime specimens are cut, the quality of the forest from the viewpoint of commercial timber is likely to decline as the inferior stock remains to reproduce (Whitten, Mustafa, and Henderson 1987: 441). From the genetic variation standpoint, it would probably make better sense to leave a random mixture of poor to excellent specimens. At the headwaters of some streams, 110 ha have been set aside as a forest reserve. If such reserves were larger, they could serve as important seed sources for re-stocking or genetic improvement in the future.

Another management technique is to cut all vines and lianas in a plot when trees are harvested, but the impact of such measures on pollinators and seed dispersal agents is unknown. In Sumatra, climbing plants are significant food sources for primates, such as orangutan and gibbons (Whitten et al. 1987: 481). It could be argued that timber companies are not in the business of managing forests for monkey populations, but at least the ecological implications of vine removal warrant further study. Whenever feasible, managed forests should serve as refuges for wildlife. Managed forest at CEMEX appears to be fulfilling this role at least partially, since jaguar cubs have been encountered by workers when preparing plots for harvesting. Another factor to consider is that vines may pump significant amounts of ground water to the canopy (Nepstad et al. 1991).

Skidders cause much less damage to remaining trees than do bulldozers, so CEMEX employs two skidders to remove logs from the forest. Skidders are equipped with large tyres rather than moving tracks and thus disturb the topsoil less than do bulldozers. The skidders drag logs to small clearings where they are cut into sections for loading on to trucks.

CEMEX began two reforestation/forest enrichment projects in 1989. Reforestation is being attempted in second growth, while enrichment planting with mahogany is being carried out in an adjacent patch of logged forest. By the end of 1992, some 200 ha were planted with a mixture of valuable timber trees. Second growth is slashed and mulched, while the larger trees are ringed. In the logged forest, par-

Table 4.9 **The annual planting rate of timber species in second-growth and logged forest at CEMEX, km 101 Santarém–Cuiabá, Pará**

Common name	Scientific name	Seedlings planted/yr
Mogno	*Swietenia macrophylla*	287,500
Cedro	*Cedrela odorata*	71,875
Cumaru	*Dipteryx odorata*	71,875
Freijó	*Cordia goeldiana*	71,875
Ipê	*Tabebuia serratifolia*	71,875

Note: Smaller quantities of andiroba, tatajuba, jatobá (*Hymenaea* sp.), piquiá (*Caryocar villosum*), gumbeira, and virola are also being planted in second growth.

allel lines are cut through the semi-open forest and timber seedlings are planted at regular intervals. Mahogany is the most commonly planted tree (table 4.9), in part because it does not occur naturally in this part of Amazonia. Only a few of the mahogany seedlings have been attacked by *Hypsipyla grandella*, a moth larva that tunnels into the growing shoot, thereby retarding growth and provoking defects in the trunk. This pest is more likely to be a problem when mahogany is planted in monospecific stands.

Although owning forest land provides some incentive for more sustainable logging practices, it remains to be seen how successful the management techniques employed by the sawmills in Pará will be, and whether the land will eventually be converted to non-forest uses. A key issue in sustainable forest management for timber production is the duration between harvests. The longer it takes for the forest to regenerate commercially harvestable timber, the less likely it is that landowners will be interested in saving their forests. The owner of São João ranch near Paragominas may have to wait decades before another sizeable harvest of timber is possible in the remaining forest stand on his property. In the Philippines, for example, 30–45 years typically pass before forests are selectively logged again (Schmidt 1987). How short one can make the cutting cycles depends on a variety of factors, such as the proximity of desirable timber species remaining to re-seed logged areas, soil fertility, the degree of damage to seedlings and soil structure, and changes in marketing opportunities for hardwoods.

One of the greatest disincentives to managing forest for timber production in Amazonia and many other parts of tropical America is that other land uses are often more profitable (Kishor and Constantino 1993). The proliferation of pioneer highways and feeder roads in Amazonia during the past three decades has made it cheaper to obtain timber along the agricultural frontier rather than to manage forests. While it is still possible to gain access to mature forests and "cream" the valuable timber, few landholders will want to invest in sustainable harvesting of timber. Rather than open any new roads in Amazonia, efforts might be made to improve existing ones by repairing bridges and side-roads. Incentives are also needed to foster attempts to manage forests for timber and other products.

Few models for sustained management of tropical forests for timber production are available to guide policy makers in Amazonia (Perl et al. 1991; Westoby 1989: 37). Members of the International Tropical Timber Agreement (ITTA) have agreed that tropical timber should be sustainably harvested by the year 2000, whereas only 1 per cent is thought to be sustainably managed today.[6] In 1991, a truck headed for the Belém port loaded with wood was stamped "Ecological Wood." A veritable industry could soon start, with organizations certifying that wood has been harvested "sustainably." Clever public relations cannot disguise the fact that the scientific underpinnings for forest management are wanting. Labels attesting to the sustainability of harvesting methods for a product may not mean much if there is not some independent review board for making such assertions. Monitoring the harvest of tropical timber to verify environmentally sound techniques will be costly.

For the time being, one can only grasp at a few cases that shed some light on the potential for harvesting timber from forests in humid tropics. In one part of Surinam, for example, selective logging with carefully planned skid trails and the poisoning of non-commercial trees can produce timber harvests of 20 m^3 per hectare every two decades (Graaf 1982). Given the dispersed nature of highly desirable timber trees (Anderson 1987), sustained management of forests in Amazonia would appear to be a low-yield operation.

International markets could be developed for some of the lesser-known timber trees, but dealers like reliable supplies in order to cultivate a new product. Considerable research is needed on potential timber trees and rational harvesting methods that offer reasonable economic returns. Of the more than 700 promising timber species in Amazonian forests, only 10 species accounted for more than 60 per cent of the saw and veneer log production in the region during the 1980s (Anderson 1987).

The Yanesha Forestry Cooperative at Palcazu in the Peruvian Amazon could provide some useful insights into sustainable timber harvesting in tropical forests. With technical assistance from the Tropical Science Centre in San José, Costa Rica, the Peruvian Foundation for the Conservation of Nature (FPCN), and the World Wildlife Fund, the Yanesha clear-cut narrow strips from 20 to 40 metres wide in the forest. In order to minimize disturbance of the topsoil and damage to remaining trees and seedlings, the Yanesha use cattle to extract timber from their 75,000 ha reserve in the Palcazu valley. A 40-year rotation is envisaged for this pilot project (Earhart 1990). Financial assistance is provided by a variety of donors, including the World Wildlife Fund and the US Agency for International Development (Perl et al. 1991: 13).

It would be premature to suggest that the Yanesha experience can serve as a model. Wood produced by such methods may be more expensive than from other timber suppliers. For the time being at least, the timber output from the Palcazu project is modest, destined mostly for artisans and local furniture makers. A contract to supply chemically treated poles for the state telephone company provides some additional income, but the entire operation is still subsidized. Furthermore, cattle pasture usually entails clearing forest, and the sawmill at the Yanesha mill is fuelled by diesel rather than waste wood. Yanesha lands are communally owned, thus making it easier to establish strips for harvesting. It could be difficult to arrange for strip harvesting on a checkerboard pattern of small, privately own lots with varying patterns of land clearance.

Start-up funds are usually necessary for pilot projects in forest management, but the acid test for sustainability is whether such ventures can be successfully weaned from external financial support. If "green" companies proliferate, or legislation restricts the importation of tropical timber harvested unsustainably, then natural forest management will have a better chance of succeeding. The Ecological Trading Company in the United Kingdom and Luthier Mercantile in California are customers for timber from the Yanesha Forestry Cooperative, but many more such companies will need to come forward to buy forest products obtained on an allegedly sustainable basis.

Sawmill linkages with other land-use systems

By-products from sawmills are used in other land-use systems. In the Santarém area, sawdust is given to farmers on both terra firma and the Amazon flood plain. The sawdust is employed to help conserve soil moisture and suppress weeds, rather than to supply nutrients.

Upland farmers mound sawdust around black pepper plants, while some vegetable growers on the Amazon flood plain scatter sawdust in tomato beds. In the Marabá area, scrap wood from some sawmills is converted into charcoal for COSIPAR, a pig-iron smelter. Sawmills benefit from this arrangement because they reduce their waste disposal problem.

Charcoal production for pig-iron smelting

Charcoal production has emerged as an important land-use activity in the Marabá area within the past decade. Furthermore, the preparation of charcoal has close linkages with other land uses, and it has the potential to alter landscapes dramatically. In most areas of Amazonia, charcoal is used extensively for cooking, in both urban and rural areas.

In order to generate more domestic employment, plans were drawn up to smelt some of the iron ore from Carajás along the railroad to Itaqui. This 900 km railroad was built in the early 1980s to export minerals, particularly iron ore and manganese, to a deep-water port near São Luis in Maranhão. All told, some 23 pig-iron smelters were planned for construction along the railroad, with charcoal as the main source of energy. In addition, charcoal is used in the reduction process. Natural vegetation was envisaged as the main source of charcoal, at least in the initial stages of production.

The spectre of 23 pig-iron smelters concentrated along a relatively thin strip of south-east Amazonia immediately sparked concern about deforestation and potentially adverse impacts on other land-use systems, such as swidden farming by small-scale colonists and indigenous groups. A single pig-iron smelter would require as much as 100,000 ha of forest for sustainable charcoal production, based on the annual production of a typical pig-iron smelter in the region and a charcoal yield of 30 tons/ha in forest.

Pig-iron smelters planned along the Carajás–Itaqui railroad could result in the destruction of 1,500 km^2 of forest each year (Anderson 1990a). On a small scale, the harvesting of native forests for charcoal makes sense, since production costs are low. On a large industrial scale, however, the vast areas of forest needed to sustain harvesting preclude other potentially more productive uses of the landscape and could lead to serious ecological degradation. In the case of pig-iron smelters along the Carajás–Itaqui railroad, for example, some of the densest groves of Brazil nut trees would be lost. At current market prices for pig-iron, plantations of fast-growing exotics, such as euca-lyptus, would not be economically viable.

How much forest will eventually be cleared to satisfy the pig smelt-ers is unclear. Iron smelting destroyed much of the oak woodlands of Sussex in England during the Middle Ages, some of which sub-sequently grew back (Perlin 1989: 168, 177, 189). Earlier, the Romans had cleared much of the forests from south-eastern England for ag-riculture and to reduce cover for hostile groups. The loss of plant and animal resources will be much greater with the disappearance of for-est along the Carajás–Itaqui railroad should all the planned pig-iron smelters come on line.

Thus far, only four pig-iron smelters have been built along the railroad, two on the outskirts of Marabá and the other two further east at Açaílandia. Only one of the pig-iron smelters near Marabá was operating in 1992. The three pig-iron smelters currently on line have not accelerated deforestation since the wood is coming from sawmills and from branches and trunks left in fields by swidden farmers (World Bank 1992: 30).

How many pig-iron smelters will be built is uncertain. Brazil's de-sire to process some of the iron ore to generate jobs is commendable, but it seems unlikely that the projected production goal of 16 million tons of pig iron a year will be reached by 2010 (Treece 1989). Even if electricity from the Tucurui dam provides much of the energy for melting the iron ore, charcoal is still needed for the reduction process.

Uncertainties about whether or not the forest would be managed on a rational basis provoked fears that large blocks of woodland would perish, thereby undercutting the subsistence base of numerous farmers and compromising future options for development and con-servation. For a variety of reasons, including a deep recession and heightened concerns about the environmental and social costs of large-scale charcoal production from the Amazon rain forest, only a handful of pig-iron smelters are currently functioning.

Before exploring the social and environmental implications of pig-iron smelters and highlighting some pertinent research questions, a brief description of current charcoal production can provide insights into interactions with other land-use systems. Charcoal-makers are at the lowest end of the socio-economic ladder, sharing this tenuous position in society with itinerant miners. Fishermen and sharecrop-pers are next on the societal ladder. Still, movement between these

Fig. 4.6   **Charcoal-maker stacking wood into an oven on a small farm. Sitio Sape-cado, vicinal Ferrovia, PA 150, km 35 south of Marabá, Pará, 13 November 1992**

"lower" strata is brisk and frequent, as people move on to other opportunities and thus leave one form of employment for another. At least some of the charcoal-makers come from Minas Gerais, a state where cerrado trees and eucalyptus plantations are converted to charcoal for the steel industry. Other charcoal-makers are from Pará and Maranhão, and have been engaged previously in a range of activities such as farming and fishing.

Charcoal-makers own no land (fig. 4.6). They work on the lots and ranches of others, and pay landlords a percentage of the value of the charcoal produced. In turn, landlords allow the charcoal-makers to live temporarily on their land, and to collect wood left over after burning forest or old second growth. Landowners often provide tangible assistance, such as a bullock and cart, power saws, and bricks to build the ovens. At Sitio Sapecado, a 90 ha property along a side-road leading from km 35 of the PA 150 highway south of Marabá, 10 ovens are in production. Charcoal-makers are generally organized into groups, which range in size depending on the number of ovens on the property; a work group can range from as few as 2 men to 20 or more. Families who accompany charcoal-makers build make-shift homes on the property, but generally do not grow any crops.

Each dome-shaped oven is designed to produce 1.5 tons of charcoal a week. Wood, cut into 1 to 1.5 metre lengths, is stacked inside the oven and then allowed to burn for two days. The temperature of the burn is controlled by blocking some of the holes in the side and bottom of the oven. After the charcoal has formed, the oven cools for three days before the charcoal is taken out. Large trucks pick up the charcoal and take it to COSIPAR, which began smelting in 1986. COSIPAR pays US$9/ton for charcoal at the "farm gate." Another pig-iron smelter in Marabá, SIMAR, is apparently slated to come back on line in the near future; if this occurs, greater competition may boost the price paid for charcoal.

Charcoal production interacts with three other main land uses in the Marabá area: swidden agriculture, ranching, and sawmills. In the first, charcoal producers remove branches and the smaller logs remaining after fields are burned for subsistence crops such as rice, maize, beans, and manioc. In this regard the removal of the wood could reduce the amount of nutrients and organic matter entering agro-ecosystems. Furthermore, scattered logs and branches help check soil erosion in swidden fields, which is particularly important in the case of steep slopes or plots cleared on sandy soils. In the case of ranching, landholders employ charcoal-makers to help defray the cost of clearing land. In exchange for preparing as much charcoal as they can, the temporary workers agree to plant pasture seed at the appropriate time, usually as the rains are beginning. Increasingly, the rancher or farmer supplies the grass seed, usually *Brachiaria brizantha*. This process is well developed in other parts of the humid tropics in Latin America, such as in the highlands of Costa Rica. Sawmills appear to be a significant source of wood for charcoal-making for use in pig-iron smelting, but hard data on the relative contribution of wood from the three land-use systems for charcoal production are lacking. One point is clear, however: forest is not currently being cut down solely for charcoal production.

Silviculture for charcoal production

In response to the requirements of IBAMA[7] that consumers of wood must either manage forest on a sustainable basis or replant, COSI-PAR has recently established a project to plant eucalyptus to supply the charcoal ovens. As of November 1992, COSIPAR had planted 400 ha of eucalyptus, mainly *Eucalyptus urophylla*, along a side-road leading from km 35 of the PA 150 highway south of Marabá. A further 800 ha of eucalyptus was slated for planting in 1993. All plantings are in second growth. Three fertilizer treatments of 65 g of triple super phosphate are applied to the trees according to the following schedule: when the seedlings are planted; at 45 days; and then again three months after planting.

It is unlikely that eucalyptus plantings for charcoal will be a viable proposition in Amazonia for the near future. At Jari, over 20,000 ha of eucalyptus have been planted for pulp production, a relatively high-value product. The abundance of forest and old second growth in the Marabá area, as well as the high cost of labour and inputs, undercut the economic viability of silviculture for charcoal. When the pioneer front has moved on and naturally occurring wood becomes more scarce, silviculture for biomass fuel might become a more attractive investment.

Two ways to help make biomass plantations more promising are to select superior germ plasm and to incorporate other crops and/or livestock. A few hectares of the COSIPAR plantation are inter-cropped with pasture, a common practice in Minas Gerais where most of the natural woodlands have long since been cleared. Nevertheless, substantial subsidies would likely be needed to accelerate eucalyptus plantings for charcoal production in the twentieth century in the Marabá area.

Perhaps natural regeneration could be managed by the addition of some quick-growing nitrogen-fixing trees, such as species of *Gliricidia*. If ashes from smelters are not returned to the land, fertilizers will eventually be needed. The economics and ecological implications of large-scale charcoal production in Amazonia are currently being investigated by CVRD in collaboration with scientists from Brazil and abroad. Large-scale monocultures for charcoal production are unlikely to become economically attractive ventures in the near term; perhaps managed second growth could satisfy some of the market for charcoal.

Another possibility would be small-scale agro-forestry, in which farmers grow fast-growing trees for charcoal alongside food and other cash crops (Shaeff 1990: 95). An advantage of such an agro-forestry approach is that it would involve many of the small farmers in the region and could be incorporated into existing farming systems. Farmers would need technical support for such a venture, however, and research would be needed on appropriate trees. Agro-forestry systems are unlikely, however, to supply sufficient charcoal for 22 pig-iron smelters, let alone many of the other enterprises in the Marabá area that draw on charcoal supplies. Some 4 million metric tons of charcoal would be needed annually to supply the planned pig-iron smelters, cement plants, and other industries during the 1990s (Shaeff 1990: 7).

Notes

1. *Veja*, 16 June 1991, p. 8.
2. "A murder in the forest," *The Economist*, 7 January 1989, p. 36; "A jungle slaying," *Time*, 9 January 1989, p. 38; "Ecologist murdered," *Nature* 337, 5 January 1989, p. 3; "Justice comes to the Amazon," *Time*, 17 December 1990, p. 76; Bendix and Liebler (1991).
3. "Coutinho quer viabilizar borracha nacional," *A Província do Pará*, Belém, Pará, 13 March 1993, caderno 1, p. 9.
4. *Environment*, September 1991, vol. 33 (7), p. 23.
5. "Radical change," *The Economist*, 16 November 1991, p. 84.
6. "Spare that tree," *The Economist*, 14 November 1992, p. 40.
7. Decree 97.682 of 10 April 1989 and IBAMA portaria 440 of 9 August 1989 stipulate that industries consuming more than 4,000 m³ of charcoal a year must make arrangements to establish and manage plantations for charcoal production (Machado 1992).

5

Silviculture and plantation crops

Agriculture, livestock raising, and silviculture are often pinpointed as major factors in the destruction of Amazonian forests. But human occupation of the region does not necessarily provoke a downward ecological spiral. Many indigenous groups have prospered with relatively sophisticated cultures for protracted periods of time in various parts of Amazonia. Answers to the difficult question of promoting sustainable agriculture in Amazonia will come from a blend of indigenous knowledge and modern, scientific input. Also, a blend of native and exotic plants will provide the mainstay for farmers, ranchers, and plantation operators. Dynamic and successful agricultural and silvicultural systems are always open to new opportunities for incorporating promising plant and animal species, wherever they may come from.

A major focus on agriculture is justified because approximately half the people in Amazonia still live in rural areas and depend on farming, ranching, plantations, and forest resources for a living. Also, a growing number of forest- and agriculture-based industries are being established in Amazonia, thereby creating employment opportunities in urban areas.

Sustainable agriculture requires flexible farming systems. No particular mix of crops or agronomic practices in a given area is likely to endure for long. New crops and varieties must be constantly introduced to raise and sustain productivity, and novel agronomic practices adopted in response to changing market and environmental conditions. Such practices are well developed in Amazonia among small-, medium-, and large-scale operators.

Sustainable agriculture is a multifaceted concept, involving both ecological and socio-economic and political dimensions (Smith 1990). A critical defect in much of the discussion about sustainable development in Amazonia, particularly as it applies to agriculture, is the lack of attention to economic realities. Ecologists provide valuable insights with regard to the role of forests in environmental stability and as food sources of pollinators, but ecological perspectives alone will not lead to sustainable development. Also, social scientists tend to stress policy and sociocultural dimensions to development; as important as these perspectives are, they need to be tempered by economic realities.

Our analysis does not suggest that technological fixes will solve sustainability issues in Amazonia. Rather, we stress the need to conserve and manage natural resources while designing agricultural systems that provide some hope of generating income for farmers, ranchers, and plantation owners.

Amazonia can be a graveyard for over-ambitious agricultural development schemes. Derelict rubber (*Hevea brasiliensis*) plantations, weed-choked pastures, and the early failure of some small farms along pioneer highways are testament to the folly of attempting to establish farming systems that are not attuned to ecological or market realities. Although ecological constraints were factors in the demise of some agricultural development schemes, mismanagement and a distorted policy of fiscal incentives are also to blame. The preponderance of ecological and socio-economic factors in farming difficulties varies with time and location. A major point here is that, with proper management and an openness to incorporating new technologies as well as learning from traditional systems, many constraints to raising and sustaining yields can be overcome. The relative success of many farms and plantations on the uplands attests to the resilience of some agricultural systems that have been deployed.

Some positive developments are under way in Amazonian agriculture and silviculture, indicating that environmental constraints are being surmounted. For example, Jari's plantations of exotic trees for pulp production appear to have turned the corner with respect to increased productivity and profitability. Cash-cropping with several perennial crops is breathing new life into the Bragantina zone east of Belém, an area once thought to be at the terminal stages of slash-and-burn farming. An emphasis on what appears to be going right for at least some Amazonian farmers and plantation operators should provide some insights into the development process and could generate helpful information for policy makers.

Our analysis of sustainable agriculture and silviculture thus focuses mainly on perennial cropping systems, mostly geared to generating cash income. An emphasis on income generation is justified by the evolutionary trend of many subsistence systems towards cash-cropping (Juo 1989). Jari's experience with pulp production, and the efforts of various companies to establish oil-palm and coconut plantations are discussed here. In subsequent chapters we explore agroforestry systems, ranching, and the potential of the flood plains for increased food production.

Silviculture for pulp

The Jari project, originally owned by the shipping magnate Daniel Ludwig, has been controversial since the ambitious project began in 1967. The immense size of the concession, 1.6 million ha, understandably fanned nationalistic feelings within Brazil. Plans to establish monocultures of fast-growing exotic trees for pulp production stirred concerns about creating ecological deserts in Amazonia and other regions.

Ludwig invested close to a US$1 billion in the Jari project before selling out to a consortium of 23 Brazilian companies and banks in 1982 (Kelly and London 1983: 282). Jari is often portrayed as a failure and as an undesirable development model for Amazonia (Browder 1989b; Parker et al. 1983; Schmink 1988b; Szulc 1986; Uhl, Jordan, and Herrera 1982), but much valuable experience has been gained at Jari that could be useful for environmentally sound development in the humid tropics.

Many of the early failures of the Jari project can be attributed to inept management and to a disregard of the scientific literature on mechanical clearing of tropical soils and silvicultural experiments (Palmer 1986). In the 1960s and the 1970s, management seemed to be operating on a revolving door principle (Kinkead 1981). Ludwig fired as many as 30 directors at Jari (Hecht and Cockburn 1989). Lack of continuity and a slowness to learn from early errors retarded Jari's progress. Under Ludwig's tenure, heavy machinery was used to clear forest for plantations of *Gmelina arborea* as well as to harvest the broad-leafed trees introduced from tropical Asia. Bulldozers and other machinery scraped away thin and valuable topsoil and compacted the subsoil (Greaves 1979).

Now plantations are harvested by hand-held power saws. Whereas in the past some steep slopes were cleared for plantations, many of these erosion-prone ravines are being allowed to revert to forest. Soil erosion no longer appears to be much of a problem in plantations at Jari. In Jamaica, the dense mat of needles in commercial stands of Caribbean pine has actually reduced soil erosion rates compared with native forests (Richardson 1982).

At first, Gmelina was envisaged as the main plantation tree for pulp production at Jari. But yield projections for this sun-loving Asian tree were not met at Jari. Gmelina produces reasonably well only on the better soils, mostly alfisols (*terra roxa*). In Thailand, where *G. arborea* is native, the species occurs in mixed deciduous forest growing on loamy soil, either calcareous or granitic (Smitinand 1989). Gmelina fares poorly on the sandier ultisols and heavily leached oxisols found in much of Jari and other parts of Amazonia, and is susceptible to insect and pest attack, such as *ceratocystis* wilt. Caribbean pine (*Pinus caribaea* var. *hondurensis*; fig. 5.1) was brought to Jari in 1973 and two species of eucalyptus (*Eucalyptus*

Fig. 5.1 **Three-year-old Caribbean pine (*Pinus caribaea* var. *hondurensis*) on third cycle. Jari, January 1990**

Fig. 5.2   **Nursery for *Eucalyptus urophylla*. Jari, January 1990**

deglupta and *E. urophylla*; fig. 5.2) were introduced in 1979 because they are fast-growing, hardier, and better adapted to poorer soils (Fearnside and Rankin 1982). By the late 1980s more eucalyptus species were being tried at Jari, including hybrids.

In 1989, Jari had some 85,000 ha in plantations. Pine and eucalyptus dominate the planted area, a reflection of the generally poor soils (JARI 1989). In December 1989, pine occupied 42,832 ha, eucalyptus covered 22,749 ha, while Gmelina was planted on 19,700 ha, the last down from a high of 64,000 ha (Palmer 1986). The proportion of new plantings to eucalyptus will continue to grow, while the relative contribution of Gmelina will decline further. Eucalyptus accounted for only 3 per cent of the plantation area in 1984 (Hornick, Zerbe, and Whitmore 1984), but by 1989 the two eucalyptus species occupied 27 per cent of the plantations. Gmelina will still be planted

115

for the foreseeable future, however, because some customers prefer its smooth paper for specialized uses, such as airline tickets (Reier 1990).

In 1989, the average yields of Jari's plantations were modest, about 13 m³/ha/year for pine, 15–17 m³/ha/year for Gmelina, and 19 m³/ha/year for eucalyptus. Nevertheless, productivity is increasing with the deployment of improved genotypes and the adoption of new agronomic practices. Eucalyptus yields of 42 m³/ha/year were not unusual by the late 1980s, and in 1990 several plots of *E. grandis* were producing 53 m³/ha/year. The latter species is so precocious at Jari that it attains 30 metres within six years. Eucalyptus yields of 60 m³/ha/year are no longer unusual in the humid tropics and are far greater than the potential of plantations in temperate climates (Evans 1986). In the mid-1980s, for example, Aracruz was regularly achieving eucalyptus yields of 70 m³/ha/year in south-eastern Brazil (WRI 1985a: 39), and, by selecting a mix of superior clones, yields reached as high as 100 m³/ha/year (Zobel, Van Wyk, and Stahl 1987: 142).

Deployment of superior genotypes is also the main strategy for increasing the productivity of plantations at Jari. Seed of *Eucalyptus urophylla* was originally obtained from Flores in Indonesia, but Jari has recently been purchasing seed from other companies in Brazil. Jari anticipates producing its own *E. urophylla* seed in the near future. The eucalyptus species employed at Jari do not coppice after cutting, thus enabling foresters to introduce fresh germ plasm after each five–seven-year cutting cycle.

Jari is drawing on the experience of Aracruz in Espírito Santo and Bahia with vegetative propagation of especially fast-growing eucalyptus material. Aracruz has planted over 60,000 ha of eucalyptus in south-eastern Brazil, much of it in clones. In 1979, for example, Aracruz had rooted 1 million eucalyptus cuttings, but by 1984 some 15 million eucalyptus clones were established. To reduce the danger of disease or pest epidemics, no more than 100 ha are planted to any one clone in the same area (WRI 1985b: 50). From 10 to 20 ha per clone appears to be the best compromise between reducing pest and disease attack and easing the task of planting and harvesting (Zobel, Van Wyk, and Stahl 1987: 213).

Similarly, Jari is conducting trials of over three dozen promising Gmelina selections in order eventually to plant various high-yielding clones in different blocks. In this manner, ecological heterogeneity will be maintained while raising yields. Gmelina cuttings root readily, thereby eliminating the need to graft on rootstock. In 1988, Jari began producing its own pine seed from controlled crosses on a 100 ha orchard near Morada Nova de Minas in Minas Gerais, an area far removed from other pine plantings and therefore free of pollen contamination.

A similar strategy of broadening the genetic base of plantations is under way on the savannas of Amapá, where AMCEL has planted 90,000 ha of tropical American pines. About 90 per cent of the plantings at AMCEL are *Pinus caribaea* var. *hondurensis*, with *P. oocarpa*, *P. caribaea* var. *Caribaea*, and *P. tecunumanii* comprising the remainder. The AMCEL plantings are cut on an eight-year cycle and the logs are sent to the nearby Jari pulp mill. In the past, germ plasm was obtained from scattered populations in Honduras, Guatemala, and first-generation plantings in Fiji and Brazil (McDonald and Fernandes 1984). AMCEL currently obtains its planting material from one of the Jari companies that maintains a nursery in Minas Gerais and from a forestry research institute (IPEF – Instituto de Pesquisas Florestais) in the state of São Paulo. The savanna soils under AMCEL management are poor in nutrients, but have suitable physical structure for silviculture and agriculture. To maintain yields, nitrogen and phosphate fertilizers are applied periodically to the soils in AMCEL's pine plantations.

On the agronomic front, weeding, control of ubiquitous leaf cutter ants (species of *Atta* and *Acromyrmex*), and fertilizers are necessary to achieve high yields. Weeds are controlled by herbicides (3 litres Roundup and 1 litre DMA per ha) and tractor mowing. In some cases, helicopters spray pre-emergent herbicides before planting. Herbicides are cheaper to use than mechanical weeding; also, unwanted plants return more quickly when they are cut. While plantations are becoming established, two herbicide applications a year are usually needed.

Leaf cutter ants are the most serious pests of recently planted Gmelina and eucalyptus. Leaf cutter ants can be serious agricultural pests in other parts of Amazonia and contiguous regions, sometimes forcing farmers to abandon fields (Butt 1970; Gonçalves 1957, 1967; Lathrap 1968; Nepstad, Uhl, and Serrão 1990). If fields are closer than 1 km apart, leaf cutter ants are more likely to find cleared areas in the forest during nuptial flights (Fautereau 1955). Jari's large, open spaces are ideal grounds for the build-up of leaf cutter ant populations.

Leaf cutter ants probably became a scourge to farmers soon after the dawn of agriculture in Amazonia. The ants have even been in-

117

corporated in mythology; the Desana of the Uaupés River, for example, believe that the "saliva" of the moon helps keep leaf cutter ants away from manioc fields (Reichel-Dolmatoff 1974: 73). *Saúva*, as the ants are called in Brazil, were reported as a common agricultural pest in the Amazon in the nineteenth century (Bates 1863: 23) and in Bahia during the sixteenth century (Sousa 1971: 173).

Traditional control measures against leaf cutter ants have been non-existent or largely ineffective. In most cases, fields seriously affected by the ants are simply abandoned. Various control measures were attempted against leaf cutter ants in Bahia during the 1500s: nests were sometimes dug up and burned; the nests were compacted to make it difficult for the ants to gain access to their subterranean chambers; or manioc leaves were spread along the ants' trails to distract them (Sousa 1971: 173). As leaf cutter ants became an increasingly serious problem in coffee groves along the Paraíba valley between Rio de Janeiro and São Paulo after 1830, fires were built by the ants' nests. Bellows were also used to force smoke into the nests, but such practices sometimes damaged the coffee bushes (Stein 1985: 217). In north-western Amazonia, leaf cutter ants are savoured as a culinary item, but human predation of *Atta* ants has not impaired their reproductive potential – a leaf cutter ant nest can contain more than 1 million individuals.

Jari staff use three pesticides to control leaf cutter ants. Mirex granules are placed by nests, while white Termicidol powder, which contains Aldrin, is doused into nests. Biabine gas is pumped into the nest galleys. The principal active ingredient in Biabine is methylbromide. Mirex has not been sprayed by air in the United States to control fire ants since 1978, a year after it was found to be a carcinogen; Amdro is now used for fire ant control in the United States, but it costs four to five times as much as Mirex (Jerry Stimac, pers. comm.). In 1990, 160 people, split up into several teams, were employed to destroy leaf cutter ant nests in Jari's plantations. Leaf cutter ant control thus requires about 1 person per 530 ha at Jari. In the late 1970s, Jari was spending US$1 million a year on the control of leaf cutter ants (Palmer 1986).

In view of the potential environmental hazards of pesticides, more research on biocontrol or less toxic control methods is warranted. The Kayapó, for example, scrape a forest vine (*Tanaercium nocturnum*, Bignoniaceae) to kill African bees five minutes prior to extracting honey from the hive (Kerr 1986). This vine can kill leaf cutter ants within a minute and, when placed in the nest, eliminates leaf cutter ants, or reduces them to such low numbers that they are no longer significant pests.

Some 100–150 kg of triple superphosphate are applied per ha to establish eucalyptus and pine plantings. In the case of Gmelina, 70 g of NPK fertilizer are applied at planting time. Pine orchards are fertilized again two to three years after planting. Experiments are under way to see if the addition of lime would reduce the need for relatively expensive phosphate fertilizer. Unfortunately, some of the lime has come from shell mounds near Santarém, thereby partially destroying some valuable archaeological sites (Anna Roosevelt, pers. comm.). Large quantities of Carboniferous limestone occur at Monte Alegre and along the middle Tapajós; such deposits could eventually be exploited for lime fertilizer.

To help raise and sustain plantation yields, Jari has created a superintendency for forestry research with a staff of 33 people. The research division is divided among several departments, including genetic improvement, silvicultural research, plant pathology, soils, plant nutrition, and native forest resources. Consultants are also employed to tackle specific problems, but an in-house scientific capacity provides continuity and greater familiarity with the overall project.

The investment in science is paying off at Jari. The pulp mill, towed from Japan in 1978, functioned mostly at a loss until the main boiler blew up in July 1988. Since the mill came back on line in March 1989, operations have been in the black. Some of the wood for pulp production is being met by bringing in Caribbean pine logs from the AMCEL plantation in Amapá, but Jari expects to be self-sufficient in wood production within a few years. From March to December 1989, the Jari mill produced 230,000 tons of pulp, mostly destined for export. By 1993, annual production of pulp at Jari had reached 330,000 tons per annum (Blount 1993).

Enormous investments were necessary at Jari to turn the corner. A 9,000 km road network was laid out, a 68 km railroad was built to transport harvested logs to the pulp mill, several residential communities were created with support services, and experiments were carried out over two decades. Jari now appears to be a sustainable operation, welcome news for the 5,500 employees and for the 60,000 people who depend indirectly on the enterprise. Plantations can clearly make a dent in rural poverty by providing employment opportunities.

Jari started becoming profitable in 1990 largely because of improved planning, research, and streamlining operations. The current management team took advantage of lessons learned during the learning curve when Ludwig held the helm at Jari. The current consortium operating Jari recently made a profit of US$5 million on pulp sales of US$160 million (Alvarenga 1991). Jari has dropped its cattle operation, including the intercropping of pasture and pine, to concentrate on its core business: pulp production. Jari terminated a highly mechanized rice operation on the Amazon flood plain, owing mainly to the high cost of controlling water levels in rice paddies using diesel pumps, and to low rice prices in the 1980s. The former rice area around São Raimundo has been sold to Grupo Uliana, and this consortium maintains a herd of 13,000 water buffalo on the flood plain. Grupo Uliana also plans to raise pirarucu (*Arapaima gigas*) in ponds and to operate a hotel emphasizing eco-tourism. The kaolin mine, in operation for over a decade, has been profitable since its inception in the mid-1970s; in 1991, the mine turned a US$12 million profit (Alvarenga 1991).

Some are still concerned that Jari is not an appropriate model for Amazonian development or that profitability does not take into account resource depletion (Vosti 1993). Jari was never intended to be the model for development in Amazonia or elsewhere. Rather it contributes to a mosaic of land uses in the region. The criticism that profits do not consider such factors as soil erosion and loss of biodiversity could be applied to most development schemes throughout the world. Overall, Jari is helping to conserve the environment by maximizing production from a relatively small proportion of the property and by taking stringent safeguards to avoid water pollution.

The idea that Jari is causing major ecological impacts, and therefore cannot be considered a model for agro-silvicultural development, is without merit. Jari anticipates clearing only 145,000 ha, less than 10 per cent of the property. Effluent from the paper mill passes through a series of large settling ponds before it is discharged into the Jari River. When the second pulp mill comes on line in the mid-1990s, the settling ponds will occupy some 450,000 m^2, roughly the area covered by 63 soccer fields.

In new plantations established inland from the left margin of the Jari River, extensive corridors of forest, at least 400 metres wide, have been left to provide faunal bridges (fig. 5.3). A similar approach is being studied in Florida to connect otherwise isolated patches of forest (Harris 1984). Only flat areas have been cleared for plantations. Forest patches provide windbreaks for young trees and firebreaks; in 1987, 600 ha of pine were lost in a lightning-caused fire.

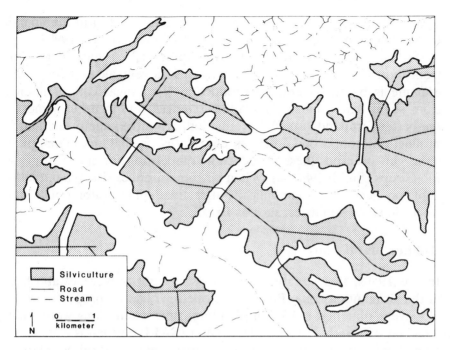

Fig. 5.3 **Corridors connecting forest in a portion of Jari's pulpwood plantations. Morro do Felipe, Amapá. Blank areas are forest**

The proposed 100 MW hydroelectric plant at the Santo Antônio falls of the Jari River was expected to be ready in the mid-1990s and will supply energy for the pulp mills. The energy needs of the mill are currently met by pulp wastes, diesel oil, and to a lesser extent fuelwood. Instead of a dam, the hydroelectric station will divert some of the Jari River through a turbine. Fisheries will not be disrupted and the scenic beauty of the basalt falls will remain intact.

Although few would argue that the vocation of Amazonia is converting all of the forest to plantations, the Jari experience could prove useful as world demand for pulp continues to rise and methanol becomes an economically viable fuel by the late 1990s. The cost of pulp production in industrial countries is increasing owing to environmental restrictions. In Scandinavia, for example, ever more stringent emission controls and pollution taxes are driving up the cost of operating pulp mills. In the north-western United States, access to some old-growth timber is being denied to protect mature ecosystems that contain endemic species. The construction costs for a modern pulp mill with a capacity of 1,500 tons of pulp a day are approaching

121

US$1 billion, so more pulp operations are likely to shift to the humid tropics where operating costs are generally lower (Benoit 1990).

Methanol can be made from fossil fuels, such as natural gas, or from biomass, particularly wood. Brazil's current alcohol fuel programme is based on ethanol production from sugar cane. Ethanol from sugar cane, maize, or manioc requires setting aside some of the better farmlands for fuel production. An advantage of methanol production from wood, such as eucalyptus, is that more marginal areas can be used, thereby reducing competition for space to grow food crops (Smith 1981b,c). When petroleum prices rise again, methanol may become an economically attractive fuel for automobiles and trucks in some countries, such as Brazil.

Rubber plantations

In the 1950s, two sizeable plantations of rubber were established in the Bragantina zone. Pirelli developed a 7,000 ha property, while Goodyear obtained a 4,500 ha holding. Both plantations were soon attacked by South American leaf blight (SALB), which is caused by an endemic fungus, *Microcyclus ulei*. Most commercial rubber plantations in the Amazon are double-grafted to reduce disease problems and to improve yields. A relative of the rubber tree, *Hevea pauciflora*, is often employed for the crown because it resists SALB. Still, yields do not compare with those prevailing in South-East Asia. At the Goodyear plantation near São Francisco in the Bragantina zone, for example, latex yields average only 300 kg/ha/yr, less than one-third of those achieved on Goodyear plantations in Malaysia and the Philippines where groves are free of SALB (Goodyear 1989: 28). Furthermore, operating costs are higher in the Amazon, particularly with respect to labour and fertilizer.

Rubber fares better as an intercrop in Amazonia, because disease pressure is less severe when the trees are dispersed among other plants. But the immediate outlook for rubber in Amazonia is dim. As mentioned in the discussion of extractive reserves, the Brazilian government is essentially eliminating all subsidies for natural rubber. At best, rubber may have a future only as an intercrop with small farmers, or on well-managed plantations in southern Brazil where disease problems are less severe.

Fiscal incentives promulgated since 1950 have spurred much of the rubber planting in Brazil. For example, SUDHEVEA (Superintendência da Borracha) was established in 1967 to promote rubber planting, to support rubber tappers, and to improve product quality. In 1989, SUDHEVEA's functions were taken over by the environment agency IBAMA (Instituto Brasileiro do Meio Ambiente e dos Recursos Naturais Renováveis) before SUDHEVEA had accomplished its goals. Besides, IBAMA is concerned more with nature preservation and wildlife regulations than with stimulating rubber production.

PROBOR (Programa de Incentivo à Produção da Borracha) was created in 1972 to help Brazil become self-sufficient in natural rubber within a decade. Yet in 1974 Brazil imported 41 per cent of its natural rubber needs, and in 1989 the proportion had climbed to 74 per cent (Goodyear 1989: 26). PROBOR was phased out in 1985, when SUDHEVEA was charged with providing technical assistance only. Even though a suite of fiscal incentives, taxes, and subsidies did little to redress the balance of imports of natural rubber to Brazil, investments were made in rubber plantations in various parts of Brazil. Today, planted rubber covers at least 40,000 ha, mostly in São Paulo, Espírito Santo, Bahia, Mato Grosso, and Pará. If rubber is to remain a viable commercial crop in Amazonia, more research will be needed on resistance to SALB, among other diseases and pests.

Oil-palm

In contrast to the rather gloomy prospects for rubber in Brazil, an exotic plantation species shows greater promise. African oil-palm is well adapted to most soils and climates in Amazonia. Pará has the largest plantings of African oil-palm in Brazil (table 5.1), but at least 50 million ha in the Brazilian Amazon are deemed suitable for the quick-growing palm (Alvim 1989). Brazil imports palm oil and the market for vegetable oils is growing. Furthermore, palm oil can serve

Table 5.1 **Area planted to African oil-palm in Brazil, 1991**

State	Area planted (ha)
Pará	32,000
Amapá	4,300
Amazonas	2,000
Bahia	15,000
TOTAL	53,300

Source: Falesi and Osaqui (1992).

123

as a substitute for diesel fuel, so both the short- and long-term prospects for oil-palm are bright.

The Bragantina zone has the oldest African oil-palm groves in Amazonia, on both small- and medium-sized holdings. The largest plantations are operated by DENPASA (Dendê do Pará, S.A.), which inaugurated an oil-processing factory along the Belém–Mosqueiro road in 1976 with fiscal incentives provided by SUDAM (Superintendência do Desenvolvimento da Amazonia). DENPASA currently operates two oil-processing factories with a capacity of 20 tons fruit/hour. DENPASA imports planting material from a British company that uses micropropagation techniques to multiply high-yielding varieties. DENPASA's 6,000 ha are mostly sandy, so fertilizers are applied according to foliar analyses. Soils are enriched with nitrogen by a thick mat of planted leguminous creepers (*Pueraria javanica* and *P. phaseoloides*; fig. 5.4). DENPASA processes oil-palm year-round and provides steady employment for about six persons per hectare.

Following the lead of DENPASA, several entrepreneurs have established three small-scale African oil-palm processing factories in the Bragantina zone near Belém and Castanhal. These oil-palm processing plants, capable of processing 6–7 tons fruit/hour, service 10–20 ha plantations, often in a cooperative arrangement. At least 3,000 ha of African oil-palm are planted on smallholdings outside of DENPASA's property. The small-scale oil-palm processing facilities use boilers fuelled by fruit stalks, cracked kernels, and wood. Fruit stalks are sometimes mulched for later distribution around oil-palms, while the pressed kernels are sold for livestock feed. Oil-palm production is thus linked to the livestock sector, and provides employment opportunities in rural areas.

A cloud nevertheless looms on the horizon for oil-palm plantations in the Bragantina zone and other parts of Latin America. Spear rot, possibly caused by a viroid or mycoplasma-like organism, appeared in the Bragantina zone in 1985. Spear rot stymied an attempt by SOCFIN to establish an oil-palm plantation near Tefé in Amazonas in the late 1970s. Only 2,000 ha of oil-palm were planted by the Belgian company near Tefé, a fraction of the original plans. In the Bragantina zone, only the DENPASA plantations have been struck by the disease as of 1990, when some 400 ha were affected. By 1992, 1,500 ha of DENPASA's plantation near Mosqueiro in the Bragantina zone had been destroyed in an effort to control spear rot.

Fig. 5.4 **Pueraria ground cover in an African oil-palm (*Elaeis guineensis*) plantation operated by DENPASA. Near Belém, 1990**

Some 7,500 ha of oil-palm in the Bragantina zone are thus in imminent danger of spear rot.

Some 200 km south of Belém, 13,900 ha of recently planted oil-palm are also at risk to spear rot. In 1989, a subsidiary of Banco Real (CRAI – Companhia Real Agroindustrial) purchased 3,340 ha of oil-palm established by Agromendes; the latter was a subsidiary of Mendes Junior, a giant construction firm, which diversified into agriculture with fiscal incentives. In 1986, Agromendes and CRAI owned some 6,000 ha of oil-palm in the vicinity of km 74 of the PA 150 highway (Barcelos et al. 1987). As of 1992, CRAI and the absorbed Agromendes, now renamed Agropalma, cultivate 9,210 ha of oil-palm on adjacent properties. Nearby, DENPASA maintains a 2,500 ha plantation of oil-palm, which is processed by Agropalma. Approximately 100 km north-east, along the PA 252 road, REASA operates a 2,500 ha oil-palm plantation. The Moju-Acará area, with 14,210 ha of oil-palm, thus had the greatest concentration of the crop in Pará in 1992.

CRAI and Agromendes plan to plant a further 10,000 ha on their 33,000 ha property. Roughly half of CRAI and Agropalma's property is slated to remain in forest in order to comply with Brazil's environmental regulations. Some 20 hybrids are planted, with an average yield of 22 tons fruit/ha/yr from the 5,000 ha of plantations in production. Even this diversity of planting material may not save the plantations from spear rot. Banco Real has invested approximately US$70 million in oil-palm along the PA 150 highway, and failure of the oil-palm plantations at CRAI and Agropalma would put 1,000 people out of work.

Inputs at the oil plantations along the PA 150 highway are kept to a minimum, and environmental impacts appear to be negligible. Agropalma maintains a 100 metre strip of forest on either side of streams on the property and plants only on relatively flat surfaces. No pesticides are used on the plantations. A company agronomist suggests that the surrounding forest and second-growth communities provide biocontrol agents (W. Padilha, pers. comm.). A lepidopteran larva, *Anteotricha* sp., started attacking oil-palm leaves in 1991, but the caterpillar is apparently controlled by a fungus. Native açaí palm (*Euterpe oleracea*) appears to be one of the pest's hosts.

Pressed fruit cake from the processing plant is recycled to the plantations, which have a ground cover of nitrogen-fixing *Pueraria*. Fertilizer applications are carefully calibrated according to foliar analyses. Provided that spear rot does not appear along the PA 150 highway, Banco Real's oil-palm plantations are likely to succeed. As in the case of the Bragantina zone, the presence of large oil-palm plantations and processing plants could eventually provide a stimulus for small-scale producers to diversify their crop base with oil-palm. Already, Pará accounts for almost two-thirds of Brazil's oil-palm production (Falesi and Osaqui 1992).

More than 20,000 ha of oil-palm established in the Huallaga valley in the Peruvian Amazon since 1967 are also threatened by spear rot (Pulgar 1987: 134). If spear rot strikes the Huallaga valley, it will deal a severe blow to the Peruvian government's efforts to find viable alternatives to coca production.

The disease, known as *amarelecimento fatal* in Brazil and *marchitez sorpresiva* in Peru, is currently managed with varying degrees of success by early identification of symptoms and prompt elimination of diseased trees. Spear rot is thought to be transmitted by insects, but fogging with insecticides would destroy beetle pollinators. The separation of oil-palm plantations by stretches of second growth and other crops may retard the spread of the disease. Black vultures (*Coragyps atratus*) relish ripe oil-palm fruits, so plantations are best kept away from large towns and cities where large populations of the vultures congregate.

Genetic resistance to spear rot is the best way to combat the disease, and a near relative of African oil-palm that grows wild along the Amazon flood plain promises to help in this regard. American oil-palm (*Elaeis oleifera*) resists spear rot and has already been used in crossing work with *E. guineensis* to reduce the latter's height and thereby facilitate harvesting. American oil-palm has also been employed by breeders to improve the oil quality of African oil-palm. Several hybrids between prostrate caiaué, as the palm is known in Brazil, and African oil-palm are under observation at a sizeable oil-palm breeding and evaluation site operated by EMBRAPA (Empresa Brasileira de Pesquisa Agropecuária) along the Urubu River north of Manaus. Caiaué's resistance to spear rot underscores the importance of conserving wild habitats in Amazonia.

Coconut

Another exotic palm, coconut, has emerged as a viable cash crop in eastern Amazonia, for both small- and large-scale producers. Fresh coconuts from smallholdings sell briskly at local markets, whereas coconuts from commercial plantations are sent to Belém and northeastern Brazil to be processed for the confectionery trade.

A Brazilian firm based in Maceio, Sócôco, is establishing a 5,000 ha coconut plantation near Belém and has planted 3,600 ha of coconut south of Belém at Acará. The plantation at Acará began in 1981 with support from the International Finance Corporation and SUDAM. Sócôco's plantations at Acará are relatively homogeneous since they contain only a few, high-yielding selections, dominated by PB 121 and PB 111, with 70 and 15 per cent of the planted area, respectively. Genetic homogeneity at Acará has not led to any serious pest or disease problems thus far. Selections planted by Sócôco contain Malayan Dwarf germ plasm, so lethal yellowing – which has ravaged coconut plantations in parts of Central America and the Caribbean –

127

Fig. 5.5 **Harvesting coconuts (*Cocos nucifera*) with a mule at the Sócôco plantation. Acará, Pará, 3 April 1991**

is not a threat. *Marchitez*, caused by a protozoan, is the main disease problem. After marchitez, the second most important cause of coconut tree mortality is lightening. An unidentified fungal disease of the leaves, called *queima de folha*, can also be a problem.

Yields at Acará on eight-year-old plantings with a density of 160 trees/ha are in the order of 10,000 coconuts/ha/yr. Fertilizer is needed because the yellow oxisols are infertile. Leaf analysis is performed in Montpellier once a year to calibrate fertilizer doses; seedlings are given 200 g urea, 300 g K, 15 g Borax, and 800 g superphosphate when planted. Salt is added to the fertilizer mix after the third year to facilitate the uptake of nutrients. Nitrogen fertilizers are no longer applied after the third year as the *Pueraria javanica* ground

Fig. 5.6 **Coconut (*Cocos nucifera*) with pueraria ground cover at the TABA plantation. Near Mosqueiro, Pará, 28 May 1990**

cover, which was introduced from Côte d'Ivoire, becomes well established. Pueraria also suppresses weeds, an important consideration in an area receiving around 3,000 mm of rain a year.

Only a small fraction of Sócôco's 17,000 ha property at Acará has been cleared. The vicinity of the plantation is not densely settled, but neighbouring communities benefit from the 600 jobs generated by the Acará coconut operation. A pasture of *Brachiaria humidicola* is maintained to supply milk for some of the employees; this pasture, already 12 years old in 1991, also supports some 50 mules, which are used to take coconuts to waiting trucks (fig. 5.5).

A 500 ha coconut plantation, operated by TABA, a regional airline, was established near Mosqueiro on the Bragantina coast without fiscal incentives. The TABA plantation contains approximately 50,000 trees and produces some 30,000 coconuts a month. The plantation is genetically heterogeneous, since most of the trees originated from seedlings collected from villages in widely scattered locations in

129

Fig. 5.7 **Coconut (*Cocos nucifera*) intercropped with lime at the TABA plantation, surrounded by forest. Near Mosqueiro, Pará, 28 May 1990**

the Bragantina zone and on Marajó. The TABA plantation is gradually becoming more homogeneous, however, as dead trees are replaced by selections made at the plantation.

The only significant pests thus far are beetles, particularly *Rincopharum palmarum*. A well-established ground cover of pueraria protects the soil and provides nitrogen to the palms (fig. 5.6). TABA is diversifying its coconut operation by experimenting with intercrops, such as lime, soursop, and guava (fig. 5.7). Also, several small reservoirs have been created to raise pirarucu, a highly valued fish in local markets.

6

Agro-forestry and perennial cropping systems

Many perennial crops are grown in agro-forestry systems, thereby diversifying sources of income for farmers. A strong trend to growing perennials is noted throughout the Amazon basin, even in the early phase of settlement. Our definition of agro-forestry embraces a mixture of perennials grown on the same plot. In some definitions of agro-forestry, annual food crops must be part of such systems. In the Brazilian Amazon, however, few instances are found where annual food crops are planted alongside perennials. Many polycultural perennial systems contain plants that provide important sources of food as well as cash income, such as banana. The agro-forestry systems explored here are found in home gardens as well as in separate fields.

Some farmers cultivate perennials as monocrops in small orchards. Sweet oranges (*Citrus sinensis*), in particular, are often grown in pure stands. Nevertheless, farmers may also have polycultural fields with a mixture of perennials, as well as diverse home gardens. The resulting farm landscapes in many areas are thus a patchwork quilt of perennial crops, annuals, pasture, second growth, and forest.

Agro-forestry and monocultural cropping with perennials investigated here are oriented strongly to markets and have not evolved primarily for food production. Although boosting the productivity of food crops is certainly desirable, attention also needs to focus on upgrading cash-cropping systems. The rural poor are not necessarily best served by focusing exclusively on food crops (Carney 1990). Nutritional gains can be achieved by increasing the income of farmers, so that they can purchase or barter for foodstuffs. In the vicinity of Ouro Preto in Rondônia, for example, farmers who cultivate perennials have generally fared better than those who rely on annual crops (Southworth, Dale, and O'Neill 1991).

Heavy reliance on annual food crops in upland areas is understandable during early phases of settlement, but yields generally decline rapidly and farmers must move on to open new patches in the forest, or intensify production on existing cleared areas by shifting to perennials, as in the Bragantina zone (Egler 1961). Annual crops, such as rice, maize, and beans, are typically cultivated during the first phase of settlement in forested areas, but continued reliance on these crops for cash and subsistence often leads to farm failures (Leonard 1989). Perennial cropping systems are helping to revive several "failed" colonization efforts in the region (Homma et al. 1992a).

Two features are typically found with successful farmers in the Brazilian Amazon: the deployment of perennial crops and/or mixed farming with livestock (Veiga and Serrão 1990). One Japanese-Brazilian with a 25 ha farm near Igarapé Açu, Pará, for example, has 4 ha in African oil-palm (*Elaeis guineensis*), 3 ha of lemon (*Citrus limon*), 3 ha of passionfruit (*Passiflora edulis*), 1 ha of "Sunrise Solo" papaya (*Carica papaya*), as well as several hectares of vegetables grown for market. Livestock provide manure for crops and aquaculture, and diversify sources of income.

Agro-forestry systems can play a vital role in helping Amazonian agriculture become more sustainable because of the wide array of environmental services they perform. For example, protecting soil from excessive soil erosion or compaction is essential to the long-term viability of land-use systems (Fernandes and Serrão 1992; Smith 1990). Agro-forestry systems are especially appropriate for the humid tropics since they address many of the ecological problems associated with farming, such as helping to conserve soil moisture and fertility (Nair 1991; Nair and Dagar 1991; Padoch et al. 1985; Peters and Neuenschwander 1988: 34). Indeed, diversity and information, rather than energy and chemicals, are the linchpins of sustainable agriculture (Ryan 1992: 35), and polycultural systems employing perennials exemplify this principle.

Diversity in space

Home gardens

Home gardens are the most diverse agro-forestry systems encountered in the Brazilian Amazon, a reflection of the desire to group numerous useful plants close to the kitchen, to offer shade, to provide a forum for trying out novel crops, and to serve as living pharmacies for treating a wide array of afflictions. A total of 74 perennial plant species, excluding ornamentals, medicinal plants, and vegetables, were found in just 31 home gardens in upland areas of the Brazilian Amazon (appendices 3 and 4). If all plants are considered, several hundred species are undoubtedly cultivated in home gardens throughout the Brazilian Amazon. Women are especially important in recruiting plants for home gardens and in experimenting with novel crops.

The home gardens of people native to the region are especially rich in species, and contain a variety of plants for food, fibre, medicine, and aesthetic pleasure. Immigrants to Amazonia, such as from the North-east region and from Japan, are also quick to adopt diverse home gardens. The number of species in home gardens ranged from four in the case of a recent arrival from Maranhão, to a high of 25 around the home of a long-time resident of Pará. The extraordinary richness of home gardens has been noted in other parts of the Amazon basin; at Santa Rosa along the lower Ucayali, for example, two home gardens had 74 and 73 annual and perennial plant species, respectively, with only 34 species in common (Padoch and de Jong 1991).

Home gardens typically contain a mixture of exotic and native species (appendix 3). Of the 74 species found in our home garden sample, approximately 46 per cent are indigenous to Amazonia and some 27 per cent are from the Old World. A precise breakdown is not possible, because the origins of some tropical perennials are obscure, and the precise identity of some of the species is uncertain. Two of the most common perennials in home gardens are from the Asian tropics: mango (*Mangifera indica*) and sweet orange. Other, more recent exotics are finding their way into backyards, such as Barbados cherry (*Malpighia glabra*), an indication of the willingness of farmers to experiment with new possibilities.

Home gardens serve as important launching pads for exotic crops. By planting a few individuals of an unknown crop in the backyard, a farmer makes a minimal investment while observing its performance and trying its products. Home gardens also serve as "low-cost" arenas for trying out new domesticates. When clearing forest or old second growth for their home-sites, farmers sometimes leave native trees if they are deemed useful. Forest vestiges often produce seedlings in home gardens, where they are tended. Another way that wild species enter the proto-domestication stage is when seedlings sprout spontaneously in house yards, either as a result of natural dispersion from surrounding vegetation or from seeds discarded by family members. Wild species are also deliberately planted, as in the case of a farmer in the Lastancia Community near Itupiranga, Pará, who planted towering buriti (*Mauritia flexuosa*) in the backyard. Buriti palm is normally found along rivers and on poorly drained savannas and its fruits contain generous amounts of vitamins A and C. Home gardens are thus propitious "hunting grounds" for promising new crops in Amazonia and could serve as important sources of germ plasm for agro-forestry and perennial cropping systems.

Several trees in forest or old second growth are deliberately left in home gardens when clearing a homestead, including jangada, embileira, piquiá (*Caryocar villosum*), babaçu (*Attalea speciosa*), and morototó (*Didymopanax morototoni*; appendix 4). Spontaneous seedlings of wild cacao (*Theobroma cacao*), Brazil nut, babaçu, and bacaba (*Oenocarpus distichus*) are sometimes protected in home gardens. The age-old process of plant domestication around homesites, often cited as one of the principal sites for crop origins, continues.

Home gardens sometimes "spill over" into adjacent fields. In some cases home gardens and cleared fields form a continuum, whereas in other instances the separation of door yard gardens and fields is abrupt. The pronounced dry season in eastern and central Amazonia is sometimes cited as the main reason farmers do not replicate the complexity of their home gardens in fields. Seedlings of perennial crops often perish before the regular rains return.

Polycultural fields

Agro-forestry configurations vary considerably throughout the Amazon, a testament to the innovative spirit of farmers. Ninety-seven distinct agro-forestry configurations were noted on small and medium-sized farms in Pará, Amazonas, Rondônia, and Acre (appendix 2). Farmers are clearly conducting experiments on a gigantic scale. Of the 97 configurations noted, only 11 were encountered on more than one occasion. The most common association, black pepper (*Piper nigrum*) and orange, was found five times in the sample of 121 fields with mixed perennial crops. The second most common combinations were manioc (*Manihot esculenta*) and banana, and manioc and orange, with four occurrences each. A strong trend towards diversifying fields with a considerable repertoire of perennial crops is thus discernible throughout the Brazilian Amazon. A remarkable diversity of agro-forestry systems is evident in areas of dynamic growth as well as in more isolated areas with traditional farmers.

Farmers deploy a range of perennials to achieve diversity in time as well as in space. Sixty species were found in 121 polycultural fields involving perennials (appendix 5). About seven species are found relatively frequently: orange, cupuaçu (*Theobroma grandiflorum*), black pepper, manioc, cacao (*Theobroma cacao*), rubber (*Hevea brasiliensis*), and banana. The first three crops, orange, cupuaçu, and black pepper, are among the most profitable cash crops. Cacao and, especially, rubber are currently declining in importance. Interestingly, Brazil nut was found in 12 agro-forestry configurations, a clear indication of the rapid transition of the giant tree from an extractive species in forest to a crop.

As in the case of home gardens, polycultural fields contain a mix of indigenous species and exotics. But agro-forestry systems in fields contain a much higher proportion of exotics than do home gardens. Only about one-third of the species found in the sampled polycultural configurations in fields are native to Amazonia – a finding that belies the oft-heard recommendation that agricultural development should focus primarily on indigenous species. Although increased attention to the native plants of Amazonia is certainly warranted, progress in raising yields and incomes for rural folk also hinges on the timely introduction of crops from other regions, and even other continents.

Nevertheless, most of the crop combinations in polycultural fields involve only two or three species. It is not surprising that polycultural fields are less diverse than home gardens; the investment is much greater in fields, so fewer risks are taken. Greater diversity in fields was noted in areas dominated by more traditional farmers. Four kilometres from Itacoatiara along the road to Manaus, Amazonas, for example, one farmer who grew up in the area maintained a field interplanted with guaraná (*Paullinia cupana*), lime (*Citrus aurantifolia*), mango, pineapple (*Ananas cosmosus*), coconut (*Cocos nucifera*), cashew (*Anacardium occidentale*), avocado *(Persea americana)*, jackfruit (*Artocarpus heterophyllus*), and guava *(Psidium guajava)*. Several Brazil nut trees and tucumã (*Astrocaryum aculeatum*) had been spared when the forest was cleared. The polycultural fields cultivated by peasants (*caboclos, colonos, pequenos produtores*) do not generally contain as rich a mixture as is often found among indigenous groups, where numerous crop species and varieties are commonly planted in a single field (Dufour 1990; Lathrap 1970: 59; Parker et al. 1983).

Diversity in agricultural systems can lead to greater "sustainability" up to a point. Greater diversity does not necessarily mean greater stability or productivity in agro-ecosystems, nor are indigenous fields always polycultural. In the most productive ecosystems, species diversity typically declines (Pimm and Gittleman 1992). Species simplicity does not necessarily lead to instability (Pimm 1984). Furthermore, some indigenous polycultural swiddens are actually dominated by one or two crops. Among the Witoto and Andoke in the Colombian Amazon, for example, manioc typically accounts for much of the planted area in fields (Eden 1988). Some indigenous groups cultivate mainly monocultural fields, such as manioc among the Kuikuru and Piaroa, and banana and plantain in the case of the Embará and Shipibo (Beckerman 1987).

As long as the mix of perennials helps protect the soil and provides some buffer to fluctuations in commodity prices and disease epidemics, reliance on two or three species for the bulk of agricultural production and income will probably work. Many of these agro-forestry systems, however, are highly dynamic, with some perennials being replaced by others after several years. Agro-forestry systems, including managed fallows, can remain productive for decades and provide appreciable income when close to markets, as along the lower Ucayali (Padoch et al. 1985).

Diversity in time

Four main crops have served as "launching pads" for agro-forestry in the Brazilian Amazon: black pepper, cacao, coffee (especially robusta coffee), and manioc (appendix 2). Interestingly, two of these mainstays of polycultural systems are exotics: coffee and black pepper. Each of the four main cash crops has served as a springboard for diversifying farming operations for different reasons – black pepper after disease took a serious toll, cacao and coffee because of a sharp drop in prices in the late 1980s, and manioc because it has traditionally served as the last crop in swidden fields before the plot is abandoned to second growth.

Instead of allowing a field to go fallow, some farmers are prolonging its useful life by opting for agro-forestry. A similar trend is noted on Borneo where some small farmers are planting perennials, such as rubber and durian, instead of allowing swidden fields to go fallow

(Brookfield, Potter, and Byron 1995). In the sample of 121 poly-cultural fields, manioc was present in 25, and the hardy tuber cultigen was the fourth most common crop in sampled polycultural fields (appendix 5). The tendency to interplant longer-lived perennials with manioc is particularly noticeable in the Santarém area (appendix 2).

Farmers know that black pepper will eventually fall victim to Fusarium wilt so they often interplant other perennials, such as pas-sionfruit or oil-palm, so that the land still produces income as the black pepper is phased out. As Fusarium symptoms become pro-gressively worse, farmers gradually replace black pepper with other perennials, such as African oil-palm, passionfruit, Barbados cherry, or cupuaçu. Even so, black pepper is still the main "money earner" for many farmers engaged in market-oriented agro-forestry systems in the Brazilian Amazon; the labour-intensive crop is the third most common component in the sample of 121 polycultural fields (appendix 5).

In this manner, farmers incorporate diversity into their cropping systems over time. Black pepper paves the way for other crops be-cause fertilizers enrich the soil and rice husks, often placed around the base of black pepper plants, help build up organic matter.

Some of the intercropped perennials are productive for only a few years, so the composition of agro-forestry systems is highly dynamic. Passionfruit, for example, normally produces for only three to five years. Longer-lived perennials are often intercropped as the passion-fruit vines mature; one farmer in Tomé-Açu, for example, has inter-cropped his passionfruit field with various timber trees. A farmer near Capitão Poço has intercropped his passionfruit with longer-lived sweet orange and annatto (*Bixa orellana*) trees (fig. 6.1). At Sitio Andiroba, near Castanhal, a 25 ha field formerly planted to passion-fruit and papaya was replanted with sweet orange after the pro-ductivity of the former intercrops declined. With periodic doses of NPK fertilizer, the 5,000 trees in the 25 ha orchard produce about 2.7 kg of oranges per tree every year.

Agro-forestry integration with aquaculture and livestock

Many farmers have prospered in the Brazilian Amazon by integrating agro-forestry with livestock and aquaculture. Only a few examples are given here to illustrate the increasing importance of cattle-raising for small farmers. Smallholders employ cattle manure to fertilize their cash crops as well as their vegetable gardens for home con-

Fig. 6.1   **Passionfruit intercropped with orange and annatto (*Bixa orellana*). Near Capitão Poço, Pará, 5 April 1991**

sumption and market. For example, a Paraense farmer along a side-road at km 105 of the Marabá–Altamira stretch of the Transamazon Highway collects cow manure to enrich potting soil for cupuaçu seedlings. This farmer, also the leader of the rural workers' syndicate for the municipality of Itupiranga, raises cattle on 25 ha of pasture; the remaining 125 ha on his lot are in crops, forest, and second growth.

At Granja Yoshirokato near Santa Isabel in the Bragantina zone, chicken manure fertilizes ponds that contain tilapia, which in turn are fed to highly prized pirarucu (fig. 6.2). When the pirarucu reach 2–4 kg, the owner sells them to other farmers and ranchers to stock ponds. Dead chickens are also fed to the carnivorous pirarucu. The medium-sized farm, which operates without fiscal incentives, also produces citrus, guava, and other fruits for the growing Belém market. Black pepper farmers in the Brazilian Amazon take advantage of chicken manure when it is available to cut down on the cost of inorganic fertilizers.

Cattle-raising is also sometimes integrated with agro-forestry and

Fig. 6.2 **Paulo Yoshirokato on his farm, Granja Yoshirokato. Along BR 316 near Santa Isabel, Pará, 28 May 1990. This farm produces a variety of fruits, poultry, and young of pirarucu and other fish for aquaculture**

perennial monocropping systems, particularly as a source of manure. On the Rio Branco ranch near Ariquemes, Rondônia, for example, cattle manure is applied to 45 ha of citrus orchards, mainly the Pêra variety of orange. Sweet orange is planted at various locations on the 7,000 ha property, half of which remains in forest. Even at the rate of 30 kg of dung per seedling, however, cattle manure is only a supplement to the commercial fertilizers needed to establish an orange grove. Orange seedlings are also given 500 g of lime and 400 g of superphosphate, together with some micro-nutrients such as zinc and sulphur, to help get them started. By diversifying their farm operations, ranchers and growers reduce fertilizer costs and are better insulated from the wild price swings typical of many commodities.

At least one Japanese-Brazilian farmer in the vicinity of Tomé-Açu is contemplating diversifying into cattle production, in part to generate manure for his perennial crops. A shift by the Japanese-Brazilian community to cattle-raising is significant, since it underscores the strong market forces favouring cattle production in Amazonia.

A farmer from Rio Grande do Sul with a 100 ha lot at km 74 of the Altamira–Itaituba stretch of the Transamazon derives a variety of benefits from his small herd of cattle. Livestock manure is used for fertilizer and to generate gas for cooking, lighting, and refrigeration. The mixed farm is planted to cacao and an assortment of other crops, and has 30 head of cattle. Dung from the cattle is fed into a rudimentary biogas digestor and the resulting methane is piped into the home to fuel a stove, two lights, and a couple of refrigerators. When the biogas digestor is cleaned out, the residue is placed on a vegetable plot.

Complementarities also exist between farmers devoted exclusively to agro-forestry and nearby cattle ranches. For example, several oil-palm factories have sprung up in the Bragantina zone to serve large and small growers. After the oil has been extracted, the pressed kernels are sold to ranchers for cattle feed. Similarly, small factories established to express castor oil sell the pressed seeds to ranchers for feed. Castor bean is a cash crop for small farmers in parts of Pará and exemplifies the strengthening integration of livestock and crop production in Amazonia.

Laissez-faire biocontrol

Few farmers routinely use pesticides on their perennial crops in the Amazon, and then only sparingly. Vegetable growers, particularly near the major cities, use the most pesticides. The high cost of pesticides is a major constraint to their use. Experience is showing, however, that growing perennials in discrete patches or in mixed cropping systems often reduces the need for pesticides. Also, patches of forest and old second growth may allow biocontrol agents to thrive, as appears to be the case with oil-palm plantations along the PA 150 road in Pará. Much research remains to be done, however, to understand the interaction of crops and pest populations, and the role of vegetation in suppressing or encouraging pests.

The owner of the Rio Branco ranch near Ariquemes, Rondônia, notes that orange trees appear more vigorous near a strip of exotic bamboo he has planted along the road dividing his property. The bamboo was originally planted for ornamental purposes, but the rancher plans to plant more near his orange plantings. Bamboo's effects on the orange orchards are unclear; the perennial grass may be benefiting the orange trees by providing a haven for predators of insect pests, or it may be serving as a windbreak. Elsewhere in pioneer areas of Amazonia, bamboo is planted as a door yard plant for construction material; Japanese-Brazilians also harvest bamboo shoots for a variety of dishes.

Innovation at Tomé-Açu

Tomé-Açu in central Pará has proved a particularly innovative pole for agricultural development in eastern Amazonia. Many of the most productive cash crops and intercropping systems in Amazonia were first tried out by Japanese farmers in the Tomé-Açu area, some 130 km south of Belém. A similar pattern of eager experimentation with perennial cash crops has been noted among Japanese farmers in the Bolivian Amazon (Hiraoka 1980b: 117).

Japanese immigrants founded Tomé-Açu in 1929, and began their malaria-stricken pioneer life by growing upland rice (*Oryza sativa*). Rain-fed rice yields were disappointing on the poor oxisols, so the Japanese settlers began planting black pepper on a commercial scale in 1947 and it soon became the main cash crop (CAMTA 1975; Staniford 1973: 46). Farmers at Tomé-Açu planted black pepper as a monocrop, and then abandoned their plantations to second growth after about a dozen years. Now farms are much more intensively managed, with few areas left to fallow.

Even though black pepper is not as dominant as formerly at Tomé-Açu and elsewhere in Amazonia, the high-value crop still provides a good return. No effective treatment for Fusarium, caused by *Fusarium solani* f. sp. *piperis*, has emerged. First reported in Pará in 1957, the fungal disease destroys black pepper plantations after about eight years. Far from "dooming" black pepper cultivation (Fearnside 1980a), however, farmers can still make handsome profits from black pepper for the first few years in spite of the ravages of Fusarium. A well-managed black pepper plantation can produce 3 kg of peppers/plant/year (Penteado 1968: 128).

Although black pepper is still grown extensively, other crops, such as cupuaçu and passionfruit, are increasingly important. Cupuaçu is the second most commonly planted crop in the sample of 121 polycultural fields (appendix 5), and Japanese-Brazilian farmers in the Tomé-Açu area are already dispatching frozen cupuaçu pulp to markets in the United States. Recently, for example, the R. W. Knudsen Company of Chico, California, began selling a "cupuassu" fruit drink containing a blend of white grape juice, mango pulp, translucent cupuassu pulp, papaya pulp, passionfruit juice, and hibiscus flower extract. Knudsen buys most of its cupuaçu pulp from Tomé-Açu, and also uses it to flavour its guanabana and calamansi juices, as well as its rain-forest fruit spreads and Rainforest Mist Spritzer (Kevin Kimbell, pers. comm.).

Tomé-Açu accounted for 327,128 kg of cupuaçu pulp produced in Pará between 1984 and 1990, approximately 60 per cent of the state total (Falesi and Osaqui 1992). Much of the cash-crop production in the Tomé-Açu area is marketed by CAMTA (Cooperativa Agricola Mista de Tomé-Açu), a co-op run by Japanese-Brazilian farmers. In 1989, passionfruit and cupuaçu accounted for 7 and 3 per cent, respectively, of CAMTA's receipts; by 1990 their proportion had grown to 23 and 8 per cent, respectively. Many farmers at Tomé-Açu have thus diversified their operations with a suite of perennial crops. Black pepper often remains the financial foundation for farmers in the Tomé-Açu area until other perennial crops become established.

A major reason that Tomé-Açu has prospered over the years is that the farmers have focused on cash crops and set up a cooperative with marketing skills and a mandate to experiment with new crops. CAMTA was formed soon after Japanese settlers arrived at Tomé-Açu, and has provided credit and marketing facilities. Flexibility in the face of constantly changing environmental conditions is the key to the success of farmers at Tomé-Açu (Barros 1990: 39). The generally well-managed CAMTA cooperative has helped farmers to adapt to shifts in markets and challenges to crop productivity. In 1988, for example, CAMTA was marketing over 25 different crops, a much more diversified base for farmers than in 1968 when black pepper accounted for 99 per cent of the co-op's sales (Barros 1990: 59, 67).

Another factor in the continued success of many farmers in the Tomé-Açu area is that facilities have been built to process some of the agricultural products for market. With support from the Japanese Development Agency (JICA), CAMTA built a plant for processing pulp from such fruits as cacao, cupuaçu, "Keitt" mango, bacuri (*Platonia insignis*), cashew, Barbados cherry, and açaí (*Euterpe oleracea*) palm. Inaugurated in 1987, the plant separates the fruit pulp, using a mixture of machinery and manual labour, freezes the pulp in plastic bags, and then sends them to major urban markets, particularly Belém. About 3 tons of passionfruit are needed to make 1 ton of juice, and the CAMTA plant processed 30 tons of passionfruit juice in 1991.

Sporadic outbreaks of cholera in the Brazilian Amazon in 1991 and 1992 temporarily dampened demand for fruit juices and ice-cream, thereby adversely affecting some growers. Generally poor hygiene standards in the region have facilitated the spread of the pathogen down the Amazon from Peru. By 1994, however, the disease appeared to have run its course. Another reason Japanese-Brazilian farmers have often fared so well is that some of them have spent months or even years working in Japan to generate savings, some of which were invested on their farms around Tomé-Açu and in the Bragantina zone. This practice was particularly common during the height of the recession in Brazil during the late 1980s and early 1990s.

Revival in the Bragantina zone

The collapse of colonization efforts in the Bragantina zone east of Belém at the turn of the twentieth century has been cited as evidence of the unfavourable environment for agricultural development in Amazonia. Although ecological constraints can certainly play a role in undercutting agricultural production, socio-economic problems are as much to blame for farm failures in the region (Falesi, Baena, and Dutra 1980). The Amazon is neither a "green hell" on the verge of turning into a "red desert" nor an Eden with a cornucopia of resources that can be heavily exploited with little regard for conservation. Rather, the region is a mosaic of environments with different constraints and potentials. Even highly leached oxisols and ultisols can be productively managed, as evidenced by dense indigenous populations in some upland areas in the distant past, and as farmers have recently demonstrated near Tomé-Açu and in parts of the Bragantina zone.

Flush with cash from the Amazon rubber boom of the late nineteenth century, the state government of Pará financed the construction of a 230 km railroad linking Belém with Bragança between 1883 and 1907 (Penteado 1968). Soils of the Bragantina zone are at least 87 per cent oxisols, the most weathered type of soils in the Amazon, and, because of the abundant rainfall (which usually exceeds 3,000 mm/year), are highly leached. Low soil fertility and poor guidance for farmers were major factors behind the failure of settlers from the drought-plagued North-east region and from Europe (Lima 1958; Penteado 1974).

Annual crop production posed great difficulties for colonists in the Bragantina zone in the early part of the twentieth century, even with the presence of a railroad linking two growing cities. Perennial crops, on the other hand, have been planted successfully in the past, such as

143

during the colonial period when productive sugarcane and cacao plantations were established for the export trade.

The mix of perennial cash and food crops has changed constantly in the Bragantina zone in response to market conditions and disease and pest attack. In the 1940s, for example, coconut, banana, orange, avocado, and guava were the most important perennial crops in the region (Penteado 1968: 15). Except for coconut, these crops have ceded space to other more profitable species. All the perennial crops important in the 1940s are still grown, but their relative contribution to the area's economy has declined. Bananas, for example, are struck by too many diseases in the Bragantina zone to be grown on a large scale. More recently, other perennial cash crops that are ecologically better suited to the generally poor soils than annual crops are spearheading an economic revival in the area.

African oil-palm, papaya, passionfruit, Barbados cherry, coconut, and citrus currently reign as the main perennial cash crops in the Bragantina zone. Oil-palm is cultivated by large operators, as described in the previous chapter, and by small-scale farmers. Some farmers with oil-palm groves on properties in the 25–100 ha range belong to Cooperativa Agricola Mixta de Santa Isabel, which processes oil-palm. Started by Japanese-Brazilians, this co-op is headquartered some 50 km east of Belém and contains members from diverse ethnic origins. In the vicinity of Belém, vegetables are grown profitably, and some communities still derive appreciable income from selling manioc flour, the region's basic staple.

Yellow passionfruit has emerged as an important cash crop in the Bragantina zone within the past decade. Passionfruit is grown as a monoculture and as an intercrop, particularly with citrus and African oil-palm. Brazil is a leading producer of passionfruit juice in the world market, and Pará has quickly emerged as the most important state in Brazil for passionfruit production (Falesi and Osaqui 1992). AMA-FRUTAS, a large passionfruit juice processing plant near Belém, recently provided a stimulus for production of the succulent fruit. Independent truckers contract with individual growers and take fresh-picked passionfruit to the processing facility, where the load is weighed and the truckers paid.

AMAFRUTAS is owned by a Swiss pharmaceutical company, CIBA-GEIGY, and the juice is exported to Europe. The appetite of Europeans and North Americans for exotic tropical fruits is growing, and more fruit-processing facilities are likely to be established in the Bragantina zone. For example, Swissair serves passionfruit sherbet between courses on some first class flights – the tip of an iceberg of potential demand for passionfruit juice in Europe. In up-market stores in London, for example, purple passionfruit from Kenya were selling briskly for US$0.50 each in December 1989.

Another indication of Bragantina's dynamic agriculture is the emergence of Barbados cherry, known locally as *acerola*, as a viable cash crop in the 1980s. Introduced by Japanese-Brazilians, Barbados cherry has become a popular fruit drink and ice-cream in Belém. The bright red berries are exceptionally high in vitamin C and the tasty pulp is frozen in plastic bags and sold in stores for home consumption, restaurants, and snack bars. Native to the West Indies and northern South America, Barbados cherry is an ideal hedgerow around fields and backyards. Belém already has over 1.2 million inhabitants and the market for Barbados cherry is growing. In 1991, the prices for Barbados cherry pulp declined somewhat in Pará as more producers came on line, but the crop is still profitable and growers rarely grow the bush as a monocrop.

Papaya, indigenous to tropical America, has been grown in Amazonia for a long time, where it also occurs as a bird-dispersed volunteer plant. Local seedling papayas are highly variable and, because they can reach the size of watermelons, often do not ship well. "Sunrise Solo," a papaya variety developed in Hawaii, has revolutionized papaya cultivation in the Bragantina zone and other parts of tropical Brazil. "Solo Sunrise" has elevated papaya from a door yard plant to a plantation crop in the Brazilian Amazon, often as an intercrop with rubber or other perennials. "Sunrise Solo" is the size and shape of a large pear, so it travels with minimal damage. Also, "Sunrise Solo" is a convenient serving size and its deep-orange flesh is widely appreciated. "Sunrise Solo" papayas from the Bragantina zone are sent to Belém and urban centres in central and southern Brazil along the asphalted Belém–Brasília highway. Market prices for "Sunrise Solo" are sufficiently high to justify mechanical preparation of the land, fertilizers, and, in some cases, irrigation. Although the Bragantina receives heavy rainfall from December to June, a week or more may pass during the dry season without a shower.

As in the case of black pepper and African oil-palm, diseases and pests are sure to raise the production cost of current hits such as passionfruit, Barbados cherry, and "Sunrise Solo" papaya. Farmers are adopting several strategies to overcome these constraints, such as multiple-cropping, the deployment of pest-resistant cultivars when available, and the testing of new crops.

Mangosteen (*Garcinia mangostana*) is one of the premier fruits of South-East Asia, but hitherto has lingered as a botanical curiosity in tropical America. Several Japanese-Brazilian farmers in the Bragantina zone have modest plantings of young mangosteen trees, which were planted in the late 1980s. The sweet, white pulp of mangosteen is finding a ready market in fashionable shopping malls in São Paulo, such as MorumbiShopping.[1]

Japanese-Brazilians, with their intensive input of family and hired labour, cooperative spirit, and keen business sense, have often been the catalysts for economic change in the Bragantina zone and some other areas of Amazonia. Other factors behind the agricultural revival of the Bragantina zone include relatively large, nearby urban markets and all-weather roads. Along the hardtop road to Vigia, for example, one Japanese-Brazilian farmer has intercropped "Sunrise Solo" papaya, orange, mangosteen, bell pepper (*Capsicum annum*), and Barbados cherry, with the latter forming a thick hedge around the field. This thriving 10 ha farm was formerly planted to black pepper.

Japanese-Brazilians are not the only innovative farmers in the greater Bragantina area, however. A former extension agent from Sergipe, a relatively dry state in the Brazilian North-east region, introduced commercial citrus cultivation to the vicinity of Capitão Poço in 1976 (fig. 6.3). Initially helped by bank loans, Antonio Soares soon found orange-growing highly profitable, and managed to increase his holdings from 25 ha to 400 ha by 1990. Close to 2 million orange trees are now planted around Capitão Poço, making it the citrus capital of Amazonia. When the nearby municipality of Irituia is included, some 3 million orange trees are planted in north-eastern Pará and these recently planted groves now supply close to 40 per cent of the state's market for orange (Falesi and Osaqui 1992).

Although São Paulo still accounts for 90 per cent of Brazil's citrus production, Amazonia's contribution (about 1 per cent of national production) is growing. Orange planting in the Bragantina zone has reached a sufficient scale to justify investments in an orange juice factory. CITROPAR plans to inaugurate an orange juice factory in the Bragantina zone in 1997 to cater for the local and regional markets. By the late 1990s, CITROPAR plans to have 1 million orange trees planted, which will be managed with technical assistance from the Faculty of Agronomical Sciences (FCAP – Faculdade de Ciências Agrárias do Pará) in Belém.

Most of the orange groves are planted to "Pêra," with smaller

Fig. 6.3 **Antonio Soares Neto in a four-year-old orange orchard. Near Capitão Poço, Pará, 5 April 1991. Mr Soares introduced commercial citrus cultivation to the Capitão Poço area**

areas devoted to the "Baianinha" and "Valencia" varieties. Some growers still plant a few of the older varieties, such as a farmer at Belterra who maintains some grafted "Selecta," introduced to Brazil in colonial times (Rosengarten 1991: 23). Many orange groves are established in old pastures or former second growth. Oranges from Capitão Poço are sent as far as Manaus and Imperatriz in the neighbouring states of Amazonas and Maranhão, respectively. Oranges are harvested all year round, thereby providing steady employment, although production peaks during the dry season.

Aware of the dangers of relying too heavily on one crop for income, some citrus growers in the Capitão Poço area are diversifying their farms. For example, 16 km from Capitão Poço, the owner of

Fig. 6.4 **Grafted, eight-year-old sweet orange in a field previously planted to pas-sionfruit and papaya. Sitio Andiroba, near Castanhal, Pará, 28 May 1990**

Sitio Rabo de Couro plans to cut back his orange acreage to make room for other crops. In 1992, the 50 ha property had 32 ha in "Pêra" orange, 7 ha in passionfruit intercropped with coconut, and an experimental 1 ha area planted to orange and cotton.

In response to the strong market for citrus products, other farming communities are seizing the opportunity of growing oranges, and to a lesser extent limes and tangerines. Near Castanhal, Pará, for example, Sitio Andiroba has established 5,000 orange trees from seedlings grafted in Capitão Poço (fig. 6.4). Several growers have taken to commercial citrus cultivation along the Manaus–Itacoatiara Highway in Amazonas; in the vicinity of Santarém, Pará; and around Rolim de Moura in southern Rondônia. Commercial orange-growing near Santarém dates to the early 1970s, when Miguel das Freiras and the Parente family began selling grafted oranges, particularly along the Santarém–Belterra stretch of the BR 163 highway.

Approximately 90 per cent of the orange groves in the Brazilian Amazon are planted to the "Pêra" variety, typically grafted on rough lemon (*limão-cravo* or *limão galego*). "Pêra" is popular because it remains juicy even when the dry season is accentuated, thus commanding a premium price when other varieties are either too dry or not producing. Still, the proliferation of "Pêra" is a risky proposition in case of a disease outbreak.[2] Some growers in Rondônia are importing grafted oranges from São Paulo, a practice that may help spread diseases such as citrus canker and CVC, a disease of unknown aetiology in southern Brazil.

The Bragantina experience is a good indicator of what is likely to happen in other areas of Amazonia as they become increasingly altered and populated. Occupation of Amazonia does not necessarily lead to a swidden tailspin with declining yields, devastation of the landscape, and rural misery. With a network of all-weather roads, sizeable urban markets, and new technologies supplied by the private and public sectors, farmers can flourish on some of the poorest soils in South America with high rainfall and intense disease and pest pressure. Intensification of land use without resorting to excessive use of agro-chemicals has helped raise living standards in rural and urban areas of the Bragantina zone.

The pioneer experience: Transamazon and Rondônia

Perennial crops are also becoming more common along the Transamazon and the Cuiabá–Porto Velho highways, both pioneered in the 1970s. Initial settlement efforts along the Transamazon were fraught with difficulties owing to such factors as settlers arriving with little if any farming experience, bureaucratic delays, and limited access to markets (Moran 1981; Smith 1982). As perennial crops, such as cacao and cashew, came into production, many farmers have prospered in the Altamira region of the Transamazon (Moran 1988b).

In Rondônia, cacao, robusta coffee (*Coffea canephora*), and even rubber, when planted as an intercrop, have emerged as important crops (Alvim 1989). The Brazilian Amazon was the first entry point for arabica coffee (*Coffea arabica*) into Brazil when coffee seeds and seedlings were brought to Pará from French Guiana in 1727. As early as 1749, Pará was exporting arabica coffee to Lisbon (Magalhães 1980: 38, 39). Coffee subsequently declined as a cash crop in Amazonia owing to poor yields until the arrival of more productive robusta coffee in the late 1970s. A few colonists keep small groves

149

Fig. 6.5 **A grove containing 100,000 bushes of robusta coffee (*Coffea canephora*) planted on two adjacent 100 ha lots. Gleba 36, lots 2 and 3, km 105 of the Altamira–Itaituba stretch of the Transamazon Highway, Pará, 10 April 1991**

of arabica coffee, mostly for domestic consumption. "Canelon" is the principal robusta coffee variety planted along the Transamazon and in Rondônia.

Robusta coffee is grown extensively on monocultural plots by some farmers in Rondônia and along the Transamazon Highway (fig. 6.5). Colonists from Espírito Santo introduced robusta coffee to the Altamira region of the Transamazon in 1972. By the late 1980s, robusta coffee had emerged as the principal cash crop in Rondônia. Low coffee prices in the late 1980s led some growers to neglect the crop. In some cases, coffee groves were simply not harvested, while in other cases, such as near Ji-Paraná in Rondônia, farmers cleared all or parts of coffee groves to make room for cotton or cattle pasture. As coffee prices began to rebound in 1993, however, more farmers are harvesting and weeding the crop. The 1994 freeze in southern Brazil further propelled coffee prices upwards on world markets, and coffee

Fig. 6.6 **Robusta coffee (*Coffea canephora*) intercropped with sweet orange and banana. Gleba 23, lot 11, km 80 of the Altamira–Itaituba stretch of the Transamazon Highway, Pará, 10 April 1991**

growers in Amazonia are sure to benefit from the resulting shortfall in production in the states of São Paulo and Paraná.

To counteract dependency on a single crop for the bulk of earnings, some farmers along the Transamazon have planted robusta coffee with other crops, such as orange and banana (fig. 6.6). Most of the coffee produced along the Transamazon is sent to Espírito Santo and São Paulo. Some colonists from southern Brazil use the discarded pulp surrounding coffee beans as an organic mulch for backyard vegetable patches.

Cacao prices also dropped in the late 1980s, prompting many farmers along the Transamazon and in Rondônia to diversify their crop base. Cacao prices plunged from a high of US$4,000 per ton in

151

the early 1980s to a low of US$800 per ton by 1989. Farmers responded by neglecting their cacao orchards and turning their attention to other crops, such as maize and citrus. Between km 80 and km 90 of the Altamira–Itaituba stretch of the highway, some cacao growers have concentrated on intensive tomato cultivation for markets in Altamira, now with close to 100,000 inhabitants, and the new boom town of Uruará at km 180 of the Altamira–Itaituba stretch of the Transamazon. Low cacao prices have prompted some farmers in parts of Rondônia and along the Transamazon to cut down orchards partially or totally.

Cacao nevertheless remains a significant cash crop along pioneer highways in Amazonia. In Rondônia, 20,000 ha of cacao have been planted in the municipality of Ariquemes, while cacao covers some 11,000 ha in the municipality of Jarú; all told, some 50,000 ha of cacao were planted in the state between 1975 and 1992. Approximately 30,350 ha of cacao have been planted within a 250 km radius of Altamira, and the area devoted to the crop is holding steady. Most of the cacao along the Transamazon is concentrated along km 70–110 of the Altamira–Itaituba stretch of the highway where fertile alfisols abound.

Spurred by concern about drought in West Africa, dry conditions in Malaysia in 1991 and 1992, a dock strike in Ghana, some pest and disease problems with cacao in Malaysia,[3] and low inventories of major chocolate manufacturers, cacao prices began to recover in the early 1990s.[4] By 1992, cacao prices had rebounded to US$1,100/ton, reaching US$1,200/ton by September 1993. By June 1994, cacao prices had climbed to US$1,400/ton. Many growers are consequently tending their orchards again, mainly by pruning branches infected with witches' broom, caused by *Crinipellis perniciosa*. This fungal pathogen first became a significant disease problem for cacao growers along the Transamazon in 1985.

One farmer near Cacaulandia, Rondônia, kept his 40 ha cacao orchard intact during the trough in cacao prices because he has two married sons living on his 250 ha farm and cacao provides employment for them. He also employs a family from Bahia as sharecroppers (*meieros*). The farmer, originally from Santa Catarina, reasoned that, if he expanded his 60 ha of pasture (*Brachiaria brizantha* and *B. humidicola*), his children would have to move on and find their own land to work. A significant reduction in the area of planted cacao coupled with an expansion of pasture could thus exacerbate social problems by increasing rural–urban migration.

When a neglected cacao orchard is once again cared for, yields soon increase. Some farmers around Cacaulandia have even secured credit to fertilize their cacao orchards, a sure indication that prices are looking up for the commodity. Most of the cacao has been planted on relatively fertile soils, so fertilizer applications are light. Cacao plantations protect the soil well; near Manaus, for example, a four-year-old cacao plantation had a thicker organic layer and better-developed root mat than nearby old-growth forest on similar soil (St. John 1985). Virtually all cacao grown in Amazonia has been planted in fields that were cleared from the forest by hand, thereby minimizing the disturbance of topsoil. One farmer near Agrovila Nova Fronteira found that cacao yields were much lower in an area formerly planted to sugarcane that had been scraped by a bulldozer compared with cacao planted in manually cleared forest or second growth.

Small-scale agro-industry is further brightening the prospects for cacao growers in parts of Rondônia and along the Altamira–Itaituba stretch of the Transamazon. Two mini-factories for preparing cacao pulp have recently been established in these pioneer zones, and a chocolate factory, employing 100 people, has been built in Altamira. Dicacau opened a cacao-processing plant at km 140 of the Altamira–Itaituba stretch of the Transamazon in 1988 with a capacity to process 400 kg of pulp a day. The cacao pulp plant employs 16 people and the frozen product is dispatched in plastic bags mostly to Belém for sale in snack bars and in supermarkets; smaller quantities are sold in Altamira and Santarém. People in the Brazilian Amazon are not accustomed to drinking juice made from cacao pulp, unlike the inhabitants of Bahia. Tastes are changing, however, and the market for cacao pulp in the North region appears to be growing.

Near Cacaulandia in Rondônia, cacao farmers successfully applied for credit from the Banco de Rondônia to build a small plant to process cacao pulp for markets along the Porto Velho–Cuiabá Highway. A decisive factor in obtaining funds for this project was the initiative of cacao growers to form an association (APRUCC – *Associação de Produtores e Criadores de Cacaulandia*) in 1989. APRUCC had some 50 members in 1992.

Diverse agro-industries, on both a small and a large scale, can thus help sustain farming efforts, particularly as growers diversify their crops. A guaraná factory in Altamira, for example, has provided a further crop option for growers along the Transamazon in the Xingu area. Bottled "Guaraná Xingu" is marketed as far away as km 108 of the Santarém–Cuiabá Highway, approximately 400 km north-west of

153

Altamira. Many of the smaller guaraná bottling plants have closed in the Amazon during the past three decades in the face of the marketing muscle of firms based in southern Brazil. Taste is always a highly personal affair, but some of the smaller operators used to put out a richer-tasting product, and it is to be hoped that "Guaraná Xingu" will be around to slake the thirst of Transamazon settlers for years to come.

Innovation with agro-forestry systems in Amazonia is thus widespread and not confined to the environs of Tomé-Açu. Given the right support, in particular efficient credit, communities of farmers from various parts of Brazil, including the North, are successfully experimenting with novel crop combinations (Barros 1990). Even without credit, Paraense communities in the Tomé-Açu area are already adopting various agro-forestry systems (appendix 2). Some of the Paraenses in the Tomé-Açu area have acquired knowledge about mixed cropping with perennials either by working for Japanese-Brazilians in the past or by observation.

The emergence of nurseries for perennial crops

Now that perennial crops are increasingly planted in fields on a commercial scale by small-, medium-, and large-scale operators alike, demand for seedlings is on the rise. Farmers are particularly eager to buy planting stock of such hot-selling crops as cupuaçu, Barbados cherry, and certain cultivars of sweet orange, particularly "Pêra." In addition to traditional networks of seed supply, mainly from home gardens, communal nurseries and private companies are increasingly stepping in to meet the growing demand for planting stock.

Communal nurseries are often fostered by NGOs as a means of fomenting social cohesion among members of rural syndicates (Sindicatos de Trabalhadores Rurais). At the Cuxiu 42 and Cuxiu 44 communities near São Domingos, Pará, for example, two communal nurseries have been established with the assistance of CAT (Centro Agro-Ambiental do Tocantins), a research-oriented NGO headquartered near Marabá. In August 1992, nine farmers were participating in the communal nursery at Cuxiu 42, which had seedlings of Brazil nut, cupuaçu, peach palm (*Bactris gasipaes*), and mahogany (*Swietenia macrophylla*).

In the Paragominas area, the World Wildlife Fund and the Ford Foundation have helped the rural syndicate to set up eight communal nurseries in seven communities. The communal nursery in Colonia del Rei some 30 km north of Paragominas, for example, has seedlings of cupuaçu, Barbados cherry, sweet orange "Pêra-Rio," ingá xicote (*Inga* sp.), soursop (*Annona muricata*), biribá (*Rollinia deliciosa*), balsa (*Ochroma* sp.), mahogany, and Job's tears (*Coix lachryma-jobi*); seeds of the latter annual grass are used to make beads. The nursery is partially thatched with fronds of inajá palm (*Maximiliana maripa*), collected from the forest. The del Rei nursery has 14 members who contribute labour while international donors help them buy fruit in markets (for their seeds) and plastic bags to start the seedlings. A watering tank has also been purchased. The Canadian government has enabled the syndicate to obtain a pickup truck, which is used to service the nurseries.

Greater attention will need to be addressed to selecting a mix of cultivars for each crop being promoted in order to reduce the dangers of genetic heterogeneity. Also, communal nurseries should strive to be self-sustaining as soon as possible, otherwise they will have to be propped up indefinitely by external donors. International donors are playing an important role as catalysts in this process, but eventually communities themselves will have to carry more of the financial and technical burden of supporting the work of nurseries.

The private sector is also stepping in to meet the rising demand for seedlings of perennial crops. Enterprising individuals sometimes organize their own small nurseries, particularly if they have ready access to a stream or river, and sell or barter some of the seedlings to neighbours (fig. 6.7). In addition, trucks periodically appear along Amazonian highways with seedlings of some perennial crops, such as coffee and sweet orange. Such operators often purchase their seedlings in central and southern Brazil, and may be introducing pests and diseases to Amazonia.

The organization of nurseries for perennial crops is a promising trend, but the success of agro-forestry operations depends on a host of factors, including research into appropriate agronomic practices and disease and pest control. One farmer near the community of São João Batista in the municipality of Itupiranga, Pará, planted approximately 100 Brazil nuts after clearing the underbrush in a patch of forest on his lot. Unfortunately for the farmer, agoutis (*Dasyprocta* sp.) allegedly absconded with all the seeds before they could sprout. The farmer is considering erecting a fence to keep out the ubiquitous rodents next time. This farmer selects seeds from large Brazil nut capsules for his door yard nursery, even though he acknowledges that large capsules and seed size do not appear to be related. Fur-

155

Fig. 6.7 **Small farmer with his nursery for peach-palm (*Bactris gasipaes*) seedlings in a banana grove. Nova Califórnia, km 155 Rio Branco–Porto Velho Highway, 16 November 1991**

thermore, a Brazil nut tree reportedly produces both large and small capsules.

Comparisons with the Old World tropics

One striking difference between the agro-forestry systems currently adopted by commercial farmers in Amazonia compared with those in tropical Asia and Africa is the paucity of intercropped annual food crops. Food crops such as maize and rice are occasionally inter-cropped in Amazonia, but rarely with perennials. Also, farmers are not currently interested in intercropping perennials to ameliorate soil, to supply fuelwood, or to provide fodder for livestock, major criteria for agro-forestry research in India (Nair and Dagar 1991). Trees are interplanted if their fruit, nuts, or timber command a high market value.

Farmers generally do not plant trees just to restore soil, provide fodder, or to establish living fences because they do not bring any immediate remuneration. For example, a farmer in the Tomé-Açu area will no longer interplant *Erythrina* with cacao to provide nitrogen and shade because the leguminous tree does not provide any tangible products. Similarly, a nearby farmer is discontinuing the practice of using *Erythrina* sp. as living stakes for black pepper because pepper yields have not increased, and because the labour costs of pruning the *Erythrina* trees are too high. Although *Erythrina* enriches the soil with nitrogen, it may compete with crops for other nutrients if planted close by. Labour costs also appear to be the main reason cattle ranchers do not use living fences; perhaps some tree species may be found that require little if any pruning.

Cash crops on the horizon

Two palm species offer the potential for heart-of-palm (palmito) production in Amazonia and other parts of the humid tropics: peach-palm and açaí. Peach-palm has been cultivated in Amazonia and other parts of lowland tropical America for thousands of years for its vitamin D rich fruits. Costa Ricans have pioneered the use of peach-palm for palmito, particularly around Guapiles, and now export significant quantities of heart-of-palm, particularly to Europe. Selections have been made that can be harvested for palmito within 18 months.

Entrepreneurs in Amazonia are also exploring the potential of peach-palm for palmito production. Both small and large landholders could benefit from growing peach-palm for the canning industry. The owner of Fazenda Carapanã, at km 86 of the Manaus–Itacoatiara Highway in Amazonas, has established an experimental plot of 0.5 ha of peach-palm for palmito production. At the moment, he is test-marketing jars of palmito in restaurants in Manaus, but plans to expand his peach-palm orchard to 30 ha, all for heart-of-palm. Palmito is prepared manually at the ranch, and by-products are fed to pigs and cattle. Cattle are also fed leaves of peach-palm, because spineless forms are used for heart-of-palm. Heart-of-palm production thus fits well with livestock production on the 150 ha ranch.

The owner of Fazenda Carapanã obtained 400 spineless seedlings of peach-palm from the National Institute for Amazonian Research

157

(INPA – Instituto Nacional de Pesquisas da Amazônia) in Manaus. INPA in turn received some of its peach-palm germ plasm from Yurimaguas in the Peruvian Amazon. At a nearby property, Fazenda Baxica, the same owner has established 250 ha of peach-palm, much of it for seed production. The owner hopes to obtain financing for a small palmito factory on the Carapanã ranch to process his own production and eventually for neighbours. He also anticipates generating income from the sale of peach-palm seedlings from the Baxica ranch. Both ranches were established exclusively for cattle-raising but, as pastures have become more difficult to maintain, the owner has diversified into perennial crops.

In addition to cattle, pig, and palmito production, Fazenda Carapanã is also expected to produce coconut, açaí, cupuaçu, Barbados cherry, and "Sunrise Solo" papaya for the Manaus market in the near future. Over the long term, the ranch may diversify further with Brazil nut and timber trees, such as mahogany and cedar (*Cedrela odorata*).

The largest plantation of peach-palm in the Brazilian Amazon is managed by Fazenda Bonal at km 70 of the Rio Branco–Porto Velho Highway (BR 364). Approximately 400,000 peach-palms have been planted on 275 ha, all for palmito production. Peach-palm seedlings are given 100 g of P_2O_5 at planting; thereafter no further fertilizer is applied except for groves set aside for seed production. A thick ground cover of *Pueraria* fixes nitrogen and helps reduce soil erosion. The red–yellow ultisols on the ranch are relatively fertile for Amazonian uplands, but some top dressing with phosphorus will likely be needed in the future. Fazenda Bonal has a small plant to bottle the heart-of-palm, which is sold mainly in São Paulo. An old wood-burning boiler from England is used to sterilize the jars, thereby reducing energy costs.

The 10,247 ha Fazenda Bonal was originally purchased to set up a rubber plantation. Rubber was first planted on the property in 1976, and now 900 ha are planted to the tree crop. But the need to double-graft for high latex production and resistance to South American leaf blight, combined with the virtual elimination of subsidies for rubber in Brazil, has signalled a need to diversify. Fazenda Bonal still plans to stay in rubber production by specializing in high-quality rubber (*folha clara brasileira*) for medical purposes, but some of the rubber trees are being cut down to make room for peach-palm. Most of the property remains in forest.

In flood-plain environments, açaí (*Euterpe oleracea*) could be planted for palmito production. Native stands of this graceful, water-loving palm produce much procured purple fruits from February to September, which are mashed and mixed with manioc flour or made into thick, carbohydrate-rich drinks and savoury ice-cream. Within the past two decades, açaí stands have been felled for palmito production, particularly north of Marajó Island. As in the case of peach-palm, açaí coppices readily if cut from the base. Plantations using rapid-growing selections might be economically feasible in some flood-plain areas near palmito factories.

Another potential cash crop for small- and medium-scale growers is superior mangoes. Several farmers in the vicinity of Tomé-Açu and Castanhal, Pará, have experimental plantings of "Keitt" mango, a selection from Florida (Smith and Popenoe 1992; Smith et al. 1992). Consumers in large Amazon cities, such as Belém and Porto Velho, pay high prices for premium mangoes, such as pear-sized "Haden" and giant "Keitt," which are trucked from southern Brazil, particularly São Paulo. Some farmers in the Brazilian Amazon have noted the large price discrepancy between locally grown mangoes, which tend to be small and fibrous, and the generally larger, less stringy commercial cultivars.

Constraints on further intensification

Our review of perennial cropping has identified some promising trends in upland agriculture in Amazonia, particularly towards systems that better protect water and soil resources, while at the same time generating income. Although agro-forestry and monocropping with perennials offer great promise to address sustainability issues in Amazonia, they can be carried too far. Cash crops can shoulder aside food production, thereby driving up local costs of basic staples. And many annual food crops, such as maize and rice, do better in more open conditions. Nevertheless, perennial cropping systems, particularly in agro-forestry configurations, are clearly helping both small- and large-scale farmers to prosper. To accelerate agro-forestry development in the region, several constraints will need to be overcome, including the paucity of agro-industries, of credit on reasonable terms, of higher-quality nurseries, and of inexpensive irrigation systems to keep seedlings alive.

Moisture stress during the often intense dry season in eastern and central Amazonia is one of the principal reasons farmers cite for not planting more perennial crops. One farmer from the community of

Lastancia east of Itupiranga, Pará, reported that he lost 1,000 coffee seedlings during the especially severe dry season in 1992. A planting of 1,000 coffee seedlings is a major investment for a resource-poor farmer with no access to credit. When farmers were asked why they did not simply extend their species-rich home gardens to their surrounding fields, a frequent response was that seedlings often do not survive the dry season. Irrigation or more drought-tolerant germ plasm would help further agro-forestry.

Greater accessibility to credit would help spur more intensive land use on both the uplands and the Amazon flood plain. A further benefit of allocating property rights, particularly during the early phase of settlement, is that it promotes equity (Schneider 1993). In Brazil, only one-fourth of agricultural credit goes to small operators, who account for 70 per cent of farm produce (Santos and Cardoso 1992). Credit policies can be misplaced and excessively subsidized agriculture can lead to abuse of resources, both natural and financial, but carefully crafted incentives could steer Amazonia into more productive agriculture. A major stumbling block for small farmers attempting to obtain credit is that they often lack title to their lands. Without such documents, banks will not lend to farmers. Redoubled efforts to provide titles to legitimate landowners would thus be an essential precursor to more widespread adoption of more intensive land-use practices.

The abundance of relatively inexpensive land in Amazonia is a major impediment to the intensification of land use (Homma, Teixeira Filho, and Magalhães 1991). The pace of opening pioneer roads has slowed considerably since the 1970s, but the temptation to forge new highways to alleviate social tensions in other regions might return as global recession eases. Incentives should be targeted towards restoring degraded land. Also, the construction of new highways should be put on hold until existing ones better serve the people living near them.

Notes

1. "Alface com griffe: por que a feira do MorumbiShopping faz successo," *Veja São Paulo*, 10 March 1993, pp. 10–12.
2. "Pesquisadores da região vão debater produção de citros," *O Liberal*, Belém, 25 August 1992, p. 2.
3. *Boletí del Cacao*, no. 5, 1993.
4. "Cocoa futures' strong technical position pushes prices to highest level in more than a week," *Wall Street Journal*, New York, 23 July 1992, p. C12.

7

Ranching problems and potential on the uplands

Pasture development in Amazonia is often mired in controversy. From the social standpoint, ranches provide minimal employment and in some cases have led to conflicts over land rights (Schmink and Wood 1992). Alarms have sounded about creating biological deserts in artificial pastures. Furthermore, pastures cleared in forest are often deemed unsustainable (Fearnside 1989b). Three prevailing myths about cattle-raising in Amazonia need to be put to rest: (1) that ranching is the domain of large landholders; (2) that cattle-raising is chiefly an artefact of fiscal incentives; and (3) that pasture formation in Amazonia is the principal cause of forest destruction.

Much of the heated debate about pastures in the region stems from the relatively recent push to open up artificial pastures in mature forest. Traditional cattle-raising on natural flood-plain meadows and on patches of savanna poses fewer ecological and cultural hazards than forest-clearing on the uplands. In the case of small- and medium-scale operators, cattle pastures are formed only after one or more cropping cycles with annual crops. Instead of returning the land to second growth, some farmers prefer to form pasture (Hébette 1991). Even some of the larger ranchers often sow rice and/or maize with pasture grasses in order to recoup some of their costs. It is thus difficult to assign with any degree of accuracy the proportion of deforestation due to cattle-raising. Whether on flood plains, savanna, or artificial pasture in upland areas, cattle have become an integral part of the regional economy. In cleared areas of Amazonia, cattle-raising is usually the dominant land-use system.

In 1985, cattle accounted for one-quarter of the agricultural production of the states of Pará and Rondônia. In the latter state, the cattle herd had grown from 7,800 head in 1970 to some 2 million by 1991 (Falesi and Osaqui 1992). SUDAM (Superintendência do Desenvolvimento da Amazônia), a regional development agency, facilitated the investment of US$880 million in cattle projects in the Brazilian Amazon between 1966 and 1978 (Dwyer 1990: 81).

Driving forces and the mythical hamburger connection

Cattle-raising is an attractive proposition in frontier areas of Latin America, including the Amazon, for a number of reasons. First, cattle are a highly liquid investment. Second, cattle can be easily walked long distances to market when roads are in poor condition. Third, sales can be delayed without major losses in most cases. Fourth, the marginal cost of establishing pasture after cropping is low for smallholders. Fifth, ranching is a low-risk operation compared with crop farming (Seré and Jarvis 1992).

Small farmers often maintain a few cattle for milk, for a quick sale when a financial crisis looms, and to provide manure for crops. For many small operators, cattle are a more secure and familiar investment than banks, whose interest rates do not always accompany inflation (Hecht 1992). Cattle-raising thus transcends farm size.

Cattle's impressive role in the regional economy is not simply an artefact of fiscal policy incentives. After it became apparent that SUDAM incentives for cattle pasture were being used primarily for land speculation and timber extraction, the federal government withdrew subsidies for pasture development in forested areas of Amazonia. This was expected to curtail pasture development in the region (Collins 1990: 42).

Even without fiscal incentives, though, cattle-raising remains the predominant land use in pioneer areas of Amazonia (Hecht 1992; Homma et al. 1992b). In Acre, for example, pasture is by far the most common vegetation in cleared areas, occupying 55 per cent of such areas in 1987 (FUNTAC 1990b). In the vicinity of Parauapebas, at the base of the Carajás range in southern Pará, cattle pasture with varying degrees of invasion by weeds accounts for about 90 per cent of the cleared land after 10 years of settlement. Settlers from the North-east region and central Brazil occupy homesteads in the 50 ha range and prefer to sow guinea grass (*Panicum maximum*) after a crop of rice because it is easier to manage. Small- to medium-scale ranches also dominate the landscape around Marabá, a Brazil nut

Fig. 7.1 **Small farm with vigorous pasture of brizantão (*Brachiaria brizantha* cv. Marandu). Sitio Biazate, Linha 601, near Theobroma, Rondônia, 18 February 1992**

town that has grown rapidly since the advent of several pioneer roads in the 1970s, and in colonization areas of Rondônia (fig. 7.1). The trend towards cattle-raising remains strong in western Amazonia and many other parts of the American tropics (Hiraoka 1980a).

A variety of cultural and socio-economic forces have propelled cattle-raising to one of the leading economic activities in both pioneer areas and long-settled parts of Amazonia. Cattle represent capital assets that can be readily sold when a crisis or opportunity arises. Cattle-raising is not labour intensive, an important consideration in rural Amazonia where the paucity of available workers is a perennial complaint. Small farmers are especially attracted to cattle-raising as one of their major land-use options because they have fewer resources to hire labour (Homma et al. 1992b).

Milk production is another powerful force behind the sowing of grasses in Amazonia. Small farmers, in particular, are keen to maintain a few cows to provide milk for the family. Small and medium-sized ranches, such as in the vicinity of Marabá, provide milk for the market as well. Large-scale operators tend to concentrate on beef production. Marabá now has two dairy plants, which send milk in plastic bags to Belém. In nearby Morada Nova along the PA 70

163

highway, Leite Carajás works with some 400 farmers and small-scale ranchers. Leite Carajás has a capacity of 35,000 litres/day, and sends milk to Marabá and cheese to Belém. Marabá has emerged as one of the more important dairying centres in Pará within the past 10–15 years. The growth of the dairy industry around a town formerly linked mainly with the Brazil nut trade is largely a result of improved road transportation to Belém along the PA 150, which opened in 1978, and of Marabá's spectacular growth from around 4,000 inhabitants in 1970 to about 150,000 in 1992.

An appreciation of beef and a predilection for cattle grazing are rooted in Iberian culture. Cattle were imported to Belém in 1644, and the first ranch was established on nearby Marajó Island in 1692 (Le Cointe 1918: 9). Cattle have thus been part of the cultural landscape of the Amazon basin for centuries.

Ranching is more prestigious than growing crops, and many pioneer settlers aspire to phase out, or reduce, their involvement in the arduous task of growing crops (Smith 1982). Cattle are easily herded to market, whereas crops may spoil in the field because transportation cannot be arranged. The precarious condition of roads and bridges after the rainy season in many parts of Amazonia results in considerable post-harvest losses.

Amazonia has been implicated in the "hamburger connection," which attributes tropical deforestation to the appetite for fast food in North America, particularly the United States (Hall 1989; Myers 1980a; Roddick 1991: 197). Yet the region has never been a significant exporter of beef. In 1982, the Brazilian Amazon supplied 0.0007 per cent of US beef consumption (Browder 1988); since then, the region has hardly been able to meet domestic demand for meat. Brazil exports mostly processed beef, such as corn beef and sausage. Amazonia is a net importer of beef in most years, and foot-and-mouth disease prevents the region from becoming a significant exporter of chilled beef to foreign markets (Hecht and Cockburn 1989: 98).

The "hamburger connection" asserts that consumers in North America are responsible for converting substantial areas of tropical forest to pasture in Latin America (Harris 1983). Rain forests in Central America were even projected to disappear by 1990, in part because of the growing appetite for fast food in the United States and Canada (Lavelle 1987; Myers 1980b). Deforestation in Central America stirred most of the controversy over the "hamburger connection," which in turn spurred protests against Burger King and prompted denials from McDonalds that foreign beef was used in their hamburgers (Nations and Komer 1987).

At its heyday in the 1970s, the "hamburger connection" was tenuous even in Central America. Beef exports from Central America peaked in 1979 at 162,000 metric tons and declined to some 61,000 tons by 1985 (Myers and Tucker 1987). Beef exports from Central America, never significant on a global scale, have now essentially dried up because of increased domestic consumption. It is clearly time to put the "hamburger connection" on the back-burner.

Domestic, rather than international, demand for beef is one of the main driving forces behind cattle production in Amazonia. Rapid urban growth in Amazonia is creating an ever-greater demand for meat and dairy products. Domestic beef markets therefore spur forest-clearing in Amazonia. In the short term at least, it often makes economic sense to convert forest to pasture. The liveweight price of cattle in Amazonia fluctuates, as with most commodities, but fattening steers remains one of the most profitable agricultural activities in Amazonia.

By 2030, 80 per cent of the population of the Brazilian Amazon is expected to live in urban areas (Vera and Alves 1985). If the projected demand for beef in Brazil of 5.6 million tons by 2000 is to be met, production will have to double (Montoro Filho, Comune, and Melo 1989). Demand for milk in Brazil is also expected to double in the 1990s. By 2000, beef consumption in Brazil is expected to exceed production by 44,000 tons (CIAT 1991: 67). As incomes rise in Manaus, beef consumption increases at a faster rate than consumption of other sources of animal protein, such as fish (Amoroso 1981). A similar pattern probably prevails in other Brazilian cities.

The need to intensify production

Given the growing demand for beef and dairy products in Amazonia, boosting the productivity of cattle and water buffalo herds becomes imperative. Particular attention is needed to raising the productivity of existing pastures and range land, while minimizing environmental damage and adverse social impacts. The demand for beef and dairy products can be met, at least for the foreseeable future, by improving production on pastures already established in cleared forest and on natural grasslands. By boosting the output of cattle and milk from existing pasture and grassland, pressure can be relieved on remaining forest areas.

Some might argue that devising low-cost technologies to improve the economic viability of cattle-raising in Amazonia will only exacerbate forest-clearing. Precisely the opposite is likely to occur. Intensification of agricultural and livestock production alone will not "save" wilderness, but it provides some manoeuvring room. At least a farmer or rancher has more options for raising crops, or leaving forest alone, if output is increased on areas already in production.

Pasture development in the uplands

The big push to open up new cattle pastures in Amazonia started in the late 1960s and was targeted at forest areas. Attracted by generous fiscal incentives promulgated in 1967, corporations started investing up to half their taxes in development projects in Amazonia. A "grass rush" of major proportions quickly ensued in eastern and southern Amazonia (Sternberg 1973). Some 15 million ha of forest, mostly in southern Pará and northern Mato Grosso, have been felled and planted to a variety of grasses since the mid-1960s.

First-generation grasses on recently formed pastures in the uplands

Fig. 7.2 **A weed-choked pasture of *Brachiaria decumbens*, formed in 1982 and last weeded in 1989. Spittlebug attacks facilitate weed invasion. Fazenda Boi Branco, near Paragominas, Pará, 4 April 1991**

Table 7.1 **Pasture grass turnover in Amazonia in response to weed and pest problems, among other factors**

First generation (1965–1975)	Second generation (1975–1982)	Third generation (1983–Present)
Panicum maximum *Brachiaria decumbens* *Hyparrhenia rufa*	*Brachiaria humidicola*	*Brachiaria brizantha* *Andropogon gayanus*

Note: All species are still cultivated in the Brazilian Amazon, but first-generation species are now much less common.

were mainly guinea grass (*Panicum maximum*), brachiaria (*Brachiaria decumbens*), and, in drier areas, jaraguá (*Hyparrhenia rufa*). Within about five years, however, weeds, resprouting trees, and compacted soils depressed the productivity of many of these new pastures. The carrying capacity of neglected pastures often fell below 1 head/ha, compared with 1.5–2 head/ha on newer, better-managed pastures. At Fazenda Boi Branco near Paragominas, Pará, for example, the carrying capacity of a 12-year-old *Panicum maximum* pasture had dropped to 0.5 head/ha until it was restored with *Brachiaria brizantha* cv. Marandu in 1990.

Pests and germ-plasm turnover

Spittlebugs (*Deios* spp.) have triggered a turnover of grasses in artificial pastures in Amazonia. In the mid-1970s, spittlebug attacks, especially by *Deios incompleta*, exacerbated weed problems in many brachiaria (*Brachiaria decumbens*) pastures (fig. 7.2). Known as *cigarrinha* in Brazil, the small bugs can spread and multiply quickly. Spittlebugs feed on the grass sap, thereby withering the pasture and allowing weeds to proliferate (Penny and Arias 1982: 65).

Spittlebugs forced ranchers to seek alternative grasses in order to recoup lost productivity. The stage was set for a second generation of pasture grasses (table 7.1). In 1976, many ranchers turned to quicuio da Amazônia (*Brachiaria humidicola*), a fast-growing grass with moderate resistance to pests. An African grass, as are all introduced pasture grasses in Amazonia, quicuio has also been widely used for erosion control along roads, railways, and electrical transmission lines. By 1982, however, some pastures of *B. humidicola* were being severely attacked by spittlebugs in the Paragominas area, possibly because of the pronounced dry season, which weakens the plants.

167

Fig. 7.3 **A 20-year-old fenced pasture of** *Brachiaria humidicola*, **fertilized five years previously with rock phosphate and superphosphate, at a rate of 75 kg/ha. Fazenda Itaqui, 54 km east of Belém on the BR 316 highway, 28 May 1990**

In wetter areas of Amazonia, such as near Belém, *Brachiaria humidicola* and to a lesser extent *B. decumbens* still resist spittlebugs. Belém and much of the adjacent Bragantina zone receive around 3,000 mm of rain annually, compared with about 1,700 mm in the Paragominas and Manaus areas where spittlebugs have wreaked havoc. At Fazenda Itaqui, 54 km east of Belém on the BR 316 highway, a 20-year-old pasture of *B. humidicola* is still productive because it is fenced, thereby allowing rotation of cattle-grazing, and is weeded and fertilized periodically (fig. 7.3). Also in the Bragantina zone, a 20-year-old pasture of *B. decumbens* cleared from second growth is still grazed because the heavy rainfall depresses spittlebug populations and because the pasture is fenced and weeded; this pasture, located at Fazenda São Judas Tadeu, 19 km from São Miguel do Guamá, has never been fertilized.

Many ranchers have been planting braquiarão (*Brachiaria brizantha* cv. Marandu) since 1983, in part to escape problems of spittlebugs. Also known as brizantão, *B. brizantha* is more vigorous than

168

Fig. 7.4 **Braquiarão (*Brachiaria brizantha* var. Marandu) in foreground is gradually replacing many pastures of first-generation grasses, such as guinea grass (*Panicum maximum*) in background with light-coloured panicles. PA 256 highway near Paragominas, Pará, 3 April 1991**

B. humidicola, provides better ground cover to suppress weeds, and currently resists spittlebugs. Although more demanding of soil nutrients and physical conditions than first-cycle *Brachiaria* species, brizantão is rapidly replacing first- and second-generation pasture grasses in many parts of the Brazilian Amazon (fig. 7.4). Third-generation pastures are generally under more intensive management.

Weeds and degraded pastures

Close to half of the artificial pastures in Amazonia are degraded (Hecht 1985; Serrão and Toledo 1988). Degradation generally refers to weed infestation, which in turn can be facilitated by pests or deteriorating soil conditions. The proliferation of weeds can be a symptom of soil exhaustion or compaction, but not always. Pastures with numerous termite mounds appear to be in poor condition. The infestation of volunteer plants can thus be a consequence of soil depletion and compaction, overgrazing, underutilization, or insufficient weeding. Weed infestation is a sure sign of poor pasture management.

169

Weeds originate from seeds dropped by birds, other animals, and the wind, and from imported seed. Stump resprouting in relatively new pastures can also quickly shade out grass. Weeds can take over relatively fertile pasture if they are not checked. Overstocking or understocking can also favour the emergence of unwanted plants in pastures. Manual clearing is the most common method of controlling weeds on an annual basis; herbicides are generally too expensive.

Dozens of unwanted plants arise in pastures in Amazonia. The composition of weedy communities varies markedly within an area and between different parts of the Amazon. A few weeds stand out as being especially troublesome. In the Manaus area, vassoura de botão (*Borreria* sp.) is a pernicious rubiaceous weed, while around Paragominas, matapasto (*Cassia* spp.), milkweed (*Asclepias* spp.), and species of *Verbena* infest some pastures. Along the PA 256 road linking Paragominas and Tomé-Açu, lacre (*Vismia guianensis*) forms virtually pure stands in some degraded pastures. In the Marabá area, babaçu palm (*Attalea speciosa*) or assar-peixe (*Vernonia* sp.) typically dominate poorly managed pastures. Some pasture weeds are an important source of food for butterflies and bees, which may in turn provide pollination services to other plants, including economic ones. The complex interactions of weed populations and pasture management warrant further study.

Pastures sown with various species of *Brachiaria* are prone to infestation with several grass weeds. Seed from the *Brachiaria* grasses is collected from the ground, whereas seed from *Panicum maximum* is gathered from the mature spikes, thus reducing the chances of weed contamination (Nepstad, Uhl, and Serrão 1991). Pastures of *Brachiaria* can be established by cuttings, but this procedure is labour intensive and can pose problems for ranchers, even though the minimum wage is only US$60/month. Furthermore, workers are often scarce in pioneer areas. At least one vigorous pasture weed, capim navalha (*Paspalum virgatum*), is thought to have entered Amazonia with *Brachiaria* planting seed (M. Simão, pers. comm.). Although *P. virgatum* is also a grass, it is much less palatable to cattle. Sapé (*Imperata brasiliensis*), the ecological equivalent of the notorious alang-alang grass (*Imperata cylindrica*) of South-East Asia, may have been introduced to some parts of Amazonia after 1970 in seed of *Brachiaria humidicola*. Both *Paspalum virgatum* and *Imperata brasiliensis* are indigenous to Amazonia; a striking feature of weeds in both pastures and fields of Amazonia is that most are native to lowland South America.

Some ranchers are aware that not all invading or resprouting plants in pastures are a nuisance. Fazenda Boi Branco near Paragominas is allowing some forest trees to resprout in pastures if they have timber value. Some leguminous pasture "weeds," such as *Mimosa sensitiva* and matapasto, enrich the soil with nitrogen. Still other volunteer plants in pastures are highly nutritious and are eaten by cattle (Camarão et al. 1990).

Pasture restoration

Given that cattle pastures are likely to remain an important fixture of the agricultural economy of Amazonia, technologies and management practices are needed to improve their productivity. Improvement of existing pastures and livestock, rather than trying to "re-educate" people not to eat beef, is also likely to be more fruitful in Central America (Nations and Komer 1983). With proper management, artificial pastures in Amazonia can be reasonably productive and sustainable (Falesi 1976; Falesi, Baena, and Dutra 1980).

Periodic upgrading with a range of technologies, such as improved germ plasm, is a key part of pasture management in Amazonia. The trend towards improved management of pastures in the region strengthened considerably in the 1980s (Serrão 1989), and remained strong in the early 1990s.

The move to restore pastures has been spurred by a number of factors. First, more technologies, particularly improved pasture grasses, are available than in the past. More productive, pest-resistant grasses have been developed through collaborative research between CIAT (Centro Internacional de Agricultura Tropical) in Cali, Colombia, and national agricultural research systems, such as Brazil's EMBRAPA (Empresa Brasileira de Pesquisa Agropecuária). Second, with a slow-down in road construction in the 1980s, less "virgin" land was available for opening new pastures. Third, land prices have been rising in many parts of Amazonia because of the slow-down in road construction and population increases (Serrão 1989).

How quickly a pasture degrades depends mainly on its management history and to a lesser extent on inherent soil fertility. Some first-generation pastures of guinea grass on alfisols (terra roxa) derived from weathered basalt in the Altamira area of the Transamazon Highway are still reasonably productive after 20 years without fertilizer, provided that they are periodically weeded and fenced to allow rotation. Some guinea grass pastures on relatively infertile ultisols

171

and inceptisols near Maracá, Roraima, were still in good shape after a decade of grazing; pastures tend to degrade when stocking rates exceed 1 head/ha (Eden, McGregor, and Vieira 1990). A guinea grass pasture at Fazenda Piquiá, some 60 km south of Paragominas, has been kept in production for 20 years in spite of the acid, infertile sandy loam on which it has formed. Fazenda Piquiá has kept its guinea grass pasture going with periodic weedings and fertilization with rock phosphate. Transported from central Brazil, rock phosphate is broadcast at the rate of 35–50 kg P_2O_5/ha.

On the other hand, a guinea grass pasture approximately two decades old at km 30 of the Marabá–Altamira stretch of the Transamazon Highway was in extremely poor shape during the 1992 dry season; overstocking and poor weed management had contributed to compaction and in some cases erosion of the relatively infertile oxisol. A regularly weeded and fenced *P. maximum* pasture on yellow oxisol near Paragominas was replaced with braquiarão after 12 years. Even with relatively careful management, the rancher considered the inputs required to keep the guinea grass pasture going would be better spent on "upgrading" to a newer grass, after mechanically loosening the soil and fertilizing with phosphorus.

At the São Judas Tadeu ranch 19 km from São Miguel do Guamá in the Bragantina zone, a 21-year-old pasture of *Brachiaria decumbens* is still grazed. This pasture was cleared in second growth and has never been fertilized, even though the soil is an oxisol. It is still productive because it is fenced, rainfall is plentiful in the 2,500–3,000 mm range, and the land has been weeded periodically.

The cost of upgrading pastures varies according to the degree of treatment and the location (table 7.2). At the high end, pasture restoration involves bulldozing weeds and logs into windrows (fig. 7.5), discing the cleared soil, fertilizing with phosphorus, sowing improved pasture grasses, erecting fences so that pastures can be rotated, and, in some cases, intercropping with forage legumes. In the mid-1980s, an investment of approximately US$150–200/ha was necessary to rehabilitate degraded pastures in areas with good road connections to major markets, such as around Paragominas (Serrão and Toledo 1988; Uhl and Vieira 1989). By the early 1990s, the cost of restoring pastures with the "full treatment" in eastern Pará had climbed to the US$230–350/ha range. In the vicinity of Manaus, increased costs for fertilizer, manual labour, and equipment rental drive up the price for upgrading pastures to the US$350–500/ha range. In Acre, restoration

Table 7.2 **Costs of restoring degraded pasture in upland areas of the Brazilian Amazon, 1991–1992**

Location	Cost (US$/ha)	Year	Observations
Nr. Manaus, Amazonas	460	1991	Mechanized, P fertilizer and intercropping with *Desmodium ovalifolium*[a]
Fazenda Vitoria, Paragominas, Pará	350	1992	Mechanized, P fertilizer and fencing
Fazenda Boi Branco, Paragominas, Pará	300	1991	Mechanized, P fertilizer (rock and super-phosphate) at 200 kg/ha
Fazenda Paraiso, Rio Gurupi, Pará	234	1991	Mechanized, P fertilizer and fencing[b]
Fazenda Modelo, km 12 PA 150 Morada Nova, Marabá, Pará	116	1992	Mechanized, fencing, but no fertilizer

a. This herbaceous legume was originally introduced to the Manaus area in 1978 by EMBRAPA as a ground cover for experimental jacarandá (*Dalbergia* sp.) plantations.
b. For a breakdown of cost per item see table 7.3.

costs average some US$400/ha, but in one case reached as high as US$800/ha.

Larger ranches may employ aircraft to accelerate seeding of their pastures. One ranch near Rio Branco, Fazenda Cipoal, for example, has employed aircraft to seed pastures with *B. brizantha*, a practice that is economically feasible only with target areas in excess of 50 ha. Private companies are the main source of seed for ranchers and farmers in Amazonia. General farming supply stores, such as Agroboi in Altamira, stock seed of several pasture grasses.

The price differential between rehabilitating existing pastures and clearing forest is important when considering land-use changes in Amazonia. In the case of the Rio Branco area of Acre, the cost of felling forest was approximately US$120/ha in November 1991. The higher the cost of pasture restoration, the more likely it is that ranchers will open forest. Research on ways to reduce the cost of pasture improvement could thus help deflect the axe from forest stands.

In spite of the relatively high cost, some 700,000 ha of artificial pasture had been rehabilitated in the Brazilian Amazon by the late 1980s, reaching approximately 1.5 million ha by 1993 (Serrão and Homma 1989, 1993). The income generated from selling timber in the

Fig. 7.5 **Restored pasture with bulldozed windrows and sown to brizantão (*Brachiaria brizantha* cv. Marandu). Near Paragominas, Pará, 4 April 1991**

Paragominas area has helped ranchers restore their pastures. Indeed, the financial incentives to clear forest for pasture have decreased in areas with sawmills and a relatively good road system; in such places, the wood is worth more than the ash fertilizer from forest burns (Buschbacher, Uhl, and Serrão 1987).

Encouragingly, the trend to upgrading pastures is widespread in the Brazilian Amazon. Artificial pastures in Amazonia are being upgraded with a variety of techniques. Fertilizers, particularly phosphorus, are usually essential. More productive and pest-resistant grasses are usually deployed, and legumes, such as *Calopogonium mucunoides*, *Pueraria phaseoloides*, and species of *Centrosema*, are sometimes interplanted for improved ground cover and to fix nitrogen. If the pasture is not bulldozed, weeds are cut and burned, but in heavily compacted sites the soil must be mechanically disced or raked to restore productivity (Serrão 1986a). As in Central America, fencing and rotation of pastures planted in former rain-forest areas can substantially increase the yield and sustainability of cattle operations (Parsons 1989).

The amount of money that ranchers and farmers invest in upgrading their pastures depends on the degree of degradation and available

Table 7.3 **Breakdown of the costs of restoring pasture on two ranches in the Brazilian Amazon**

Item	Observations	Ranch A (US$/ha)	Ranch B (US$/ha)
Bulldozing debris into windrows	Ranch A bulldozed in rainy season when rental rates are lower	45	40
Discing with tractor	Two discings are typically needed at 1 ha/hr	45	40
Phosphate fertilizer		45	None
Brizantão seed	Seed and sowing costs; ranch A application rate was 16 kg/ha, ranch B application rate was 12 kg/ha	36	15
Clean-up and burning	Moving large logs, firing windrows	35	None
Fencing	Enclosing 50 ha plots at cost of US$1,400 per km of fence	28	21
TOTALS		234	116

A: Fazenda Paraiso, Rio Gurupi, Pará, 1991
B: Fazenda Modelo, km 12, PA 150 Morada Nova–Belém, 1992

resources. At the lower end, small-scale farmers, such as colonists along the Transamazon Highway with 100 ha lots, simply cut and burn weeds in pasture and seed with braquiarão. Larger operators often opt for hiring a bulldozer, and purchase fertilizer and barbed wire for fences.

Phosphorus deficiency is common in Amazonian soils and managing P levels in soils is essential to maintaining the productivity of pastures. When available phosphorus declines in soils, weeds usually proliferate (Falesi 1992). Although Brazil is virtually self-sufficient in phosphate, costs of the mineral fertilizer remain high in the Brazilian Amazon. Phosphate fertilizer is one of the major items in the cost of upgrading pastures (table 7.3). In the vicinity of Belém, which has among the cheapest prices for fertilizer in Amazonia, superphosphate fertilizer cost US$180/ton in May 1990. Simple superphosphate is usually applied to pastures at the rate of 1 ton per 5 ha. Large distances between factories in central and southern Brazil elevate the cost of fertilizers for ranchers and farmers in the North region. In spite of these high costs, however, ranchers increasingly employ fertilizers to upgrade the productivity of their pastures.

Earlier predictions that ranchers in the Brazilian Amazon would eschew phosphate fertilizers because of their high cost (Fearnside

1980b) have not come to pass. Between a fifth and a quarter of the first-cycle pastures in the Brazilian Amazon have been upgraded, many with phosphate fertilizer. To prolong the effect of phosphate fertilizer, some ranchers use a combination of superphosphate and rock phosphate. Substantial deposits of phosphate at Maicuru near Santarém, estimated at 100 million tons, may eventually reduce the cost of this important nutrient for ranchers and farmers. However, these phosphate deposits are deep and in a thin band, which will drive up extraction costs.

The restoration treadmill

Restored pastures provide an immediate productivity boost. How much time elapses between each major upgrading of a pasture depends on a host of factors, including the state of finances of the ranch and grazing pressure. Weeds are usually cut and burned every one to four years, but some five to ten years typically elapse before fertilizers need to be applied.

Upgraded pastures in the Paragominas area appear to be profitable, even though they often require fertilizer every five years (Mattos, Uhl, and Gonçalves in press; Nepstad, Uhl, and Serrão 1991). On Fazenda Sinuelo at km 23 of the Rio Branco–Porto Velho Highway, a seven-year-old *B. brizantha* pasture has been weeded only once, shortly after the grass seed germinated, and has not needed any fertilizer. On infertile oxisols in the Paragominas area, several ranches have not had to fertilize their brizantão pastures after five years.

With adequate care, pastures of *B. brizantha* are reasonably productive. Well-managed brizantão pastures on moderately fertile ultisols near Rio.Branco, Acre, permit cattle to reach 500 kg within three years. At Fazenda Boi Branco near Paragominas, superior Nelore stock can attain 350 kg within 18 months when grazing on well-managed brizantão pasture and supplemented by chopped elephant grass mixed with mineral nutrients (fig. 7.6). At Fazenda Paraiso on the Rio Gurupi, Pará, cattle typically gain 144 kg per year on brizantão pastures without supplemental feed.

Restoration of pastures is not a one-shot affair. Inevitably, rehabilitated pastures require more fertilization as well as new forage species or varieties. For all its favourable attributes, for example, brizantão is no panacea for improving pastures in Amazonia. When

176

Fig. 7.6 **Owner of Fazenda Boi Branco, Gastão Carvalho, with Nelore cattle raised on brizantão (*Brachiaria brizantha* cv. Marandu) pasture and fed supplemental commercial rations and elephant grass. Near Paragominas, Pará, 4 April 1991**

planted on poor soils, for example, productivity is likely to fall off without periodic fertilization with phosphorus. Furthermore, *Brachiaria brizantha* may be allelopathic, thus diminishing the chances of successful interplanting with forage legumes.

Another factor mitigating against a long tenure for *Brachiaria brizantha* var. Marandu in many areas of the Amazon basin is that pest populations are likely to change. For example, one small patch of *Brachiaria brizantha* pasture on Fazenda Rio Branco near Ariquemes, Rondônia, appeared to be suffering from spittlebugs in February 1992. If such proves to be the case, then spittlebugs have evolved a new race, thus putting at risk the large areas planted to *B. brizantha*. As in the case of silviculture and field crops, pasture ecosystems in Amazonia are highly dynamic, thus requiring a continued research effort to maintain their long-term productivity.

Scale and pace of rehabilitation

Small- to medium-scale ranchers appear to be most actively upgrading artificial pastures throughout Amazonia. In 1991, ranches with restored pastures were observed along the Manaus–Itacoatiara road; the Transamazon Highway from the Altamira area to km 80 of the Altamira–Itaituba stretch; the highway linking Tomé-Açu and Paragominas (PA 256); the Belém–Brasília Highway from Paragominas to Belém; the road from the Belém–Brasília Highway to Capitão Poço, Pará; and the Rio Branco–Porto Velho Highway in Acre. In 1993 and 1994, rehabilitated pastures were observed along BR 364 and associated side-roads in Rondônia and along the Obidos–Oriximiná Highway. At least a quarter of the ranches observed along the above roads had all or some of their pastures under improved management. Ranchers in northern Mato Grosso are also actively upgrading their pastures.

How fast the restoration of pastures in Amazonia proceeds hinges largely on market signals and fiscal policies, since technologies for pasture improvement are no constraint. Relatively low market prices for beef in 1989 and 1990 discouraged investment in pasture improvement. In addition, hyperinflation in Brazil, which reached 60 per cent a month by February 1990, dampened the investment needed to improve the productive capacity of businesses and industry.

Prior to Collor de Melo's presidency in March 1990, the federal government was offering financial instruments (Letras Financeiras do Tesouro) that paid rates of return greatly in excess of inflation to help finance the burgeoning deficit. Working with commercial banks, investors with as little as US$100 were obtaining an unsecured rate of return of about 3 per cent every 24 hours in February 1990 through this financial instrument. Over US$50 billion was tied up in "overnight" deposits in early 1990, funds that could be used more productively to improve pastures and other enterprises. Fiscal measures were taken after March 1990 to dampen inflation and eliminate the "overnight" option, but investors switched to 30-day notes.

Inflation dropped dramatically with the introduction of a new currency, the *real*, in July 1994. The architect of the *plano real*, Fernando Henrique Cardoso, was elected President of Brazil in October 1994, and the investment climate will likely improve for upgrading pastures and other agricultural enterprises.

Modest fiscal incentives are available for pasture improvement from the Amazon Regional Development Bank (BASA – Banco da Amazônia, S.A.). BASA taps funds from the Fundo Constitucional de Financiamentos do Norte (FNO) for this purpose. To qualify, ranchers must intercrop pastures with nitrogen-fixing *Pueraria* in an effort to improve their sustainability. Few ranchers appear to have taken advantage of BASA loans for this purpose, partly because *Pueraria* does not withstand much trampling by cattle. Stocking rates have to be

Fig. 7.7 **Shells of Brazil nut (*Bertholletia excelsa*) mixed with cattle manure for fertilizing pasture. Fazenda Rio Doce, 46 km east of Belém on the BR 316 highway, Pará, 28 May 1990**

carefully controlled when *Pueraria* is intercropped, and not all ranches have established expensive fencing to rotate pastures carefully.

Further research, fresh germ plasm, and new management techniques will be required to keep pastures sustainable over the long term. As in the case of agro-forestry systems, a better inventory of existing practices by farmers and ranchers might uncover promising avenues for further development. The owner of Fazenda Baixa Verde, located at km 46 of the Rio Branco–Porto Velho stretch of BR 364, is restoring 2,500 ha of pasture in stages using maize as an intercrop to reduce costs. At Fazenda Rio Doce, 46 km east of Belém on the BR 316 highway, Brazil nut (*Bertholletia excelsa*) shells from factories in Belém are recycled on to pastures after they have been mulched for several months with cattle manure (fig. 7.7). Other ranchers in eastern Amazonia are experimenting with grain crops as a phase in pasture rehabilitation (Veiga 1986).

179

Intercropping pasture with perennials

The notion of planting perennial trees in pastures, or along their margins, is attractive on many counts. First, it would diversify income for ranchers. Second, a more ecologically diverse landscape would ensue, with possible benefits for some wildlife. Third, nutrients and water would be sequestered from soil layers out of reach of grasses, thereby improving the productivity of the land and increasing evapotranspiration, particularly in the dry season. Fourth, depending on the species employed, soils could be replenished with nitrogen. Fifth, cattle would benefit from shade, and would concentrate dung around the trees, thereby fertilizing them.

Although the benefits of intercropping pastures with fruit, nut, or timber trees, and of encircling them with living fences, are well recognized, few ranches have implemented such practices. Annual crops are often planted before a pasture is established, or during the initial stages of restoration, but they are phased out as the grass becomes established. Jari discontinued its pasture/Caribbean pine operation to concentrate on pulp production.

Ranchers are reluctant to try intercropping pasture with perennials because of management concerns. Management intensity would necessarily increase as the operation diversifies. Most ranchers lack the knowledge base to work with an assemblage of perennials. The cost of fencing off tree seedlings so that they are not damaged by cattle is a concern. Fire, a common management tool to reduce weeds, would also damage tree seedlings.

Small farms are likely to be the first successful testing ground for intercropping pastures with trees and bushes. Small farmers often have experience with both livestock and a mixture of crops. Land tenure is an important dimension here: only if the farmers own the land are they likely to invest in perennials and other long-term conservation measures (Vosti 1991).

For the most part, ranchers in the Brazilian Amazon are not currently interested in agro-forestry systems that incorporate pasture grasses with perennial crops. A few medium-scale ranchers intercrop rubber with pasture, such as in the vicinity of Tomé-Açu, but ranchers generally prefer to concentrate on pasture or pasture–legume intercrops. At Fazenda Aruanã near Itacoatiara an attempt was made to intercrop Brazil nut trees with pasture: Brazil nut trees were initially planted at 20 metre intervals, but the pasture was already degraded when the Brazil nut seedlings were planted and the effort to combine beef and Brazil nut production on the same land was discontinued because of weed problems. A decision was made to double the planting density of Brazil nut trees instead of trying to combine them with cattle grazing. The rancher is still in the business of producing beef and Brazil nuts, but on different parcels of his property. Approximately 4,000 ha of Brazil nut trees have been planted at Fazenda Aruanã at 10 metre intervals. Most of the Brazil nut trees have been grafted in an effort to ensure higher yields, but 12-year-old trees are still not producing adequately, possibly because of pollination or soil fertility problems.

For larger ranches, the first "breakthrough" in diversifying the pasture landscape is likely to come with living fences. Fence posts have to be replaced every four to five years, mainly because of termite damage. If suitable species can be found that do not require expensive labour for pruning, ranchers are likely to adopt living fences, as in Costa Rica, where at least 57 plants are employed as living fences (Sauer 1979).

Most of the living fence species in Costa Rica are native to Central America and were already adapted to agricultural conditions since they are also volunteers in open sites. The practice of using living fences pre-dates the Spanish Conquest in Costa Rica. Suitable candidates for living fences in Amazonia might come from the native second-growth flora, from indigenous groups, or from other tropical regions.

On-farm and on-ranch experiments are ideal ways to introduce new technologies. In the vicinity of Paragominas, the Brazilian agricultural research service (EMBRAPA) and Woods Hole Research Center in Massachusetts are collaborating with a rancher to test the suitability of rehabilitating pastures with various intercropped fruit trees.

Pasture intercropping raises a host of research issues. Allelopathic interactions can thwart some intercrops. Perennials are long-term investments, but market conditions can shift unpredictably. For example, low latex prices have forced the owner of Fazenda Rio Branco near Ariquemes, Rondônia, to cut down rubber intercropped on 750 ha of his 2,000 ha of pasture. The mix of perennials suitable for any given area will depend on soil conditions, allelopathic behaviour, rainfall patterns, and marketing infrastructure, among other factors.

Intercropping with leguminous ground cover

Although a number of ranchers introduce some herbaceous legumes to their pastures, particularly when they are being upgraded, this practice is not as well developed as it could be. The advantages of intercropping pasture with a leguminous ground cover are well known – increasing soil nitrogen levels, provision of a nutritious forage, and, in areas with a pronounced dry season, increased food for cattle – but few artificial pastures in Amazonia are systematically planted with legumes. Less than 5 per cent of the sown pastures in Amazonia include planted herbaceous legumes (Serrão 1986a).

Two main reasons appear to account for the slow adoption of intercropped legumes in pasture. First, the introduction of a leguminous ground cover implies new management practices. Weeds are frequently suppressed in pastures by fire, so legumes can be destroyed when pastures are "cleaned." Another management issue with forage legumes is that they can become weedy and interfere with crops. *Pueraria* and mucuna preta (*Mucuna aterrima*) can spread quickly; *Pueraria* is known as the notorious kudzu vine in Florida and Georgia. Also, while legumes are becoming established, careful attention to grazing pressure is usually needed. Second, farmers may not have used the appropriate germ plasm for their soils and climate.

The push to experiment with leguminous ground cover in Amazonian pastures is nevertheless well under way. In addition to trials conducted by EMBRAPA in collaboration with CIAT, many ranchers are experimenting with legumes on their own. The manager of Sementes Garanhão in Marabá, for example, reports an increasing demand for seeds of *Pueraria*, mucuna preta, and soja perene (*Glycine wightii*) from local ranchers (Borba, pers. comm.). Sementes Garanhão has seed production facilities in Mato Grosso do Sul and also buys seed from other producers in the south-central state. The owner of Fazenda Nova Aurora on the outskirts of Quatro Bocas further north in Pará has established experimental plots intercropping brachiarão with soja perene and mucuna preta.

Research carried out by EMBRAPA's cerrado research centre (CPAC – Centro de Pesquisa Agropecuária do Cerrado) in conjunction with CIAT scientists has identified a number of different strategies for improving pastures, some of which may soon pay off for ranchers in Amazonia. For drier areas of Amazonia, *Stylosanthes guianensis* holds promise because it withstands drought well and provides valuable forage when pasture grasses are suffering from moisture stress. This waxy-leafed legume is a native of the cerrado and parts of the Amazon; it is at home in areas with long dry seasons and is adapted to poor, acid soils. Poor seed production will need to be overcome and trials in various parts of Amazonia will have to be carried out before *S. guianensis* can be recommended for planting in the North region. Another promising candidate for Amazonian pastures is *Arachis pintoi*. This relative of the groundnut quickly establishes a lush green carpet, and is thus particularly appropriate for bunch grasses, such as *Panicum maximum*. A further advantage of the legume is that it produces abundant seed, tolerates drought and shade, and is eaten eagerly by cattle (J. Spain, pers. comm.).

Savannas

In upland areas, extensive *campos* in Roraima and Amapá and smaller patches of native grassland in Rondônia, Amazonas, Pará, and Amapá cover at least 20 million ha and have supported low-density cattle populations for centuries (Eden 1990: 3; Moura 1989: 92; Pires-O'Brien 1992; Serrão 1986b). The impressive extent of savannas in some areas is due in part to human activities, both at present and in remote times. Edaphic factors, such as poor drainage caused by a clay hardpan near the surface, create a core of natural grassland much of which has expanded after burning.

In the distant past, hunters and gatherers ignited savannas to facilitate hunting, and some indigenous groups still follow this practice (Smith in press). Cattle were first introduced to the savannas of Roraima in 1787, and by 1930 some 300,000 head of cattle roamed the annually torched grassland (Rivière 1972). Ranchers ignite the *campos* in the dry season to promote more succulent and nutritious growth when the rains come. Only fire-hardy tree species, such as *Curatella americana*, survive in grasslands that are annually torched. The carrying capacity of such rangeland is low, but could be improved by new management techniques, such as interplanting with more nutritious forage species (Braun and Ramos 1959). Flood-plain pastures along the Amazon are much more productive, but they are only seasonally available. Some 50 million ha of savanna and flood-plain meadows are currently underutilized by livestock (Serrão 1989), an area two-and-a-half times greater than planted pastures in deforested areas of the uplands. Stocking rates on "natural" or non-planted grasslands could increase from the current 6 million head of cattle and water buffalo to at least 30 million without cutting down any trees (Serrão 1990). The potential and pitfalls of ranching on the flood plain are explored in more detail in the following chapter.

183

8

Land-use dynamics on the Amazon flood plain

The extensive flood plains of alluvium-rich rivers in northern South America represent one of the last major frontiers for expanding food production in Latin America. Currently, the cerrados of central Brazil are being developed more intensively to become important granaries. Although more gains are expected from cultivating these seasonally dry areas, the sinuous flood plains of the Amazon and Orinoco river basins have been largely neglected by researchers and development planners (Goulding, Smith, and Mahar in press.).

The flood plains of silt-laden rivers have historically been the most productive farming environments in Amazonia. Although flood plains account for less than 4 per cent of the region, they have traditionally provided most of the food for rural and urban inhabitants of the Amazon. The most fertile flood plains are along "white water" rivers, such as the Amazon and Madeira, which occupy some 190,000 km², an area bigger than many countries. Clear and black water rivers, such as the Tapajós and Negro, respectively, are much less propitious for agricultural development because their waters contain little sediment and their flood plains are mostly porous sand. The flood plains of black and clear water rivers are best left in forest, to provide food and refuge for resident and migratory fishes.

Crop production holds particular promise on the flood plains (*várzeas*) of turbid, white water rivers. Annual rejuvenation of these flood-plain soils permits much higher yields than is typically achieved on upland sites. Yearly floods also destroy weeds and permit a fresh beginning for each cropping season. Water transportation is also cheaper than hauling cargo by truck, bus, or pickup on the uplands.

184

Annual crop production in upland areas poses many more problems (Fearnside 1987). Soils are generally too poor for sustained annual cropping without the use of fertilizers and weed control. Organic mulches are usually expensive to acquire and apply. Currently, the only annual crops that justify the use of fertilizers are vegetables when planted close to urban areas. Many upland sites are steep and prone to soil erosion, in contrast to the relatively flat flood plains.

An aquatic breadbasket

Manioc (*Manihot esculenta*), a basic staple in Amazonia, is grown extensively along the Amazon flood plain as well as on other alluvial soils. Varieties have been selected that can be harvested within 6–8 months, before rising waters inundate fields. Although the growing season is shorter than on the uplands, yields are often better than in interfluvial areas because of the generally superior soils. Manioc yields on *várzea* soils are in the 16–40 tons/ha range (Pickles 1942), which is appreciably higher than on uplands where yields are usually between 10 and 20 tons/ha.

Although manioc harvests on the *várzea* are generally bountiful, diseases sometimes depress yields. As in the case of uplands, several fungi attack manioc roots, particularly species of *Diplodia*, *Scytalidium*, *Fusarium*, and *Phytophthora*. Moist conditions in flood-plain environments foster the development of fungi. Collaborative research between CIAT (Centro Internacional de Agricultura Tropical), the Centre for Research on Manioc and Beans (CNPMF – Centro Nacional de Pesquisas de Mandhioca e Fruticultura) in Bahia, and the EMBRAPA stations in Belém and Manaus has identified 12 root rot-resistant clones, two of which were released to *várzea* farmers in 1990 ("Mãe Joana" and "Zolhudinha"), and a third (EMBRAPA-8) in 1992 (CIAT 1992).

Even without fertilizer, rice (*Oryza sativa*) yields on the Amazon flood plain average 3,000 kg/ha (Camargo 1948), whereas they rarely reach much more than 1,000 kg/ha on the uplands. Some of the deep-water rice varieties selected by farmers in parts of Thailand might be appropriate for the Amazon flood plain, thereby permitting two crops of the nutritious cereal a year.

In spite of the higher yields of annual food crops on the flood plain, scope still exists for further boosting yields through more productive varieties and improved management. Disease and pest resistance would be a high priority, in order to reduce the need for pesticides that could enter aquatic food-chains.

For some time now, people have talked about the enormous potential of the Amazon flood plain for increased food production, but this promise is still largely unrealized. Most of the food consumed in the large cities of the Amazon, such as Belém, Manaus, and Santarém, comes from central and southern Brazil and, to a lesser degree, upland sites in Amazonia. The main crops grown on the Amazon flood plain in Brazil are manioc, maize, beans, squashes, and some vegetables. Much of the agricultural production is for domestic consumption; limited quantities of manioc flour, maize, and vegetables are sold in nearby towns and villages.

The apparent lack of an agricultural "boom" on the Amazon flood plain is perplexing, but is probably due to a combination of factors. The flood plains have been largely neglected by fiscal incentives and rural extension. Electricity is still a rarity, thus impeding the development of agro-industry. Although riverine transportation is cheaper, flood-plain farmers often do not have access to a regular boat service to sizeable markets. In spite of such drawbacks, a few interesting developments are under way along the middle Amazon that provide glimpses of what might be possible for the future development of this last great agricultural frontier of South America.

An important lesson that can readily be drawn from agricultural experiments under way along the Amazon flood plain is that it is important to start on a small scale and monitor progress and possible environmental problems. Jari attempted a large-scale mechanized and irrigated rice operation on the Amazon flood plain that failed. Although yields were higher than with traditional methods, costs were much higher, owing in part to the expense of pumping to control water levels in the rice fields. The Jari rice operation included aircraft and large combine harvesters, an enormous investment with high upkeep costs in the Amazon. In the end, rice prices were not high enough to sustain the operation. Jari's rice experiment lasted only about a decade.

A cereal merchant in Santarém has been experimenting with mechanized rice production on the Amazon flood plain since the early 1990s, but with much more modest inputs. About 800 ha of the flood plain near Alenquer were prepared by tractor for rice in 1994; although floods came early that year, thereby destroying some of the crop, yields average 6 tons/ha, about twice those achieved by resource-poor farmers on the Amazon. The increased yield was made possible by combining modern varieties and NPK fertilizer applied at the relatively low rate of 70 kg/ha. The cereal merchant, a native of Ceará in the Brazilian North-east region, markets his flood-plain rice in Fortaleza, the capital of his native state, and plans to expand production.

Although this cereal merchant is likely to face future setbacks, he may well succeed. He runs a profitable cereal-drying and warehousing operation in rapidly growing Santarém. He has the financial resources to withstand the trial-and-error period of this new venture. Besides, a precedent for successful mechanized rice production on white water flood plains in Amazonia has already been set in Roraima. In this northern state, farmers from Rio Grande do Sul have mechanized and irrigated parts of the Rio Branco flood plain, another silt-laden river. Produce is marketed in the boom town of Boa Vista. Interestingly, it is outsiders who are experimenting with higher-input rice production in Amazonia.

Efforts to mechanize maize production on the Amazon flood plain have not been as successful. A Belém-based rancher with a 5,000 ha property on Ilha do Ituqui near Santarém was attracted to the idea of becoming a maize farmer because of a sizeable poultry operation in Santarém. Wisely, the rancher in question started on a small scale rather than risk too many of his resources or squander fiscal incentives. A total of 70 ha of flood plain were prepared with a tractor and planted to an open-pollinated variety of maize (BR 5107) at Fazenda São Sebastião in 1992. A floating barge was used to pump river water on to the crop while it was growing. The irrigation schedule was set at twice a week during the first 20 days, and about every 8 days from the 20th day until the plants started flowering, when irrigation was halted. No herbicides or pesticides were used, but small amounts of K fertilizer were applied. The owner of this ranch obtained financial support from the Banco da Amazônia for equipment purchases, and yields were expected to be about 8 tons/ha.

The maize harvest on Fazenda São Sebastião in early 1993 was only 3 tons/ha, not nearly as bountiful as expected. A proliferation of weeds, such as matapasto (*Senna reticulata*), and slack adherence to the watering schedule were deemed responsible for the lacklustre yields. For future growing seasons at low water, the rancher plans to deploy herbicides to control weeds. If this practice proves economically feasible, the rancher plans to expand the honed "technological package" to neighbouring small farmers. The rancher will prepare fields and loan irrigation equipment in exchange for a percentage of the harvest.

Although cereal yields might be relatively high on modern farms, several resource management issues arise from the intensification of cereal production on the Amazon flood plain. First, weeds may increase with continuous cultivation. Even with annual floods that generally destroy most herbs, weed populations could proliferate. The extent to which large-scale herbicides can adversely affect aquatic food-chains is unknown at this time. It might make more sense to adopt some of the tall, traditional maize varieties on the Amazon flood plain, which usually outpace weeds and rising floods, at least until the harvest is completed. Second, soil structure could change without a fallow period. The dynamics of weed populations and soil texture warrant study here. It may prove necessary to allow fields to revert periodically to fallow for a year or two to restore soil structure and suppress weed populations.

Soybeans (*Glycine max*) might prove a suitable cash crop for flood-plain farmers in the future, if well-adapted varieties are developed. Currently, Paraná and Rio Grande do Sul are the main soybean-producing states in Brazil. Lesser quantities of the pulse are grown on the cerrado, including transitional areas with forest in southern Rondônia. The municipal governments of Santarém and Juriti in particular have expressed keen interest in promoting soybean production on the Amazon flood plain.

Although greater food production is possible on flood plains, especially along the Amazon, Madeira, Purus, and Juruá, large-scale clearing of *várzea* forest would likely disrupt some major fisheries. Over three-quarters of the fish important in commerce and subsistence depend directly or indirectly on flood-plain forests for food (Goulding 1980). Hence the need to focus efforts on designing more intensive cropping systems on already cleared areas.

The collapse of jute and the emergence of market gardening

For decades, jute (*Corchorus* spp.) reigned supreme as the main cash crop along the middle Amazon. Introduced to the Amazon by Japanese farmers in 1931 (Biard and Wagenaar 1960), jute is well adapted to the rich soils of the flood plain and found a ready market in northeastern and southern Brazil, particularly to sack sugar and coffee. In recent years, however, competition from synthetic fibres, particularly polypropylene, has undercut the market for jute. In Brazil, petroleum-derived polypropylene bags are one-third to one-half the price of jute bags, and are now widely used for many commodities, particularly for groundnuts, potatoes, and onions (Thigpen, Marongiu, and Lasker 1987). A second factor in the decline of jute is the shift to bulk handling of many commodities, particularly sugar, grains, and soybeans. Finally, producers in Bangladesh have driven down the price of jute fibre because of their relatively low operating costs; they now provide close to half of all jute traded on world markets.

One symptom of jute's decline in Brazil is the shrinking number of factories working with the material. No jute-pressing plants remain in Santarém and Juriti, formerly important processing centres for the crop. In 1991, the Brazilian government eliminated import tariffs for jute imported from Asia. The area planted to jute is thus shrinking along the Amazon, and farmers are searching for other sources of income. Many have turned to fishing on a more intensive scale and to livestock raising. Others are searching for more viable cash crops.

Vegetables have emerged as one of the most promising options for flood-plain farmers seeking a replacement crop for jute. With the spectacular growth of cities, demand for a wide variety of vegetables, particularly tomato, lettuce, cabbage, cucumber, bell pepper, okra, and spring onions, has increased dramatically (fig. 8.1). Traditionally, people in Amazonia have not eaten many vegetables (Shrimpton and Giugliano 1979), but customs are changing with the rise of the middle class in urban areas and the influx of people from other regions (Von der Pahlen et al. 1979). Salads are now much more commonly served in homes, restaurants, and fast-food outlets in Amazonian cities.

All the vegetables grown on the *várzea* are produced by small farmers with heavy reliance on family labour. Women and children help transplant, weed, and harvest vegetables. Wage labourers, paid the equivalent of US$1 a day including lunch, also find employment on small vegetable farms, particularly for harvesting tomatoes.

Vegetable plots are typically fenced to keep out cattle and water buffalo. The high return on vegetables apparently pays for the investment in fences. Many farmers have purchased diesel pumps to irrigate their vegetable plots; in some cases, several families have cooperated to buy and maintain portable irrigation pumps. Farmers along Paraná Cachoeri near Oriximiná have built raised platforms so that they can grow vegetables year-round. One such farmer has 70 raised platforms in production, ranging in length from 20 to 50 metres.

The experience of vegetable growers along Paraná Cachoeri illus-

Fig. 8.1   **Farmer on the Amazon flood plain with a pile of cattle manure for fertilizing an assortment of vegetables. São Cirico de Urucurituba, near Santarém, Pará, 18 November 1992**

trates the importance of markets and linkages with other land-use systems. "Cured" cattle manure is the planting medium in raised vegetable beds. Cattle dung is used uncut, after at least a month of storage. Thus cattle production on the Amazon flood plain can be a blessing or a bane of vegetable growers. Most of the vegetables produced along Paraná Cachoeri are taken by boat to Porto Trombetas to feed workers and their families associated with the bauxite-mining company, Mineração Rio Norte. "Mineração," as the mining operation is known locally, has chartered as many at two jets a month from São Paulo to provide the company town with vegetables. Flights are now down to once a month, in part owing to vegetable production along the Paraná Cachoeri.

Although the spread of vegetable farming along the Amazon flood plain is undoubtedly improving rural incomes and employment opportunities, as well as helping to improve the vitamin and fibre content of diets in urban areas, market gardening raises some ecological issues. Vegetable production, particularly in the tropics, is renowned for the heavy use of agro-chemicals, particularly pesticides. Apart from possible poisoning of farmers and workers owing to inappropriate handling of pesticides and insufficient washing of vegetables by consumers, the use of such chemicals in flood plains raises the spectre of contamination of fish, the most important source of animal protein for the regional population.

If vegetable farming increases, as seems likely, insecticides could start finding their way into aquatic food-chains and contaminate fish. At the moment, mercury levels in fish are a regional concern as a result of gold-mining activities. But gold mining has declined dramatically since the late 1980s, accompanying the worldwide plunge in gold prices. A preoccupation with mercury contamination could blind public health officials to the "sleeper" issue of potentially dangerous levels of insecticides in some fish species in certain areas.

One way to counteract the use of insecticides would be to deploy pest-resistant varieties. At the moment, vegetable growers in the Santarém area are purchasing seed produced in Minas Gerais and Rio Grande do Sul, or imported from Denmark. Pest pressure is less severe in the subtropical and temperate climates where the vegetable varieties are developed. Vegetable growers in Amazonia would undoubtedly benefit from more research on varieties adapted to the intense onslaught of diseases and pests characteristic of the humid tropics. A broad-based research agenda would include integrated pest management systems, such as resistant varieties, biocontrol of pests and diseases, and improved agronomic practices, such as crop rotation.

Flood-plain orchards

At first glance, flood plains might appear to be inappropriate for perennial crops. Although flood plains seem flat from the air, they are a complex of ridges, swales, and broad terraces. Some parts of the flood plain may be swamped for seven months or more, while higher portions may be under water for a month or less. Still other areas of the flood plain may be inundated only every 5–15 years or so during exceptional floods. Subtle but significant differences in topography create many micro-environments for different crops.

Many economically viable perennials are suited to the varied drainage conditions of flood plains in Amazonia. At least 80 species of perennials are grown in home gardens of the middle Amazon flood plain (Smith in prep.). Some of the plants are relatively well known, such as the palms açaí (*Euterpe oleracea*) and buriti (*Mauritia flexuosa*), while others are in the process of domestication. Home gardens contain a wealth of species and varieties adapted to the Amazon flood plain, some of which could be grown on a larger, commercial scale.

Açaí palm, for example, is already an important component of riverine vegetation in many parts of Amazonia, particularly in the estuarine area, but is not common along the middle Amazon. Açaí is harvested from natural and planted stands for its fruit and heart-of-palm (Anderson 1990b). Açaí fruit finds a ready market in both rural and urban areas, where it is mixed with manioc flour to make a thick, purple porridge; taken with water as a refreshing "milk" shake; and made into ice-cream. More flood-plain forests could be enriched with this graceful palm to boost food production and diversify sources of income, particularly near the mouth of the Amazon.

Numerous other native fruit trees thrive on the flood plains of white and clear water rivers, such as buriti palm, cajá (*Spondias mombim*), and cacao. Extensive stands of buriti palm are found along the upper Amazon, particularly between Leticia and Iquitos, but they are being felled to harvest the vitamin C-rich fruits. Improved harvesting techniques, and replanting devastated areas with this towering palm, would help ensure plentiful supplies of nutritious buriti fruit for generations to come.

Indigenous nuts, such as sapucaia (*Lecythis pisonis*), are a common backyard tree on the middle Amazon flood plain. Sapucaia also occurs in the remaining forest patches and could be planted more extensively in orchards and second-growth communities. Specimens of sapucaia on the flood plain are much shorter than populations in upland forests, so the nut cases can be harvested before the lid falls off and bats abscond with the nuts. Sapucaia rivals the better-known Brazil nuts in taste; indeed, to some, sapucaia nuts are creamier and more savoury than their distant cousin, the Brazil nut.

Although some time might be required before desirable selections of sapucaia are available for more widespread planting, other perennial crops well adapted to the flood plain could be promoted for planting in polycultural orchards or single stands. Cupuaçu, for example, thrives on higher parts of the flood plain, and could become a viable cash crop along the Amazon, particularly if floating pulp-processing plants could be established. With the help of simple freezers, upland-based farmers' and growers' associations are marketing ever-increasing quantities of cupuaçu for the ice-cream and juice trade. Flood-plain farmers are being bypassed by the cupuaçu boom; small, barge-based agro-industrial plants combined with cheap water transportation could help rectify the situation. Large, low-fibre selections of mango, such as "Kent" and "Keitt," might also help flood-plain farmers boost their incomes.

Tree crops thus provide many benefits and warrant more attention on the *várzea*. Labour costs are lower than for most annual crops, and discarded or rotten fruit and nuts provide food for fish. Several species of forest trees are tended in home gardens for fish bait, such as tarumã (*Vitex cymosa*) and catauari (*Crataeva benthami*), and some of them could be grown in larger agro-forestry fields to supply upland-based fish farmers. Within the past two decades, fish culture has progressed to the point that some pond-raised species are already reaching the market, as in the case of tambaqui (*Colossoma macropomum*) from ranches in the vicinity of Rio Branco, Acre. Tambaqui is one of the most commercially valuable fish in Amazonia and, although an omnivore, depends heavily on fruits and seeds in the wild. In fish ponds, tambaqui thrives on starchy rations, but its flavour is reputedly not the same as wild tambaqui. Fish farmers might well be interested in buying fruits and nuts favoured by tambaqui to improve flavour and conditioning, particularly just before the fish are harvested for market.

Livestock in conflict with crops and fisheries

The most acute threat to the integrity of forests along the Amazon flood plain is livestock raising, particularly cattle and water buffalo. Ranchers and small farmers alike fell trees to create pasture at low water and to promote floating meadows at high water. Cattle and water buffalo wreak havoc in farmers' fields at low water. Even fences will not keep out powerful water buffalo, which can easily swim around barriers.

The driving forces behind cattle and water buffalo raising are similar to those on uplands, explored in the previous chapter. As on terra firma, some small farmers are opting to raise cattle, even if they occasionally damage crops. Water buffalo are still the domain of larger ranchers, however. In time, though, water buffalo will likely be taken up by some smallholders, as they have in many parts of tropical Asia.

The convergence of market and cultural forces is likely to further propel livestock raising on the *várzea*. Short of unleashing a Jurassic Park, no policy action is likely to rid the flood plain of cattle and water buffalo; cattle and water buffalo have become an integral part of the culture and economy of the Amazon flood plain. It is the scale of ranching that is triggering concern. Given that large livestock are here to stay on the flood plain, ways must be found to improve productivity while minimizing environmental damage and social conflicts. After reviewing the potential of flood-plain meadows, possibilities for raising native animals for food are explored.

Flood-plain meadows

Small cattle herds have been kept along the flood plains of major white water rivers, such as the Amazon, for centuries. At low water, zebu cattle are let out to graze on lush new growth, where they fatten up for market and produce milk for cheese-making. During the flood season, ranchers and small farmers have three options for safeguarding their herds during the season of deprivation: floating corrals, small pens along the interface between uplands and the flood plain, or upland pasture.

The first two options are generally employed by small operators. Livestock placed in floating corrals (*marombas*) or pens (*caiçaras*) are fed floating grasses (Sternberg 1953). Other operators lease or own pasture on terra firma. Cattle transhumance is common along the Amazon, particularly in the mid-section. Sometimes ranchers own land both on flood plains and on uplands (fig. 8.2). In other cases, particularly among smaller operators, pasture is often rented at certain times of the year. For example, one rancher with 280 ha of land along Ramal Andirobalzinho near Alter do Chão, Pará, keeps 70 head of cattle on 30 ha of weed-infested upland pasture from April to September, then transports his cattle to the Amazon flood plain. Truck and boat charges amount to US$4/head, while the lease of flood-plain pastures is US$2/head. The availability of lush *várzea* pasture is a major reason few ranchers have invested in pasture improvement in the Santarém area.

Partially submerged water buffalo are able to feed directly on the floating meadows. Water buffalo are admirably adapted to the fluctuating water levels and the native grasses of Marajó Island and stretches of the middle to lower Amazon (fig. 8.3). Only a small fraction of the estimated 11 million ha of flood-plain pasture available

Fig. 8.2 **Ranch on an upland bluff overlooking the Amazon flood plain with grazing sheep. Km 4 of the Itacoatiara–Manaus Highway, Amazonas, 15 November 1991**

in the Amazon is effectively utilized by livestock. Although the carrying capacity of flood-plain meadows is generally higher than that of upland pasture, cattle can take advantage of them for only roughly 4–8 months. Improved management, such as enrichment planting with legumes and fencing, could boost the productivity of ranching on flood plains while reducing damage to adjacent fields and lakes.

Water buffalo were introduced to Brazil in the late nineteenth century, and now exceed 800,000 head, mostly in the lower Amazon (Alvim 1990; Mahadevan 1974; NRC 1981: 2). Marajó Island alone is reputed to have half a million water buffalo (Leal 1990). Water buffalo take an average of three years to reach 350 kg, while cattle take four years to reach the same weight in Amazonia. Also, water buffalo can remain on the flood plain longer than cattle during the flood stage.

Although raising cattle along flood plains is considered more environmentally benign than ranching in upland forest, some environmental and social costs are incurred. Ranchers sometimes clear parts of the flood-plain forest to create more grassland at low water. Rather than keep cattle on barges or in sheds kept above the water line by stilts, some of the larger operators often clear adjacent up-

195

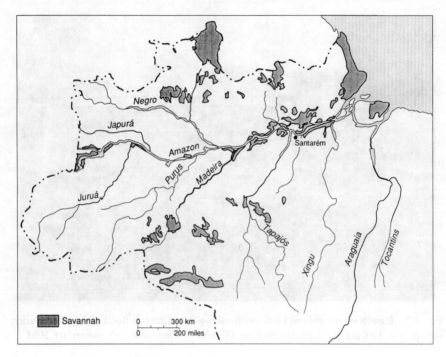

Fig. 8.3 **Riverine and upland savanna in Amazonia (Sources: adapted from Eden 1990: 3; Pires and Prance 1985)**

lands to maintain the cattle during the flood stage. This lateral trans-humance reduces the amount of forest cleared because cattle are kept on artificial pasture only for some three to five months. Nevertheless, forests are cleared to raise beef, when fish protein can be produced much more cheaply by leaving the forest cover.

Both cattle and water buffalo can interfere with small-scale farmers' efforts to grow food crops, especially vegetables. Conflicts between farmers and ranchers occasionally flare up on Careiro Island near Manaus and along other sections of the Amazon. Farmers erect fences at their own expense to keep out cattle, even though ranchers are supposed to be liable for any damage to crops. Conflicts between ranchers and small farmers is likely to increase in the future unless management systems are worked out to the benefit of all stake-holders on the flood plain. Various options are worth exploring such as living fences, designating certain islands for crop or livestock pro-duction, and improving the forage of existing flood-plain pastures so that cattle and water buffalo are less tempted by nearby fields.

Alternatives to cattle

Our analysis of cattle and water buffalo production in Amazonia does not imply that other systems of raising animal protein do not deserve more support, particularly for research. Indeed, sheep and goats appear to be increasingly raised by small- and medium-scale operators in Amazonia, in part because they are less demanding in terms of feed and veterinary care. Non-conventional animals for meat production also warrant further study, such as agouti (Smith 1974a), paca (Myers 1990; Smythe 1991), and capybara (Ojasti 1991), all indigenous rodents with widely appreciated flesh.

A major impediment to raising capybara, which is still found on the Amazon flood plain in spite of extensive hunting, is the legal restriction on maintaining wild animals in captivity. One farmer near Santarém keeps about a dozen capybara for domestic consumption and for sale or exchange to neighbours. Under the current legal framework and under-staffed wildlife protection agencies, capybara can be hunted to local extinction with no effective protection from authorities, while ranchers can clear forest for cattle and water buffalo with virtual impunity. But a small farmer wishing to raise capybara, instead of cattle, is subject to fines. If a farmer is caught trying to sell capybara meat in an urban market, he or she could be imprisoned. A ready market exists for capybara; it makes sense to provide incentives for raising them in captivity. The social and ecological benefits of raising the native rodent would warrant an exception to the prevailing law on keeping wild animals in captivity.

Some species of turtle, particularly *Podocnemis expansa*, which can reach 50 kg when mature, could also be raised commercially in ponds (Smith 1974b, 1979). Aquaculture is appropriate for riverine and upland areas, but more research is needed on disease control, dietary requirements, and breeding for precocious weight gain, among other traits. In the early 1970s, a rancher near Juriti, Pará, took advantage of fiscal incentives from the regional development agency, SUDAM (Superintendência do Desenvolvimento da Amazônia), to stock an Amazon flood-plain lake with 70,000 hatchlings of *Podocnemis expansa*. Few if any tartaruga, as the turtle is known locally, remained in the lake at Fazenda Lago Pretinho by 1994. Future efforts to raise turtle in semi-captivity should be backed by credible scientific research to verify reproduction and growth rates so that sustainable harvests can be set.

Pond-raised pirarucu (*Arapaima gigas*) will soon reach the market, particularly in Pará. Upland ranchers have been among the leaders in trying out aquaculture with pirarucu and other fish species in Amazonia. Ironically, no aquaculture is under way on the Amazon flood plain, presumably because it is still cheaper to harvest wild stocks of fish. Nevertheless, some incentives for raising fish in cages or pens in lakes and small channels might pay off. Experience on the uplands has demonstrated that private sector involvement in research is essential to improve the R&D process.

Setting the stage

To reap the potential of flood plains for improving food production and rural incomes, more land-use surveys are needed to assess current uses, settlement patterns, and soil and vegetation types (Hiraoka 1989). An approach that combines fieldwork with remote sensing and GIS (Geographic Information Systems) would provide planners with a better sense of the land capability for different agricultural systems.

Greater accessibility to credit would help spur more intensive use of the land. In Brazil, only one-fourth of agricultural credit goes to small operators, who account for 70 per cent of farm produce (Santos and Cardoso 1992). Credit can be abused and heavily subsidized agriculture is an onus for society and often leads to inefficiencies and adverse environmental impacts, such as overuse of agro-chemicals. But carefully crafted incentives could encourage farmers to use such relatively benign technologies as solar-powered irrigation systems using windmills or photovoltaic pumps, and enable farmers to erect strong fences and purchase tree seedlings. Farmers on the flood plain and uplands would surely benefit from improved access to credit.

A major stumbling block for small farmers in their attempts to obtain credit is that they often do not have title to their land. Without documents establishing land ownership, banks will not consider granting agricultural loans. Redoubled efforts to provide titles to legitimate landowners would greatly facilitate efforts to promote more intensive and environmentally benign land-use practices. Without a clear system of property rights, few farmers will be motivated to conserve natural resources (World Bank 1992). For the most part, land conflicts are rare on the Amazon flood plain because land ownership is generally well recognized, even without official documentation. Still, lending agencies usually require title to the property to secure loans. If it is not feasible to distribute land titles to people who farm, fish, and/or raise livestock on the flood plain in the near future, then the exigency of land titles could perhaps be waived. In such cases, the state or federal government might offer a guarantee to the lending institution to cover any losses should the farmer default.

With a careful assessment of the potential and pitfalls of harnessing natural resources on the Amazon flood plain, this critically important environment could make a much greater contribution to the welfare of people living in Amazonia. A headlong rush to "develop" the Amazon flood plains, akin to some of the settlement and engineering schemes perpetrated on the uplands in the 1970s and 1980s, could lead to a bitter harvest. Although many ecosystems along the Amazon have already been dramatically altered by human activities, with proper management their long-term productivity could be greatly improved.

9

Trends and opportunities

Amazonia is so heterogeneous, with so many poles of development
and environmental change scattered across the vast basin, that it is
difficult to sum up trends and opportunities adequately. Our main
message is that, in spite of the many difficulties encountered in moving towards sustainable development and conservation of resources,
many positive trends are under way that auger well for the long-term
future of the region.

Particularly impressive is the entrepreneurial spirit of so many
small-, medium-, and large-scale operators as they try new approaches to managing farms, ranches, plantations, and mineral operations. Across the board it is clear that individuals, cooperatives,
growers' associations, and corporations are not prepared simply
to wait for the government to tackle problems for them; rather they
are prepared to seek their own solutions within their resource
constraints.

Environmental degradation

Amazonia has clearly not entered the critical stage with regard to
environmental destruction. Deforestation is confined mainly to an arc
stretching along the southern and eastern fringe of the Amazon, and
along the mid to lower Amazon river (fig. 9.1). The only major ecosystem seriously threatened in the region is the Amazon flood-plain
forest, particularly from Manaus to the mouth of the Xingu. Overall,
only 10 per cent of Amazonia's forests are currently cleared (Brown
and Brown 1992).

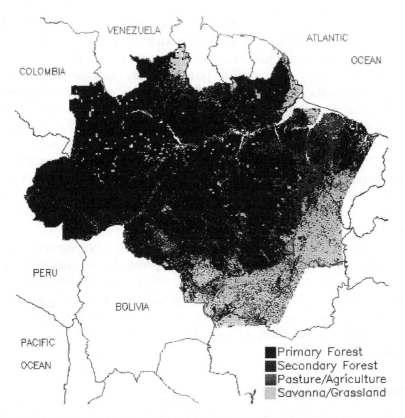

Fig. 9.1 **Cleared areas in the Brazilian Amazon are concentrated in an arc from Rondônia in the south-west to south-eastern Pará (Sources: adapted from Stone 1992; Stone and Schlesinger 1992 – courtesy of P. A. Lefebvre, Jr., The Woods Hole Research Center)**

Although the impacts of environmental changes under way in Amazonia appear to be confined to the regional or local scale, the forces of destruction are likely to increase in the future. Brazil's population is growing by some 3 million people a year, and efforts to open up Amazonia for settlement and development will inevitably intensify.

With a return to a democratic form of government in Brazil, pent-up social pressures for land reform and more jobs will surely lead to greater migration currents and the opening up of forest to settlement and development projects. Indeed, threats to parks and reserves are increasing during the transition to full democracy, as politicians seek to curry favour with voters, both poor and rich, by "liberating" forest areas for occupation.

201

Some forms of environmental degradation grow worse over time, whereas others improve as a country develops (Steer 1992). If incomes continue to rise in Amazonia, then urban sanitation is likely to improve. Installing or upgrading potable water and sewerage systems is a high priority for the state of Pará, for example. With hundreds of millions of dollars from the Inter-American Development Bank, Belém is bringing safe drinking water to hundreds of thousands of residents. Air pollution in cities generally becomes worse then gradually improves with rising incomes. Also, deforestation and encroachment generally diminish as living standards improve (Steer 1992). There is nothing automatic about these trends; they still hinge on the commitment and foresight of policy makers and funding agencies.

The underlying rationale here – and it is the key assumption – is that only by addressing the need to improve living conditions can concerns about environmental degradation be adequately addressed (World Bank 1992). Although some would argue that higher levels of consumption bring their own environmental problems, few would argue that the Amazon can be "saved" by restricting economic growth.

Wealth and well-being

In the aggregate, wealth in the Amazon region is increasing. Per capita income in the Brazilian Amazon leaped from US$204 in 1970, to US$1,192 by 1980, and US$1,509 by 1990 (Costa 1990). In the 1980s, economic growth in most parts of Brazil slowed, but the North region's economy grew by an average of 5.8 per cent per annum (Costa 1992).

Other social indicators suggest that living conditions overall have improved in the Brazilian Amazon. Life expectancy at birth in the North region has been rising steadily since the 1930–1940 period, when it was 39.8 years, to 63.1 years by 1970–1980, when it even surpassed the national average (Wood and Carvalho 1988: 93). Also, the Brazilian Amazon has the least difference in life expectancy at birth by monthly household income. Infant mortality in the Brazilian Amazon has dropped from 117.1 per thousand in 1960 to 72.3 in 1980 and 47 in 1988 (Costa 1990, 1992). Improved access to medical services, schooling, and potable water has contributed to the overall improvement in well-being in the Brazilian Amazon over the past half century (Wood and Carvalho 1988: 101). By 1980, 78.9 per cent of the population over the age of 5 in the Brazilian Amazon could read and write, up from 48.1 per cent in 1960 (Costa 1990). Other social indicators that improved in the Brazilian Amazon during the 1970s and 1980s include literacy rates, household income, and access to electricity.

Impressive strides in improving infrastructure notwithstanding, some segments of society in the North region have apparently not benefited as much as others. Some signs suggest that the gap between the poor and rich has grown in the North over the past two decades (Costa 1992). The numbers of urban poor have grown spectacularly, and are arguably one of the most serious social problems confronting development planners in the region. Still, it appears that the poor are better off in absolute terms than in the past.

Other segments of Amazonian society have benefited little if at all from the impressive investments in improving infrastructure and services in the region. Overall, indigenous groups have not reaped many rewards from economic development in the region. And some small-scale farmers occupying areas with no land titles have been driven off the land by new proprietors. Rural inhabitants in remote headwaters remain essentially cut off from social services and outside employment opportunities.

Nevertheless, both rural and urban poor generally have better access to services and educational and job opportunities than their parents had when they were young. Except in a few isolated areas, environmental degradation has not yet seriously undermined the long-term capacity of the landscape to cater for the needs of future generations.

Progress towards improved well-being slowed in the 1980s and early 1990s in response to inflationary pressures in Brazil and a downturn in rates of growth in the global economy. When inflation reached over 1,000 per cent a year by the close of the 1980s, very few segments of the economy were expanding. Few data are available to ascertain whether the inhabitants of Amazonia suffered a decline in well-being in the early 1990s. More likely, improvements in indicators such as life expectancy levelled off, or rose much more slowly.

Environmental degradation has not progressed on a sufficiently large scale to undercut economic development at this point. Poverty in the region is still by and large a problem of access to better roads, schooling, and medical care, rather than putting out environmental brushfires.

Vulnerability

Although environmental deterioration is not as alarming as is often portrayed in the media, and well-being and incomes are generally improving in the region, the stakes are ever higher. As more Amazonian ecosystems are altered to make room for people and development projects, nutrient recycling pathways are interrupted, heat and water fluxes may change, and other unseen ecological chain reactions may be taking place. Some plant and animal species are surely slipping into extinction with every burning season. How many keystone species are being lost? The toll may not become obvious for generations to come. The assumption here is that, as forest and aquatic environments are increasingly altered, human activities could become increasingly vulnerable to ecological surprises.

As Amazonia is increasingly occupied and the tempo of resource extraction increases, management inputs will have to increase accordingly. As farmers switch from extensive slash-and-burn systems to more intensive cropping patterns in response to population pressure and rising land values, even more sophisticated management is needed. Traditional agro-forestry systems are certainly complex, but modern mixed cropping patterns must also make adjustments to market conditions as well as shifting biotic pressures. Modern farms are characterized by a more rapid turnover of crop varieties and other technologies, all of which require a finely tuned agricultural research and development system. Farmers could become vulnerable to serious production shortfalls if the R&D pipeline becomes inefficient (Plucknett and Smith 1986).

Fine-tuning the policy environment

One of the greatest obstacles to raising standards of living for both the urban and rural poor is improved infrastructure, particularly better roads. Whereas the opening of pioneer roads reduces the incentive to intensify production because new lots can be acquired readily and cheaply, paving existing roads improves land values and marketing opportunities (Southworth, Dale, and O'Neill 1991). The cost of goods in urban areas is also reduced. A moratorium on major new road-building activity would allow better consolidation of gains in existing cleared areas, and reduce wasteful land-use practices.

Another imperative to ensure the future of Amazonian forests and other natural habitats is to balance conservation efforts between the local, community level and the public sector. A decentralized approach to environmental protection can be effective only up to a point. The ultimate fate of parks and reserves will be decided by local people; unless they are involved in land-use regulations and the selection and management of protected areas, few reserves are likely to survive much into the twenty-first century. If local communities are convinced that it is in their material interest to conserve natural resources, they will be motivated to help safeguard their natural resource endowment.

Empowerment should begin at the individual farm and community level, with municipal governments also involved in planning and overseeing protected areas. State and federal agencies are needed to help formulate broader conservation strategies and provide expertise in protecting and managing reserves. Funds for conservation should therefore flow as directly as possible to the field level, rather than slowly filtering down through various levels of bureaucracy in capital cities. A top–down approach to conservation often leads to slow disbursements, with their value eroded by rampant inflation. Rather than a punitive approach, conservation should be promoted by incentives, including payments for not cutting down forest in some cases.

International donors and development organizations need to recognize, however, that a "grass-roots" approach to conservation is not a panacea. "Grass roots" must include all players on the landscape, not just poor farmers or community organizations. This means the interests of powerful landholders, such as ranchers, should be considered when devising conservation plans. The well-to-do are not necessarily against preserving the environment, any more than all small farmers are naturally predisposed to managing natural resources rationally. As discussed in an earlier chapter, some of the best-protected forest in Amazonia is in private hands. Sawmill operators, plantation owners, and ranchers – as well as small farmers, indigenous peoples, and disenfranchised groups – should be brought into the local dialogue about conservation objectives. The task of building a consensus for action plans to preserve habitats and manage natural resources will often be difficult, as different groups must compromise and be sensitive to each other's concerns.

The notion that empowering communities will necessarily lead to "sustainable" development and wise management of resources warrants careful scrutiny. A community may overexploit resources owing to insufficient information about the natural history of the plants and animals concerned, or because of a desire to generate income for various projects. The conservation of ecosystems will require a co-ordinated effort over large distances, and no evidence has emerged that community groups can manage such a task.

Decentralization of environmental protection will thus not ensure the survival of forest reserves and other protected areas. Local governments can change, or the agendas of community groups might shift in response to emerging market opportunities. A change of mayors can signal a different philosophy towards the environment and even the handing over of protected areas to people without land or to the wealthy. Disbursements should always be contingent on respect for conservation programmes. To the extent that conservation efforts are built on the foundation of self-interest for broad segments of the society, and incentives are used rather than punitive measures, then prospects for safeguarding a substantial portion of Amazonia's biodiversity are improved.

A team approach

A better integration of research efforts across the many institutions conducting research within and outside of Amazonia would also help further our understanding of biodiversity patterns, sustainable agricultural practices, and the potential and impact of new technologies. Networking is poorly developed among Amazonian research institutions, ranging from basic and applied science to university centres. Networking could help avoid redundancy and could make more efficient use of resources, particularly important in countries with limited resources (Plucknett, Smith, and Ozgediz 1990).

Fortunately, innovative farmers and ranchers and skilled researchers are adopting and developing new technologies to help overcome constraints to raising and sustaining agricultural and silvicultural yields in Amazonia. Although much more research and testing of agricultural technologies developed at scientific institutes and in farmers' fields are needed, there is reason for hope that many tracts of Amazonia's unique forests will survive.

This dynamic nature of Amazonian agriculture, so important for the cultural and ecological integrity of the region, is not new. Farming systems have been evolving in Amazonia since the first fields were cleared at least 10,000 years ago. Peoples in Amazonia have always been open to new crops and resource management strategies. Maize made an early entry into Amazonia, while other crops were incorporated by indigenous groups in the region after contact with Europeans, such as plantain by the Yanomamo in northern Amazonia, and sugarcane by the Jivaro, the Chácabo of the Bolivian Amazon, and the Maku of north-western Amazonia (Boom 1989; Boster 1983; Milton 1984). Only the pace of change has quickened, particularly in the twentieth century.

If properly managed, a wide range of agricultural and silvicultural activities are possible in the region. Both small-scale farmers and corporate operations are achieving sustainable yields in various parts of the basin. The continued vitality of Amazonian agriculture will rest on controlling inflation, a deeper understanding of the natural history of Amazonian ecosystems, including man-made environments, and greater support for research at agricultural research stations, basic and applied research institutes, and the growing universities in the region.

To further research on the many pressing sustainable development issues, much broader cooperation will be required by research organizations and NGOs in the region. Closer working ties need to be forged along several dimensions: between research organizations; between NGOs; and between research organizations and NGOs (Blake 1992). Although NGOs often have many advantages, such as flexibility and their links to grass-roots causes, they usually lack the capacity for scientific research. Sustainable development in Amazonia, as in any region, will require long-term commitment to research in many fields among various institutional players. Exciting opportunities lie ahead for allying the strengths of NGOs with research organizations in seeking solutions to the complex problems facing people and the environment in Amazonia.

With restricted funds for research, citizens of Amazonia can ill afford scientific institutes going their own ways, with little regard for the activities of other organizations involved in research and extension. Even if a flood of funding suddenly became available, it might not be spent wisely if viable research priorities and programmes have not been worked out.

Fortunately, research institutions in the region increasingly recognize the need to coordinate their efforts better. One sign of this positive trend is the creation of the Regional Commission for Research

207

in Amazonia (CORPAM – Comissão Coordenadora Regional de Pesquisas na Amazônia) in 1989. CORPAM advises the President of Brazil on research and training needs for the region and involves a range of institutions, from universities to development agencies.

Stronger collaborative links also need to be developed among NGOs. The very ease with which NGOs can be formed, essentially with a phone, fax, copier, and portable computer, can quickly overload the system. The spectacular growth of NGOs, reviewed in chapter 3, has been largely fuelled by exterior donors in response to their distrust of government agencies. By 1989, NGOs from industrial countries were distributing an estimated US$6.4 billion to developing countries (Livernash 1992), and countries with territory in Amazonia received a good share of this largess. But little effort has been made to encourage consolidation, or at least closer cooperation to avoid redundancy. Donors must accept some responsibility for possibly superfluous organizations with poorly defined agendas and questionable efficacy in Amazon basin countries.

Perhaps the weakest link in the research field is cooperation between NGOs and government research organizations, such as the agricultural research institutions, scientific institutes, and research-oriented universities. Ironically, many NGOs are flush with funds from foreign donors, but are devoid of any expertise to carry out research. The funds being channelled to NGOs in Brazil would be sufficient to pay off the external debt of several smaller developing countries, such as Uruguay.[1]

Conservation and sustainable development

The survival of forests is critical for the long-term options for Amazonian development. But reliance on parks or reserves alone to safeguard the diversity of Amazonian ecosystems will not succeed. Only 2 per cent of the Brazilian Amazon is within the boundaries of parks or reserves and, as is the case in most developing countries, many areas designated for protection have been violated by loggers, miners, ranchers, and farmers. Even with debt-for-nature swaps or other mechanisms to increase park land in Amazonia, only small islands of forest and other Amazonian ecosystems are likely to be incorporated into reserves. Although efforts to set aside and safeguard parks and reserves must continue, they should be coupled with a broader strategy to improve living standards in countries with a stake in Amazonia.

What happens outside the boundaries of parks and reserves will largely determine their fate. The yields of farms, ranches, and plantations in Amazonia must be raised and sustained if large tracts of the region's forests are to survive. By intensifying production in already cleared areas, the need to open up new areas will be reduced.

The chances that sizeable tracts of forest will survive in the twenty-first century will also improve if ways can be found to harvest their resources without destroying them. Extractive activities should be envisaged as a supplement to more conventional activities, at least in the short term. Poverty is the greatest enemy of Amazonian forests and, unless ways can be found to make forests "pay" for themselves, they will remain highly vulnerable.

Given the inevitable pressure to develop and occupy the Amazon further, careful management of forest resources and agricultural activities will become ever more urgent. Although research is under way on many fronts to further our understanding of Amazonian eco-systems and socio-economic processes, much more needs to be learned if the region's resources are to be managed on a sound basis.

Note

1. *Jornal do Brasil*, Rio de Janeiro, 13 December 1990, 1° caderno, p. 16.

Appendices

Appendices

Appendix 1 **Scientific names of plants (exclusive of ornamentals, medicinal plants, and vegetables) growing in 31 home gardens and agro-forestry systems in 121 poly-cultural fields involving perennials in upland areas of the Brazilian Amazon, and their occurrence in second growth or forest**

Common name[a]	Scientific name	Garden	Field	Second growth	Forest
Açaí	*Euterpe oleracea*	+			+
African oil-palm	*Elaeis guineensis*		+		
Ameixa	*Eugenia cumini*	+			
Andiroba	*Carapa guianensis*		+		+
Annatto	*Bixa orellana*	+	+		
Arabica coffee	*Coffea arabica*	+			
Avocado	*Persea americana*	+			
Azeitona	*Roucheria punctata* (?)	+			
Babaçu	*Attalea speciosa*	+		+	+
Bacaba	*Oenocarpus distichus*	+	+	+	+
Bacuri	*Platonia insignis*		+	+	+
Banana	*Musa* sp.	+	+		
Barbados cherry	*Malpighia glabra*	+	+		
Biribá	*Rollinia deliciosa*	+	+		
Black pepper	*Piper nigrum*	+	+		
Brachiarão	*Brachiaria brizantha*		+		
Brachiaria	*Brachiaria decumbens*		+		
Brazil nut	*Bertholletia excelsa*	+	+	+	+
Breadfruit	*Artocarups altilis*	+			
Buriti	*Mauritia flexuosa*	+			+
Cacao	*Theobroma cacao*	+	+		+
Caimito	*Pouteria caimito*	+			
Calabash gourd	*Crescentia cujete*	+			
Canela	*Miconia sp.* (?)	+			
Capsicum pepper	*Capsicum frutescens*	+	+		
Carambola	*Averrhoa carambola*	+			
Caribbean pine	*Pinus caribaea*		+		
Cashew	*Anacardium occidentale*	+	+	+	
Cedar	*Cedrela odorata*	+	+		+
Coconut	*Cocos nucifera*	+	+		
Common bean	*Phaseolus vulgaris*	+	+		
Cotton	*Gossypium* sp.	+			
Cumaru	*Dipteryx* sp.	+		+	+
Cunambi	*Ichthyothere cunabi*	+			
Cupuaçu	*Theobroma grandiflorum*	+	+		+
Cupuí	*Theobroma speciosum*	+			+
Embileira	?	+		+	+
Erythrina	*Erythrina* sp.		+		
Freijó	*Cordia goeldiana*		+		+
Gandu	*Cajanus cajan*		+		

213

Common name[a]	Scientific name	Garden	Field	Second growth	Forest
Genipap	*Genipa americana*	+			
Giant granadilla	*Passiflora quadrangularis*	+			
Grosela[b]	*Eugenia uniflora* (?)		+		
Guaraná	*Paullinia cupana*		+		
Guava	*Psidium guajava*	+	+		
Guinea grass	*Panicum maximum*		+		
Ingá	*Inga* sp.	+			
Ingá-açu	*Inga cinnamomea*	+			
Ingá-cipó	*Inga edulis*		+		
Jackfruit	*Artocarpus heterophyllus*	+			
Jangada	?	+			
Jarana	*Holopyxidium jarana*		+		+
Lima	*Citrus* sp.	+			
Lime	*Citrus aurantifolia*	+			
Lemon grass	*Cymbopogon* sp.	+			
Macacaúba	*Platymiscium ulei*	+			+
Mahogany	*Swietenia macrophylla*		+		+
Maize	*Zea mays*		+		
Malay apple	*Eugenia malaccensis*	+			
Mamelo	*Aparisthmium cordeatum* (?)	+			
Mamey	*Mammea americana*		+		
Mango	*Mangifera indica*	+	+		
Manioc	*Manihot esculenta*	+	+		
Morototó	*Didymopanax morototoni*	+		+	
Mountain soursop	Annona montana	+			
Mucajá	*Acrocomia sclerocarpa*	+		+	
Muruci	*Byrsonima crassifolia*	+			
Oiticica	*Licania tomentosa* (?)	+			
Orange	*Citrus sinensis*	+	+		
Pajurá	*Couepia bracteosa*	+			+
Palhateira	*Clitoria racemosa*		+		
Papaya	*Carica papaya*	+	+	+	
Passionfruit	*Passiflora edulis*	+	+		
Peach-palm	*Bactris gasipaes*	+	+		
Pineapple	*Ananas cosmosus*	+	+		
Piquiá	*Caryocar villosum*	+	+		+
Pitinga	*Eugenia uniflora* (?)	+			
Pitomba	*Talisia esculenta*	+			
Quicuio	*Brachiaria humidicola*		+		
Robusta coffee	*Coffea canephora*		+		

Common name[a]	Scientific name	Garden	Field	Second growth	Forest
Rough lemon	*Citrus jambhiri*	+			
Rubber	*Hevea brasiliensis*	+	+		+
Soursop	*Annona muricata*	+			
Sugarcane	*Saccharum*	+	+		
Sweet potato	*Ipomoea batatas*	+	+		
Sweetsop	*Annona squamosa*	+			
Tamarind	*Tamarindus indica*	+			
Tangerine	*Citrus reticulata*	+			
Taro	*Colocasia esculenta*		+		
Tobacco	*Nicotiana tabacum*	+	+		
Tropical almond	*Terminalia catappa*	+			
Tucumã	*Astrocaryum vulgare*	+	+	+	+
Tutaruba	?		+		
Uxi	*Endopleura uchi*	+			+
Watermelon	*Citrulus lanatus*		+		
Yellow mombim	*Spondias mombim*	+			

a. For local names of plants see appendices 3 and 5.
b. Grosela may be the same species, *Eugenia uniflora*, as pitinga (or pitanga) below.

Appendix 2   Ninety-seven agro-forestry configurations observed in 121 polycultural fields involving perennials in upland areas of the Brazilian Amazon, 1988–1992

Crops[a]	Location
African oil-palm, black pepper	Bragantina, Pará
Arabica coffee, coconut	Ramal CEMEX, km 101 Santarém–Rurópolis, Pará
Arabica coffee, ingá	Bragantina, Pará
Arabica coffee, maize	Km 104 Altamira–Itaituba, Transamazon
Avocado, mamey	Tomé-Açu, Pará
Banana, black pepper, manioc	Km 40 Santarém–Curuá Una, Pará
Banana ("Peruará," "Nanica"), cupuaçu, pineapple, papaya[b]	Ricardo Ribeiro, Sitio Sapecado, vicinal Ferrovia, km 35 PA 150 Marabá–Xinguara, Pará
Banana, orange, mango	Km 18 Santarém–Curuá Una, Pará
Banana, passionfruit	Nr. Ariquemes, Rondônia; Tomé-Açu, Pará
Banana, cupuaçu, Brazil nut	Araras, km 35 Transamazon, Marabá Estreito, Pará
Banana, passionfruit	Km 14 Ariquemes–Jarú, Rondônia
Banana, cupuaçu, pineapple, Brazil nut, mango, tangerine, açaí, piquiá, jackfruit, tutaruba[c]	José Brito's lot, Lastancia, municipality of Itupiranga, Pará
Banana ("Peruara"), cupuaçu, papaya, manioc ("Juriti"), ingá, sweetsop, grosela, mango ("Arara," "Dois kilos"), coconut, pineapple, lime, avocado	José Brito's lot, Lastancia, municipality of Itupiranga, Pará
Banana, peach-palm, cupuaçu	Side-road from km 155 BR 364, Rio Branco–Porto Velho
Barbados cherry, manioc	Colonia del Rei, Ramal Maritaca, km 128 BR 10, Pará
Black pepper, biribá, Brazil nut,[b] mango, azeitona, guava, robusta coffee ("Conilon"), pineapple	Raimundo Carneiro, São Benedito, side-road from km 77 Santarém–Rurópolis, Pará
Black pepper, Brazil nut, mango[d]	Km 172 Santarém–Rurópolis, Pará
Black pepper, cacao	Ramal Anauerá, nr. Quatro Bocas, PA 256, Pará
Black pepper, manioc	Boa Esperança, km 43 Santarém–Curuá Una, Pará
Black pepper, coconut	Miguel Pires, km 68 Santarém–Rurópolis, Pará
Black pepper, coconut, açaí	Ramal da Jupuba, PA 252, Pará
Black pepper, coconut, peach-palm, passionfruit	Ramal da Jupuba, PA 252, Pará
Black pepper, cupuaçu	Ramal Anauerá, nr. Quatro Bocas, PA 256, Pará; nr. Tailândia, PA 150, Pará

Crops[a]	Location
Black pepper, orange	Nr. Capitão Poço, Pará; nr. Tomé-Açu, Pará; nr. Tailândia, PA 150, Pará; Ramal Jambu-Açu, PA 252, Pará; Mojuí dos Campos, Pará
Black pepper, orange, manioc, watermelon	Ramal da Jupuba, PA 252, Pará
Black pepper, rubber, orange, cupuaçu, coconut, cashew	Juliano Pereira, Comunidade Boa Esperança, km 70 Santarém–Rurópolis, Pará
Black pepper, pasture	Nr. Theobroma, Rondônia
Black pepper, cupuaçu, freijó, arabica coffee ("Mocha")	Trav. Bragantina, nr. Forquilha, PA 256, Pará
Black pepper, avocado, mango, freijó, açaí, cashew	Trav. Bragantina, nr. Forquilha, PA 256, Pará
Black pepper, andiroba, coconut, freijó	Trav. Bragantina, nr. Forquilha, PA 256, Pará
Black pepper, açaí, cupuaçu, arabica coffee ("Bourbon"), yellow mombim	Ramal Anauerá, nr. Quatro Bocas, PA 256, Pará
Brachiaria pasture, Caribbean pine	Bragantina, Pará
Quicuio pasture, annatto	Bragantina, Pará
Cacao, açaí	Tomé-Açu, Pará (2 farms)
Cacao, biribá	Cacaulandia, Rondônia
Cacao, Brazil nut	Tomé-Açu, Pará (2 farms)
Cacao, Brazil nut, freijó	Tomé-Açu, Pará (2 farms)
Cacao, cedar	Tomé-Açu, Pará
Cacao, cedar, avocado, uxi	Ramal Anauerá, nr. Quatro Bocas, PA 256, Pará
Cacao, cupuaçu	Ramal Anauerá, nr. Quatro Bocas, PA 256, Pará
Cacao, freijó	Tomé-Açu, Pará (2 farms)
Cacao, guava[e]	Km 82 Altamira–Itaituba, Transamazon
Cacao, mahogany	Tomé-Açu, Pará
Cacao, rubber	Tomé-Açu, Pará (2 farms); Fazenda São Jorge, Ramal Murumuru, side-road from km 33 Santarém–Curuá Una, Pará
Cacao, rubber, tangerine, guava	Nr. Jarú, Rondônia
Cacao, mango, açaí, Erythrina, arabica coffee, palhateira, Brazil nut, cupuaçu, andiroba	Trav. Bragantina, nr. Forquilha, PA 256, Pará
Cashew, taro, sweet manioc, guava	Km 104 Altamira–Itaituba, Transamazon
Cashew, mamey, bacuri, sweetsop	Tomé-Açu, Pará
Cashew, annatto, Barbados cherry, mango, banana ("Catavé"), papaya, jackfruit, gandu, cupuaçu, coconut, ingá-cipó, orange, tangerine, avocado, bitter manioc ("Jai-bara")	Colonia del Rei, Ramal Maritaca, km 128 BR 10, Pará
Coconut, cupuaçu	Km 3, Agrovila Coco Chato–Itupiranga, Pará

Crops[a]	Location
Coconut, passionfruit	Capitão Poço, Pará
Coconut, orange	Km 178 Manaus–Itacoatiara, Amazonas; km 74 Rurópolis–Santarém, BR 163, Pará; km 10 and km 22 Santarém–Curuá Una, Pará
Coconut, lime, soursop, guava	Taba plantation, nr. Mosqueiro, Pará
Cupuaçu, banana	Km 104 Altamira–Itaituba, Transamazon
Cupuaçu, freijó	Tomé-Açu, Pará
Cupuaçu, peach-palm	Side-road from km 155 BR 364, Rio Branco–Porto Velho
Cupuaçu, macacaúba, mahogany	Tomé-Açu, Pará
Cupuaçu, peach-palm, Brazil nut	Side-road from km 155 BR 364, Rio Branco–Porto Velho
Cupuaçu, orange, black pepper, rubber	Km 81 Altamira–Itaituba, Transamazon
Guinea grass, pineapple	Lourenço Araujo's lot, Lastancia, municipality of Itupiranga, Pará
Jackfruit, avocado, rubber, cupuaçu, cacao	Km 80 Altamira–Itaituba, Transamazon
Mango, cattle pasture	Km 73 Manaus–Itacoatiara, Amazonas
Manioc, banana ("Branca," "Perua," "Casada" at Souza home)	Estrada 6, Belterra, Pará; km 62 Santarém–Curuá Una, Pará; km 151 Manaus–Itacoatiara, Amazonas; Nenas Souza, km 46 Santarém–Rurópolis, Pará
Manioc, banana, cupuaçu, peach-palm, Brazil nut	Side-road from km 155 BR 364, Rio Branco–Porto Velho
Manioc, banana, cupuaçu, papaya	Estrada 10, Belterra, Pará
Manioc ("Jibarinha"), cupuaçu, sweet potato	Elias Magres, São João Batista, municipality of Itupiranga, Pará
Manioc, cupuaçu, orange ("Serra d'água"), avocado	Casa 16, Estrada 10, Belterra, Pará
Manioc (sweet: "Boliviana"), maize, banana ("Baié," "Anajá," "roxo")	Sergio Freitas, km 56 Santarém–Rurópolis, Pará
Manioc, jarana[f]	Francisco Lira, Comunidade Cipoal, km 15 Santarém–Rurópolis, Pará
Manioc, orange	Estrada 10, and casa 10, Estrada 6, Belterra, Pará; Francisco Lira, Comunidade Cipoal, km 15 Santarém–Rurópolis, Pará; km 21 Santarém–Curuá Una, Pará
Manioc, papaya	Km 60, Santarém–Curuá Una, Pará
Manioc, passionfruit	Casa 10, Estrada 6, Belterra, Pará
Orange, robusta coffee ("Conilon"), coconut, rubber, cacao	Juliano Pereira, Comunidade Boa Esperança, km 70 Santarém–Rurópolis, Pará
Orange, Brazil nut, cupuaçu, banana, cacao, annatto, biribá, avocado, jackfruit, sweetsop	Estrada 6, Belterra, 2.6 km from the Santarém–Rurópolis Highway

Crops[a]	Location
Orange, manioc	Colonia del Rei, Ramal Maritaca, km 128 BR 10, Pará
Orange, manioc, rubber	Km 70 Manaus–Itacoatiara, Amazonas
Orange, cotton	Capitão Poço, Pará
Orange, cupuaçu	Casa 10, Estrada 6, Belterra, Pará
Orange, passionfruit	Nr. Igarapé-Açu, Bragantina; near Tomé-Açu, Pará; Francisco Lira, Comunidade Cipoal, km 15 Santarém–Rurópolis, Pará
Orange, pineapple, tangerine	Colonia del Rei, Ramal Maritaca, km 128 BR 10, Pará
Orange, cattle pasture	Km 73 Manaus–Itacoatiara, Amazonas
Orange, rubber	Km 70, km 110, and km 112 Manaus–Itacoatiara, Amazonas
Passionfruit, African oil-palm	Bragantina, Pará
Passionfruit, Barbados cherry	Granja Soc, km 35 Santarém–Curuá Una, Pará
Peach-palm, guaraná	Nr. Jarú, Rondônia
Robusta coffee, rubber	Side-road from km 155 BR 364, Rio Branco–Porto Velho
Robusta coffee, common bean	Km 104 Altamira–Itaituba, Transamazon
Robusta coffee, mahogany, cedar	Side-road from km 155 BR 364, Rio Branco–Porto Velho
Robusta coffee, rubber, tangerine, guava	Nr. Theobroma, Rondônia
Robusta coffee, rubber, biribá	Nr. Jarú, Rondônia
Robusta coffee, cacao, avocado	Km 104 Altamira–Itaituba, Transamazon
Robusta coffee, mahogany, pineapple, coconut	Colonia del Rei, Ramal Maritaca, km 128, BR 10, Pará
Rubber, black pepper	Bragantina, Pará; Capitão Poço, Pará
Rubber, brachiarão pasture	Nr. Ariquemes, Rondônia
Rubber, cacao	Km 70 BR 364, Rio Branco–Porto Velho
Rubber, passionfruit	Nr. Vila Forquilha, PA 256, Pará
Tangerine, rubber	Nenas Souza, km 46 Santarém–Rurópolis, Pará

Note: Crops are listed in approximate order of current importance in terms of production and income, although this order is difficult to ascertain in many cases. Commodity prices fluctuate and agro-forestry systems are highly dynamic, with some crops on the verge of being phased out while others are just coming on line.

a. For scientific names of plants see appendix 1.
b. Spontaneous.
c. Wild fruit tree spared when the forest was cut.
d. The few Brazil nut and mango trees are spontaneous.
e. Farmer reports that this is not a good combination because of guava's aggressive root system and competition for water.
f. Forest tree left standing; used for making fence posts.

Appendix 3. Seventy-four plant species (exclusive of ornamentals, medicinal plants, and vegetables) found in 31 home gardens in upland areas of rural Pará, 1992

Plant[a]	Local name of fruit	Home gardens	Amazon native	Native to neotropics	Old World native
Açaí	Açaí	10	+		
Ameixa	Ameixa	4			+
Annatto	Urucu	15	+		
Arabica coffee	Café	14			+
Avocado	Abacate	16		+	
Azeitona	Azeitona	2	+		
Babaçu	Babaçu, côco	3	+		
Bacaba	Bacaba	5	+		
Banana	Banana	15			+
Barbados cherry	Acerola	2		+	
Biribá	Biribá	8	+		
Black pepper	Pimento do reino	6			+
Brazil nut	Castanha do Pará	6	+		
Breadfruit	Fruta-pão	1			+
Buriti	Buriti	1	+		
Cacao	Cacao	10	+		
Caimito	Abiu	1	+		
Calabash gourd	Cuia	5		+	
Canela	Canela	1	+		
Capsicum pepper	Pimenta	5	+		
Carambola	Carambola	2			+
Cashew	Caju	19		+	
Cedar	Cedro	1	+		
Coconut	Côco	16			+
Common bean	Feijão	1		+	
Cotton	Algodão	7		+	
Cumaru	Cumaru	1	+		
Cunambi	Cunambi	1	+		
Cupuaçu	Cupuaçu	21	+		
Cupuí	Cupuí	1	+		
Embileira	Embileira	1	+		
Genipap	Jenipapo	3		+	
Giant granadilla	Maracujá-açu	1		+	
Guava	Goiaba	18		+	
Ingá	Ingá	6		+	
Ingá-açu	Ingá-açu	1	+		
Jackfruit	Jaca	15			+
Jangada	Jangada	1	+		
Lima	Lima	4			+
Lime	Limão	14			+
Lemon grass	Capim santo	1		+	+
Macacaúba	Macacaúba	2	+		

221

Plant[a]	Local name of fruit	Home gardens	Amazon native	Native to neotropics	Old World native
Malay apple	Jambo	7			+
Mamelo	Mamelo	1	+		
Mango	Manga	27			+
Manioc	Mandhioca, macaxeira	5		+	
Morototó	Morototó	1	+		
Mountain soursop	Araticum	1		+	
Mucajá	Mucajá	2	+		
Muruci	Muruci	8		+	
Oiticica	Oiticica	1		+	
Orange	Laranja	25			+
Pajurá	Pajurá	1	+		
Papaya	Mamão	10		+	
Passionfruit	Maracujá	4		+	
Peach-palm	Pupunha	13	+		
Pineapple	Abacaxi	11		+	
Piquiá	Piquiá	1	+		
Pitinga	Pitinga	1	+		
Pitomba	Pitomba	2	+		
Robusta coffee	Café	2			+
Rough lemon	Limão-cravo	3			+
Rubber	Seringa	1	+		
Soursop	Graviola	9	+		
Sugarcane	Cana	4			+
Sweet potato	Batata doce	1		+	
Sweetsop	Ata	1		+	
Tamarind	Tamarindo	1			+
Tangerine	Tangerina	14			+
Tobacco	Fumo	1		+	
Tropical almond	Castanhola	1			+
Tucumã	Tucumã	1	+		
Uxi	Uxi	1	+		
Yellow mombim	Cajá, taperebá	6	+		

Sources of information on crop origins: Cavalcante (1991); Smith et al. (1992).
a. For scientific names of plants see appendix 1.

Appendix 4 **Locations and composition of 31 home gardens (exclusive of ornamentals, medicinal plants, and vegetables) sampled in upland areas of rural Pará, 1992**

Owner/location	Species composition[a]	No. of species
Vicente Souza, Lastancia, Itupiranga Municipality, Pará	Cashew, coconut, cupuaçu, guava, jackfruit, mango, manioc, orange, papaya, pineapple, sweet potato, tamarind, tangerine	13
Raimundo Pereira de Souza, Lastancia, Itupiranga Municipality, Pará	Annatto, arabica coffee, banana, capsicum pepper, cashew, guava, mango, orange, pineapple, tangerine	10
José Brito, Lastancia, Itupiranga Municipality, Pará[b]	Annatto, avocado, cacao, capsicum pepper, cashew, cotton, cupuaçu, guava, mango, manioc, muruci, oiticica, orange, papaya, peach-palm, soursop, tropical almond	17
Francisco Geronimo do Nascimento, Lastancia, Itupiranga Municipality, Pará	Arabica coffee, biribá, black pepper, buriti, cacao, cashew, cedar, coconut, cotton, cupuaçu, embileira, guava, jangada,[d] lima, Malay apple, mango, pineapple, piquiá,[d] yellow mombim	19
Lourenço Araújo, Lastancia, Itupiranga Municipality, Pará	Annatto, arabica coffee, avocado, banana ("Casada"), cashew, coconut, cotton, guava, lime, orange, papaya	11
Manoel França de Sousa, São João Batista, Itupiranga Municipality, Pará[b]	Ameixa, arabica coffee, avocado, black pepper, cacao, cashew, cupuaçu, guava, ingá, jackfruit, lime, mango, macacaúba, orange, pineapple, rough lemon, tangerine	18
José Ribeiro, São João Batista, Itupiranga Municipality, Pará	Ameixa, arabica coffee, avocado, babaçu, biribá, black pepper, Brazil nut, cacao, calabash gourd, coconut, cupuaçu, guava, lima ("Branca," "Rosa"), mango ("Anana," "Bacuri," "Comum," "Mangita," "Tucum"), orange, soursop, tangerine ("Do Sul," "Mixirica"), yellow mombim	18
Ricardo Ribeiro, Sitio Sapecado, vicinal Ferrovia, km 35 PA 150 Marabá–Xinguara, Pará	Annatto, banana ("Peruara," "Nanica"), common bean, Brazil nut, cacao, cupuaçu, mango, manioc (bitter cvs: "Carema," "Jaibara," "Cacao"; sweet cv: "Uruim"), orange, tobacco	10

223

Appendix 4

Owner/location	Species composition[a]	No. of species
Francisco Lira, Comunidade Cipoal, km 15 Santarém–Rurópolis, Santarém Municipality, Pará[b]	Açaí, avocado, banana ("Baié," "Casada," "Roxa"), biribá, black pepper, cacao, calabash gourd, cupuaçu, guava, lime, mango, muruci, orange, papaya, peach-palm, rough lemon, tangerine	17
Juliano Pereira, Comunidade Boa Esperança, km 70 Santarém–Rurópolis, Santarém Municipality, Pará[b]	Annatto, avocado, azeitona, banana ("Branca"), biribá, cupuaçu, jackfruit, lima, lime, mango, morototó,[e] orange, papaya, peach-palm, soursop, tangerine	16
Raimundo Carneiro, Comunidade São Benedito, 7 km along side-road from km 77 Santarém–Rurópolis, Santarém Municipality, Pará	Annatto, arabica coffee, avocado, azeitona, banana ("Branca," "Prata," "Roxa"), Barbados cherry, biribá, Brazil nut, breadfruit, capsicum pepper, cashew, coconut, cupuaçu, cumaru, cupuí, guava, jackfruit, lemon grass, Malay apple, mango, mountain soursop, orange ("China"), pineapple, sugarcane ("Mansa"), tangerine	25
Sergio Freitas, Sitio Santo Antonio, km 56 Santarém–Rurópolis, Santarém Municipality, Pará[b]	Annatto, arabica coffee, avocado, babaçu,[f] bacaba,[f] biribá, Brazil nut,[f] cacao, cashew, cotton, cupuaçu, guava, jackfruit, mango, orange, papaya, peach-palm, pineapple, pitomba, rough lemon, tangerine, yellow mombim[f]	22
Nenas Souza, km 46 Santarém–Rurópolis, Santarém Municipality, Pará[b]	Açaí, annatto, avocado, babaçu, banana ("Branca," "Perua," "Roxa"), cacao, calabash gourd, coconut, jackfruit, muruci, macacaúba, orange, papaya, peach-palm, soursop, sugarcane	16
Miguel Pires, km 68 Santarém–Rurópolis, Santarém Municipality, Pará[b]	Açaí, annatto, arabica coffee ("Catu"), bacaba, banana ("Casada"), Barbados cherry, calabash gourd, capsicum pepper, cashew, coconut, cotton, cupuaçu, guava, genipap, ingá, jackfruit, mango, orange ("Pêra"), papaya, peach-palm	20
Araras, km 35 Transamazon, Marabá–Estreito, Pará	Black pepper, cashew, coconut, cupuaçu, guava, jackfruit, mango, pineapple, sugarcane	9
Cuxiu 42, São Domingos, Pará	Cashew, cupuaçu, mango, orange	4

Owner/location	Species composition[a]	No. of species
Colonia del Rei, Ramal Maritaca, km 128 BR 10, Pará	Cashew, manioc, passionfruit, pineapple	4
Colonia del Rei, Ramal Maritaca, km 128 BR 10, Pará	Ameixa, annatto, avocado, banana ("Prata"), cacao, cupuaçu, guava, jackfruit, lime, mango, orange, passionfruit, tangerine	13
Colonia del Rei, Ramal Maritaca, km 128 BR 10, Pará[b]	Avocado, cashew, coconut, cupuaçu, ingá, jackfruit, lime, papaya, passionfruit, pineapple, sugarcane, tangerine	12
Ramal Anauerá, nr. Quatro Bocas, PA 256, Pará[b]	Açaí, ameixa, annatto, arabica coffee ("Bourbon," "Mocha"), Brazil nut, cashew, cupuaçu, lime, mamelo, mango, orange, peach-palm, uxi	13
Nr. Tailândia, PA 150, Pará	Arabica coffee, avocado, banana ("Maçá"), cashew, coconut, cupuaçu, guava, jackfruit, mango, muruci, orange, pineapple, robusta coffee	13
Ramal Jambu-Açu, PA 252, Pará[b]	Açaí, banana ("Costela de vaca"), guava, ingá, lime, Malay apple, mango, orange	8
Ramal Jupuba, PA 252, Pará[b]	Açaí, biribá, cashew, coconut, cotton, cunambi,[g] guava, ingá, Malay apple, mango, orange, peach-palm, robusta coffee	13
Agrovila Coco Chato, km 42 Marabá–Altamira, Transamazon, Pará	Annatto, cashew, genipap, mango, manioc	5
Casa 16, Estrada 10, Belterra, Pará[b]	Annatto, arabica coffee, avocado, bacaba, banana ("Cascuda," "Najá"), calabash gourd, cupuaçu, genipap, lima, lime, Malay apple, mango, muruci, orange, peach-palm, rubber, yellow mombim	17
Casa 10, Estrada 6, Belterra, Pará[b]	Açaí, avocado, bacaba, banana ("Baié"), cupuaçu, jackfruit, lime, Malay apple, mango, mucajá, muruci, orange, peach-palm, soursop, tangerine	15
Km 47 Santarém–Cuiabá, Pará	Arabica coffee ("Mocha"), coconut, jackfruit, lime, mango, orange, peach-palm, soursop	8

Owner/location	Species composition[a]	No. of species
Sitio Porto Novo, Curuá-Una Reservoir, Pará[c]	Annatto, arabica coffee ("Mocha"), bacaba, cashew, coconut, ingá (da corda), jackfruit, lime, Malay apple, mango, mucajá, muruci, orange, soursop, tangerine	15
San Sebastian, Curuá-Una Reservoir, Pará[b]	Açaí, annatto, avocado, banana ("Branca," "Casca verde"), black pepper, capsicum pepper ("Pimenta do cheiro"), cashew, coconut, guava, lime, mango, papaya, passionfruit, soursop, sweetsop, tangerine	16
Boa Esperança, km 43 San-tarém–Curuá-Una, Pará[b]	Açaí, banana ("Branca"), biribá, cacao, canela, carambola, coconut, cupuaçu, jackfruit, mango, muruci, orange, peach-palm, pitinga, pitomba, soursop, tucumã, yellow mombim	18
Ramal Andirobalzinho, nr. Alter do Chão, Pará[b]	Açaí, arabica coffee, avocado, Brazil nut, caimito, canela, coconut, cotton, cupuaçu, giant granadilla, guava, ingá-açu, lime, mango, orange, pajurá, peach-palm, pineapple, tangerine, yellow mombim	20

a. For scientific names of plants see appendix 1.
b. Husband and/or wife born in Pará.
c. Husband and wife born in Amazonas.
d. Spared when forest cut down.
e. Spared when second growth cut down.
f. Spontaneous.
g. Piscicide.

Appendix 5   **Sixty plant species observed in 97 agro-forestry configurations in 121 polycultural fields involving perennials in upland areas of the Brazilian Amazon, 1988–1992**

Plant[a]	Local name of fruit	Fields	Amazon native	Native to neotropics	Old World native
Açaí	Açaí	7	+		
African oil-palm	Dendê	2			+
Andiroba	Andiroba	2	+		
Annatto	Urucu	3	+		
Arabica coffee	Café	6			+
Avocado	Abacate	9		+	
Azeitona	Azeitona	1	+		
Bacuri	Bacuri	1	+		
Banana	Banana	20			+
Barbados cherry	Acerola	3		+	
Biribá	Biribá	4	+		
Black pepper	Pimento do reino	26			+
Brachiarão	Brachiarão	1			+
Brachiaria	Brachiaria	1			+
Brazil nut	Castanha do Pará	12	+		
Cacao	Cacau	23	+		
Caribbean pine	Pinheiro	1		+	
Cashew	Caju	5		+	
Cedar	Cedro	3	+		
Coconut	Côco	16			+
Common bean	Feijão	1		+	
Cotton	Algodão	1			+
Cupuaçu	Cupuaçu	29	+		
Erythrina	Erytrina	1		+	
Freijó	Freijó	8	+		
Gandu	Gandu	1		+	
Grosela	Grosela	1		+	
Guaraná	Guaraná	1	+		
Guava	Goiaba	6		+	
Guinea grass	Colonião	1			+
Ingá	Ingá	2		+	
Ingá-cipó	Ingá-cipó	1		+	
Jackfruit	Jaca	4			+
Jarana	Jarana	1	+		
Lime	Limão	2			+
Macacaúba	Macacaúba	1	+		
Mahogany	Mogno	4	+		
Maize	Milho	2		+	
Mamey	Abricó	2		+	
Mango	Manga	9			+
Manioc	Mandhioca	25		+	
Orange	Laranja	32			+

227

Plant[a]	Local name of fruit	Fields	Amazon native	Native to neotropics	Old World native
Palhateira	Palhateira	1	+		
Papaya	Mamão	5		+	
Passionfruit	Maracujá	12		+	
Peach-palm	Pupunha	6	+		
Pineapple	Abacaxi	7		+	
Piquiá	Piquiá	1	+		
Quicuio	Quicuio	1			+
Robusta coffee	Café	9			+
Rubber	Seringa	21	+		
Soursop	Graviola	1	+		
Sweet potato	Batata doce	1		+	
Sweetsop	Ata	3		+	
Tangerine	Tangerina	6			+
Taro	Taro	1			+
Tutaruba	Tutaruba	1	+		
Uxi	Uxi	1	+		
Watermelon	Melancia	1			+
Yellow mombim	Cajá, taperebá	1	+		

a. For scientific names see appendix 1.

References

Abelson, P. H. 1990a. Uncertainties about global warming. *Science* 247: 1529.

—— 1990b. Global change. *Science* 249: 1085.

Adis, J. 1990. Thirty million arthropod species – too many or too few? *Journal of Tropical Ecology* 6: 115–118.

Agarwal, A. and S. Narain. 1991. A case of environmental colonialism. *Earth Island Journal*, Spring: 39–40.

Alcantara, E. 1991. A ciência afasta o perigo do desastre global. *Veja* 24(41): 78–44.

Allegretti, M. H. 1989. Reservas extrativistas: Uma proposta de desenvolvimento da floresta amazônica. *Pará Desenvolvimento* 25: 3–29.

—— 1992. Reconciling people and the land: The prospects for sustainable extraction in the Amazon. In Theodore E. Downing, Susanna B. Hecht, Henry A. Pearson, and Carmen Garcia-Downing (eds.), *Development or destruction: The conversion of tropical forest to pasture in Latin America*. Boulder, CO: Westview Press, pp. 249–254.

Almeida, A. L. O. 1992. Colonização na Amazônia: Reforma agrária numa "fronteira internacional." In *Perspectivas da Economia Brasileira, 1992*. Rio de Janeiro: IPEA, pp. 605–634.

Alvarado, A. 1990. Cuentas a Sting. *La Nación* (San José, Costa Rica), 14 June.

Alvarenga, T. 1991. Arquivo desprezado. *Veja*, 13 November: 50–53.

Álvares-Afonso, F. M. 1992. Rondônia: Ocupação, crescimento e organização agrária. Paper presented at the Primeiro Encontro Internacional Sobre Alternativas para a Agricultura Itinerante, Porto Velho, Rondônia, Brazil, 16–21 February.

Alvim, P. 1989. Tecnologias apropriadas para a agricultura nos trópicos úmidos. *Agrotrópica* 1(1): 1–22.

—— 1990. Agricultura apropriada para o uso contínuo dos solos na região Amazônica. *Espaço, Ambiente e Planejamento* 2(11): 3–71.

—— 1991. Non-chemical approaches to tropical tree crop disease management in the case of rubber and cacao in Brazil. Paper presented at a World Bank conference on Agriculture Technology: Current Policy Issues for the International Community and the World Bank, Airlie House, Virginia, 21–23 October.

References

Amoroso, M. C. M. 1981. Alimentação em um bairro pobre de Manaus, Amazonas. *Acta Amazonica*, supplement 9(3): 1–43.

Anderson, A. 1972. Farming the Amazon: The devastation technique. *Saturday Review* 40: 61–64.

Anderson, Anthony B. 1987. Forest management issues in the Brazilian Amazon. Report to the Ford Foundation, New York.

───── 1989. Estratégias de uso da terra para reservas extrativistas da Amazônia. *Pará Desenvolvimento* 25: 30–37.

───── 1990a. Smokestacks in the rainforest: Industrial development and deforestation in the Amazon basin. *World Development* 18(9): 1191–1205.

───── 1990b. Extraction and forest management by rural inhabitants in the Amazon estuary. In Anthony B. Anderson (ed.), *Alternatives to deforestation: Steps toward sustainable use of the Amazon rain forest.* New York: Columbia University Press, pp. 65–85.

Anderson, Anthony B., Peter H. May, and Michael J. Balick. 1991. *The subsidy from nature: Palm forests, peasantry, and development on an Amazon frontier.* New York: Columbia University Press.

Anderson, C. 1990. Methyl chloride gas implicated. *Nature* 348: 377.

Atkin, J. 1993. Tropical timber. *Economist*, 13 February: 8.

Ayres, J. M. and C. Ayres. 1979. Aspectos da caça no alto Rio Aripuanã. *Acta Amazonica* 9(2): 287–298.

Ayres, J. M., D. M. Lima, E. S. Martins, and J. L. K. Barreiros. 1991. On the track of the road: Changes in subsistence hunting in a Brazilian Amazon village. In John G. Robinson and Kent H. Redford (eds.), *Neotropical wildlife use and conservation.* Chicago: University of Chicago Press, pp. 82–92.

Balée, W. 1989. The culture of Amazonian forests. *Advances in Economic Botany* 7: 1–21.

Barbira-Scazzocchio, Françoise (ed.). 1980. *Land, people and planning in contemporary Amazonia.* Center of Latin American Studies, Occasional Publication No. 3. Cambridge: Cambridge University.

Barcelos, Edson, Abílio R. Pacheco, Antonio A. Müller, Ismael J. M. Viégas, and Paulo B. Tinôco. 1987. *Dendê: Informações básicas para seu cultivo.* Belém, Brazil: Empresa Brasileira de Pesquisa Agropecuária, Unidade de Execução de Pesquisa de Ambito Estadual.

Barnett, T. P. 1990. Beware greenhouse confusion. *Nature* 343: 696–697.

Barros, Sally M. 1990. Sustainability and social adaptation in the Brazilian Amazon: The Japanese of Tomé-Açu, 1929–89. M.A. thesis, University of California, Berkeley.

Barrow, C. J. 1987. The environmental impacts of the Tucuruí Dam on the middle and lower Tocantins River basin, Brazil. *Regulated Rivers* 1: 49–60.

───── 1988. The impact of hydroelectric development on the Amazonian environment: With particular reference to the Tucuruí project. *Journal of Biogeography* 15: 67–78.

Barthem, R. B., M. C. L. B. Brito, and M. Petrere. 1991. Life strategies of some long-distance migratory catfish in relation to hydroelectric dams in the Amazon Basin. *Biological Conservation* 55: 339–345.

Bates, Henry W. 1863. *The naturalist on the River Amazons*, vol. 1. London: John Murray.

Bayley, P. B. 1989. Aquatic environments in the Amazon Basin, with an analysis of carbon sources, fish production, and yield. *Can. Spec. Publ. Fish. Aquat.* 106: 399–408.

Bayley, P. B. and M. Petrere, Jr. 1990. Amazon fisheries: Assessment methods, current status and management options. In D. P. Dodge (ed.), *Proceedings of the International Large River Symposium*, Can. Spec. Publ. Fish. Aquat. Sci., vol. 106: 385–398.

Becker, Bertha K. and Claudio A. G. Egler. 1991. *Brazil: A new regional power in the world-economy*. Cambridge: Cambridge University Press.

Beckerman, S. 1987. Swidden in Amazonia and the Amazon rim. In B. L. Turner and S. B. Brush (eds.), *Comparative farming systems*. New York: Guilford, pp. 55–94.

Benchimol, Samuel. 1991. Amazônia interior: Apologia e holocausto. Manuscript.

―――― 1992a. *Amazônia: A guerra na floresta*. Rio de Janeiro: Civilização Brasileira.

―――― 1992b. ECO–92: Borealismo ecológico e tropicalismo ambiental. In José Marcelino Monteiro da Costa (ed.), *Amazônia: Desenvolvimento ou retrocesso*. Belém, Brazil: Edições CEJUP, pp. 17–39.

Bendix, J. and C. M. Liebler. 1991. Environmental degradation in Brazilian Amazonia: Perspectives in US news media. *Professional Geographer* 43: 474–485.

Bennett, C., G. Budowski, H. Daugherty, L. Harris, J. Milton, H. Popenoe, N. Smith, V. Urrutia, and E. Beltrán. 1974. Interaction of man and tropical environments. In Edward G. Farnworth and Frank B. Golley (eds.), *Fragile ecosystems*. New York: Springer-Verlag, pp. 139–182.

Benoit, E. 1990. Through the mill: Globalization, higher capital requirements and renewed environmental concern may lower the cyclicality of the world's forest products industry. *Financial World* 159(4): 39–44.

Biard, J. and G. Wagenaar. 1960. Crop production in selected areas of the Amazon Valley. *FAO ETAP Report* 1254: 1–47.

Biller, Dan. 1994. *Informal gold mining and mercury pollution in Brazil*. Policy Research Working Paper 1304, Policy Research Department, Public Economics Division, World Bank, Washington, D.C.

Blake, R. O. 1992. Challenges for global agricultural research. *Finance & Development* 29(1): 30–31.

Blinder, A. S. 1992. What wasn't on the Rio agenda? A little common sense. *Business Week* 3261(591): 12.

Blount, J. 1993. Brazil tree farm uses rain forest and also saves it. *Christian Science Monitor* (Boston), 27 April: 10.

Bodmer, R. E. 1990. Fruit patch size and frugivory in the lowland tapir (*Tapirus terrestris*). *Journal of the Zoological Society of London* 222: 121–128.

―――― 1991. Strategies of seed dispersal and seed predation in Amazonian ungulates. *Biotropica* 23(3): 255–261.

Bodmer, R. E. and J. M. Ayres. 1991. Sustainable development and species diversity in Amazonian forests. *Species* 16: 22–24.

Bodmer, R. E., T. G. Fang, and M. L. Ibanez. 1988. Ungulate management and conservation in the Peruvian Amazon. *Biological Conservation* 45: 303–310.

231

References

—— 1991. Primates and ungulates: A comparison of susceptibility to hunting. *Primate Conservation* 9: 79–83.

Bonalume, R. 1989a. Rain forests: Destruction area disputed. *Nature* 339: 86.

—— 1989b. Amazonian forests: Burning continues, slightly abated. *Nature* 339: 569.

—— 1991. Deforestation rate is falling. *Nature* 350: 368.

Boom, B. M. 1989. Use of plant resources by the Chácobo. *Advances in Economic Botany* 7: 78–96.

Boster, J. 1983. A comparison of the diversity of Jivaroan gardens with that of the tropical forest. *Human Ecology* 11(1): 47–68.

Bramble, B. J. 1987. The debt crisis: The opportunities. *Ecologist* 17(4/5): 192–199.

Braun, E. H. G. and J. R. A. Ramos. 1959. Estudo agrogeológico dos campos Puciara-Humaitá, Estado do Amazonas e Território Federal de Rondônia. *Revista Brasileira de Geografia* 21(4): 443–497.

Braunschweiler, H. 1991. Provisionary report for the Conselho Nacional de Desenvolvimento Científico e Tecnológico-CNPq about the project of mercury load in the Tucurui Lake and surrounding areas. Belém, Brazil: Instituto de Pesquisas Ecológicas da Amazônia.

Brklacich, M., C. R. Bryant, and B. Smit. 1991. Review and appraisal of concept of sustainable food production systems. *Environmental Management* 15(1): 1–14.

Brooke, J. 1991. A road better not taken: Brazil's plan to colonize the Amazon comes up short. *Gainesville Sun* (Gainesville, FL), 25 August: 9B.

Brookfield, Harold, Lesley Potter, and Yvonne Byron. 1995. *In place of the forest: Environmental and socio-economic transformation in Borneo and the eastern Malay Peninsula.* Tokyo: United Nations University Press.

Browder, J. O. 1988. The social costs of rain forest destruction: A critique and economic analysis of the "hamburger debate." *Interciencia* 13(3): 115–120.

—— 1989a. Lumber production and economic development in the Brazilian Amazon: Regional trends and a case study. *Journal of World Forest Resource Management* 4: 1–19.

—— 1989b. Introduction. In John O. Browder (ed.), *Fragile lands of Latin America: Strategies for sustainable development.* Boulder, CO: Westview Press, pp. 1–8.

—— 1992. The limits of extractivism: Tropical forest strategies beyond extractive reserves. *Bioscience* 42(3): 174–181.

Brown, Jr., K. S. and G. G. Brown. 1992. Habitat alteration and species loss in Brazilian forests. In T. C. Whitmore and J. A. Sayer (eds.), *Tropical deforestation and species extinction.* London: Chapman & Hall, pp. 119–142.

Brown, L. R. 1991. The new world order. In L. R. Brown, A. Durning, C. Flavin, H. French, J. Jacobson, N. Lenssen, M. Lowe, S. Postel, M. Renner, J. Ryan, L. Starke, and J. Young (eds.), *State of the world: A Worldwatch Institute report on progress toward a sustainable society.* New York: W. W. Norton, pp. 3–20.

Bryson, R. A. 1989. Will there be a global "greenhouse" warming? *Environmental Conservation* 16(2): 97–99.

Bunker, S. G. 1985. *Underdeveloping the Amazon: Extraction, unequal exchange, and the failure of the modern state.* Urbana, IL: University of Illinois Press.

Bunyard, P. 1987. The significance of the Amazon basin for global climatic equilibrium. *Ecologist* 17(4/5): 139–141.

———— 1989. Guardians of the Amazon. *New Scientist*, 16 December: 38–41.

Buschbacher, R. J., C. Uhl, and E. A. S. Serrão. 1987. Large-scale development in eastern Amazonia, case study no. 10: Pasture management and environmental effects near Paragominas, Pará. In Carl F. Jordan (ed.), *Amazonian rain forests: Ecosystem disturbance and recovery: Case studies of ecosystem dynamics under a spectrum of land use intensities.* New York: Springer-Verlag, pp. 90–99.

Bush, M. A., D. R. Piperno, and P. A. Colinvaux. 1989. A 6,000 year history of Amazonian maize cultivation. *Nature* 340: 303–305.

Butt, A. J. 1970. Land use and social organization of tropical forest peoples of the Guianas. In J. P. Garlick and R. W. Keay (eds.), *Human ecology in the tropics.* London: Pergamon Press, pp. 33–49.

Byrne, G. 1988. Let 100 million trees bloom. *Science* 242: 371.

Caccia, C. 1991. Reducing CO_2 emissions. *Environment* 33(6): 2–3.

Camarão, A. P., M. Simão Neto, E. A. S. Serrão, I. A. Rodrigues, and C. Lascano. 1990. *Identificação e composição quimica de especies invasoras de pastagens cultivadas consumidas por bovinos em Paragominas, Pará.* Boletim de Pesquisa 104. Belém, Brazil: Empresa Brasileira de Pesquisa Agropecuária.

Camargo, F. C. 1948. Terra e colonização no antigo e novo Quaternário da Zona da Estrada de Ferro de Bragança, Estado do Pará, Brasil. *Boletim do Museu Goeldi* 10: 123–133.

CAMTA. 1975. *Relatos históricos da Cooperativa Agrícola Mista de Tomé-Açú.* Tomé-Açu, Pará, Brazil: Cooperativa Agrícola Mista de Tomé-Açu.

Carney, J. 1990. *Triticale production in the central Mexican highlands: Smallholders' experiences and lessons for research.* CIMMYT Economics Paper 2, Mexico, D.F.

Cavalcante, Paulo B. 1991. *Frutas comestíveis da Amazônia.* Belém, Brazil: Edições CEJUP.

CGBD. 1989. Marketing non-timber tropical forest products: Prospects and promise. A workshop report of the Consultative Group on Biological Diversity in cooperation with Cultural Survival, Inc., Harvard University, Cambridge, MA, 7 November.

Chandless, W. 1866. Ascent of the River Purus. *Journal of the Royal Geographical Society* 36: 86–118.

Churchill, A. A. and R. J. Saunders. 1991. Global warming and the developing world. *Finance and Development* 28(2): 28–31.

CIAT. 1991. *CIAT in the 1990s and beyond: A strategic plan, Supplement.* Cali, Colombia: Centro Internacional de Agricultura Tropical.

———— 1992. *Report 1991, Cassava Program.* Cali, Colombia: Centro Internacional de Agricultura Tropical.

Cleary, David. 1990. *Anatomy of the Amazon gold rush.* Iowa City, IA: University of Iowa Press.

Cohen, Jennifer K. 1990. Emerald of the Amazon: Journalistic interpretation of the Brazilian rain forest, 1969–1990. M.A. thesis, University of Texas, Austin, TX.

Colinvaux, P. A. 1987. Amazon diversity in light of the paleoecological record. *Quaternary Science Reviews* 6: 93–114.

———— 1989. Ice-age Amazon revisited. *Nature* 340: 188–189.

Collins, Mark. 1990. *The last rain forests: A world conservation atlas.* New York: Oxford University Press.

233

References

Costa, J. M. M. 1990. A ecologia e o desenvolvimento da Amazônia. *O Liberal* (Belém), 17 June: 18.

——— 1992. Impactos econômico-territoriais do atual padrão de ocupação da Amazônia. In José Marcelino Monteiro da Costa (ed.), *Amazônia: Desenvolvimento ou retrocesso*. Belém, Brazil: Edições CEJUP, pp. 40–115.

Crist, R. E. 1963. Los Bolivianos emigran al este. *Américas* 15(5): 33–37.

——— 1967. Quelques aspects des migrations humaines et de la colonisation en Amérique Latine. In *Les problèmes agraires des Amériques Latines, Paris, 11–16 Octobre 1965*. Paris: Colloques Internationaux du Centre National de la Recherche Scientifique, pp. 501–510.

Cutrim, E. 1990. Dynamic Amazon weather. Paper presented at the annual meetings of the American Association for the Advancement of Science (AAAS), New Orleans, 15–20 February.

Denevan, W. M. 1992. The pristine myth: The landscape of the Americas in 1492. *Annals of the Association of American Geographers* 82: 369–385.

Denslow, J. S. 1988. The tropical rain-forest setting. In Julie S. Denslow and Christine Padoch (eds.), *People of the tropical rain forest*. Berkeley, CA: University of California Press, pp. 25–36.

Dickinson, R. E. 1987. Introduction to vegetation and climate interactions in the humid tropics. In Robert E. Dickinson (ed.), *The geophysiology of Amazonia: Vegetation and climate interactions*. New York: Wiley, pp. 3–10.

——— 1989. Implications of tropical deforestation for climate: A comparison of model and observational descriptions of surface energy and hydrological balance. *Philosophical Transactions of the Royal Society of London. B. Biological Sciences* 324: 423–431.

Dourojeanni, M. J. 1974. Impacto de la producción de la fauna silvestre en la economia de la Amazonia Peruana. *Revista Florestal del Perú* 5(1–2): 15–27.

Dufour, D. L. 1990. Use of tropical rainforests by native Amazonians. *Bioscience* 40: 652–659.

Dwyer, Augusta. 1990. *Into the Amazon: The struggle for the rain forest*. San Francisco: Sierra Club Books.

Earhart, J. J. 1990. Peruvian Indians work to save forest home. *Focus* (World Wildlife Fund) 12(4): 5.

Eden, Michael J. 1988. Crop diversity in tropical swidden cultivation: Comparative data from Colombia and Papua New Guinea. *Agriculture, Ecosystems and Environment* 20: 127–136.

——— 1990. *Ecology and land management in Amazonia*. London: Bellhaven Press.

Eden, Michael J., W. Braz, L. Herrera, and C. McEwan. 1984. *Terra preta* soils and their archaeological context in the Caquetá basin of southeast Colombia. *American Antiquity* 49: 124–140.

Eden, Michael J., D. F. M. McGregor, and N. A. Q. Vieira. 1990. III. Pasture development on cleared forest land in northern Amazonia. *Geographical Journal* 156(3): 283–296.

Egler, E. C. 1961. A zona Bragantina no Estado do Pará. *Revista Brasileira de Geografia* 23(3): 527–555.

Eidt, R. C. 1962. Pioneer settlement in eastern Peru. *Annals of the Association of American Geographers* 52: 255–278.

—— 1966. Economic features of land opening in the Peruvian Montaña. *Professional Geographer* 18(3): 146–150.

EMBRAPA. 1989. *O papel da EMBRAPA na Amazônia: Pesquisa para o desenvolvimento com conservação ambiental.* Brasília: Empresa Brasileira de Pesquisa Agropecuária Brasileira.

ESG. 1990. Estrutura do poder nacional para o ano 2001. Brasília: Escola Superior de Guerra.

Evans, J. 1986. Tropical forest plantations. *Anais do Primeiro Simpósio do Trópico Umido, Belém, Pará, 12 a 17 de novembro de 1984, vol. II, Flora e Floresta.* Brasília: Empresa Brasileira de Pesquisa Agropecuária, pp. 37–50.

Falesi, Italo C. 1976. *Ecosistema de pastagem cultivada na Amazonia Brasileira.* Boletim Tecnico. Belém, Brazil: Empresa Brasileira de Pesquisa Agropecuária.

—— 1992. Efeitos da queima da biomassa florestal nas características do solo da Amazônia. In José Marcelino Monteiro da Costa (ed.), *Amazônia: Desenvolvimento ou retrocesso.* Belém, Brazil: Edições CEJUP, pp. 140–162.

Falesi, Italo C. and H. Osaqui. 1992. Projeto de investimento e desenvolvimento da agroindústria na Amazônia. Paper presented at Simpósio Internacional sobre Cenário de Desenvolvimento Sustentável na Amazônia: Alternativas Econômicas e Perspectivas de Cooperação Internacional, Belém, Brazil, 17–19 March.

Falesi, Italo C., Antonio R. C. Baena, and Saturino Dutra. 1980. *Consequências da exploração agropecuária sobre as condições físicas e químicas dos solos das microregiões do nordeste paraense.* Boletim de Pesquisa 14. Belém, Brazil: EMBRAPA – Centro de Pesquisa Agropecuária do Trópico Umido.

FAO. 1990. *Conservation and sustainable development in the Amazon region.* Interdepartmental Task Force on the Amazon, Working Paper, Food and Agriculture Organization, Rome.

—— 1991a. *Criteria, instruments and tools for sustainable agriculture and rural development.* FAO/Netherlands Conference on Agriculture and the Environment, 's-Hertogenbosch, Netherlands, 15–19 April, Main Document No. 4. Rome: Food and Agriculture Organization.

—— 1991b. *Population, environment and sustainable agriculture and rural development.* FAO/Netherlands Conference on Agriculture and the Environment, 's-Hertogenbosch, Netherlands, 15–19 April, Miscellaneous Document No. 2. Rome: Food and Agriculture Organization.

Fautereau, E. 1955. Étude d'écologie humaine dans l'aire Amazonienne. *Journal de la Société des Americanistes* 44: 99–130.

Fearnside, Philip M. 1980a. Black pepper yield prediction for the Transamazon Highway of Brazil. *Turrialba* 30(1): 35–42.

—— 1980b. The effects of cattle pasture on soil fertility in the Brazilian Amazon: Consequences for beef production sustainability. *Tropical Ecology* 21(1): 125–137.

—— 1986. *Human carrying capacity of the Brazilian rainforest.* New York: Columbia University Press.

—— 1987. Rethinking continuous cultivation in Amazonia. *Bioscience* 37: 209–213.

—— 1989a. Deforestation in Brazilian Amazonia: The rates and causes of forest destruction. *Ecologist* 19: 214–218.

———— 1989b. Extractive reserves in Brazilian Amazonia: An opportunity to maintain tropical rain forest under sustainable use. *Bioscience* 39: 387–393.

———— 1989c. Manejo florestal na Amazônia: Necessidade de novos critérios na avaliação de opções de desenvolvimento. *Pará Desenvolvimento* 25: 49–59.

Fearnside, Philip M. and J. Rankin. 1982. The new Jari: Risks and prospects of a major Amazonian development. *Interciencia* 7(6): 329–339.

Fernandes, E. C. M. and E. A. S. Serrão. 1992. Protótipo e modelos agrossilvipastoris sustentáveis. In *SIMDAMAZÔNIA: Seminário internacional sobre meio ambiente, pobreza e desenvolvimento da Amazônia, Belém, 16 a 19 de fevereiro de 1992*. Belém, Brazil: Secretaria de Estado de Ciência, Tecnologia e Meio Ambiente, pp. 245–251.

Ferreira, E. J. G. 1984. A ictiofauna da represa hidrelétrica de Curuá-Una, Santarém, Pará, I–lista e distribuição das Espécies. *Amazoniana* 8(3): 351–363.

Flavin, Christopher. 1989. *Slowing global warming: A worldwide strategy*. Paper 91. Washington, D.C.: Worldwatch Institute.

Foresta, Ronald A. 1991. *Amazon conservation in the age of development: The limits of providence*. Gainesville, FL: University of Florida Press and Center for Latin American Studies.

Fowler, Gary and Pat Mooney. 1990. *Shattering: Food, politics, and the loss of genetic diversity*. Tucson, AZ: University of Arizona Press.

Fuge, R., N. J. G. Pearce, and W. T. Perkins. 1992. Mercury and gold pollution. *Nature* 357: 369.

FUNTAC. 1990a. *Diagnóstico das indústrias de serraria de Rio Branco*. Rio Branco, Brazil: Fundação de Tecnologia do Estado do Acre.

———— 1990b. *Monitoramento da cobertura florestal do estado do Acre: Desmatamento e uso atual da terra*. Rio Branco, Brazil: Fundação de Tecnologia do Estado do Acre.

Gentry, A. H. and J. Lopez-Parodi. 1980. Deforestation and increased flooding of the Upper Amazon. *Science* 210: 1354–1356.

Glacken, Clarence J. 1967. *Traces on the Rhodian shore*. Berkeley, CA: University of California Press.

Godfrey, B. J. 1990. Boom towns of the Amazon. *Geographical Review* 80: 103–117.

———— 1992. Migration to the gold-mining frontier in Brazilian Amazonia. *Geographical Review* 82(4): 458–469.

Gonçalves, C. R. 1957. Observações sôbre as saúvas da Amazônia. *Rev. Soc. Bras. Agron.* 12(3–4): 43–52.

———— 1967. As formigas cortadeiras da Amazônia, dos géneros "Atta" Fabr. e "Acromyrmex" Mayr (Hym., Formicidae). *Atas do Simpósio sôbre a Biota Amazônica* 5: 181–202.

Goodland, Robert J. A. and Howard S. Irwin. 1975. *Amazon jungle: Green hell to red desert?* Amsterdam: Elsevier.

Goodman, B. 1993. Drugs and people threaten biodiversity in Andean forests. *Science* 261: 293.

Goodyear. 1989. *Revista Goodyear, Edição especial, 50 anos*. São Paulo, Brazil: Goodyear.

Goulding, Michael. 1980. *The fishes and the forest*. Berkeley, CA: University of California Press.

—— 1981. *Man and fisheries on an Amazon frontier*. The Hague: W. Junk.

—— 1989. *Amazon: The flooded forest*. London: BBC Books.

—— 1993. Flooded forests of the Amazon. *Scientific American* 266(3): 114–120.

Goulding, Michael, Nigel J. H. Smith, and Dennis Mahar. In press. *Floods of fortune: Ecology and economy along the Amazon*. New York: Columbia University Press.

Graaf, N. R. 1982. Sustained timber production in the tropical rainforest of Suriname. In J. F. Wienk and H. A. deWit (eds.), *Proceedings of the joint workshop on management of low fertility acid soils of the humid tropics*. San José, Costa Rica: IICA.

Gradwohl, Judith and Russel Greenberg. 1988. *Saving the tropical forests*. Washington, D.C.: Island Press.

Greaves, A. 1979. *Gmelina* – Large scale planting, Jarilandia, Amazon Basin. *Commonwealth Forestry Review* 58(4): 267–269.

Gribel, R. 1990. The Balbina disaster: The need to ask why? *The Ecologist* 20(4): 133–135.

Grove, R. 1990. The origins of environmentalism. *Nature* 345: 11–14.

Hall, Anthony. 1978. *Drought and irrigation in North-East Brazil*. Cambridge: Cambridge University Press.

—— 1989. Agrarian crisis in Brazilian Amazonia: The Grande Carajás Programme. *Journal of Development Studies* 23(4): 522–552.

Hansen, J. E. and A. A. Lacis. 1990. Sun and dust versus greenhouse gases: An assessment of their relative roles in global climate change. *Nature* 346: 713–719.

Harmon, M. E., W. K. Ferrell, and J. F. Franklin. 1990. Effects on carbon storage of conversion of old-growth forests to young forests. *Science* 247: 699–702.

Harris, Larry. 1984. *The fragmented forest: Island biogeography theory and the preservation of biotic diversity*. Chicago: University of Chicago Press.

Harris, M. 1983. The revolutionary hamburger. *Psychology Today* 17(10): 6–8.

Hébette, J. 1991. O Centro Agroambiental do Tocantins: Propostas e desafios. *Proposta* 48: 32–37.

Hecht, Susanna B. 1985. Environment, development and politics: Capital accumulation and the livestock sector in eastern Amazonia. *World Development* 13(6): 663–684.

—— 1992. Logics of livestock and deforestation: The case of Amazonia. In Theodore E. Downing, Susanna B. Hecht, Henry A. Pearson, and Carmen Garcia-Downing (eds.), *Development or destruction: The conversion of tropical forest to pasture in Latin America*. Boulder, CO: Westview, pp. 7–25.

Hecht, Susanna B. and Alexander Cockburn. 1989. *The fate of the forest: Developers, destroyers, and defenders of the Amazon*. London: Verso.

Hemming, John. 1978. *Red gold: The conquest of the Brazilian Indians, 1500–1760*. Cambridge, MA: Harvard University Press.

—— (ed.). 1985a. *Change in the Amazon basin: Man's impact on forests and rivers*. Manchester: Manchester University Press.

—— (ed.). 1985b. *Change in the Amazon basin: The frontier after a decade of colonisation*. Manchester: Manchester University Press.

—— 1987. *Amazon frontier: The defeat of the Brazilian Indians*. Cambridge, MA: Harvard University Press.

References

Henderson-Sellers, A. 1987. Effects of change in land use on climate in the humid tropics. In Robert E. Dickinson (ed.), *The geophysiology of Amazonia: Vegetation and climate interactions*. New York: Wiley, pp. 463–493.

Heriarte, Mauricio. 1964. *Descriçam do estado do Maranham, Para, Corupa, Rio das Amazonas (1662)*. Austria: Akademische Druck, Verlagsanstalt Graz.

Hicks, James F., Herman E. Daly, Shelton H. Davis, and Maria L. Freitas. 1990. *Ecuador's Amazon region: Development issues and options*. Discussion Papers 75. Washington, D.C.: World Bank.

Hiraoka, Mario. 1980a. Settlement and development of the Upper Amazon: The East Bolivian example. *Journal of Developing Areas* 14: 327–347.

—— 1980b. *Japanese agricultural settlement in the Bolivian Upper Amazon: A study in regional ecology*. Latin American Studies 1, Special Research Project on Latin America, University of Tsukuba, Sakuramura, Ibaraki, Japan.

—— 1989. Agricultural systems on the floodplains of the Peruvian Amazon. In John O. Browder (ed.), *Fragile lands of Latin America: Strategies for sustainable development*, Boulder, CO: Westview Press. pp. 75–101.

Hiraoka, Mario and S. Yamamoto. 1980. Agricultural development in the Upper Amazon of Ecuador. *Geographical Review* 70: 423–445.

Hogan, K. B., J. S. Hoffman, and A. M. Thompson. 1991. Methane on the greenhouse agenda. *Nature* 354: 181–182.

Holling, C. S. 1986. The resilience of terrestrial ecosystems: Local surprise and global change. In W. C. Clark and R. E. Munn (eds.), *Sustainable development of the biosphere*. Cambridge: Cambridge University Press, pp. 292–317.

Holloway, J. 1991. Biodiversity and tropical agriculture: A biogeographic view. *Outlook on Agriculture* 20(1): 9–13.

Holt, Jeremy. 1992. *The Brazil nut market*. London: Amazonia Trading Company Ltd.

Homma, Alfredo K. O. 1989a. A extração de recursos naturais renováveis; O caso do extrativismo vegetal na Amazônia. Ph.D. dissertation, Universidade Federal de Viçosa, Viçosa, Minas Gerais, Brazil.

—— 1989b. Perspectivas da economia extrativista vegetal na Amazônia. Belém: EMBRAPA, unpublished report.

—— 1990a. A questão do desmatamento na Amazônia. *Folha de São Paulo*, 7 July: C 5.

—— 1990b. Deixem Chico Mendes em paz. *Veja*, 19 December: 106.

—— 1990c. *A dinâmica do extrativismo vegetal na Amazônia: Uma interpretação teórica*. Belém, Brazil: Empresa Brasileira de Pesquisa Agropecuária, Centro de Pesquisa Agropecuária do Trópico Umido.

—— 1992a. Os limites de atuação das ONGs. *Economia Rural* 3(3): 10–12.

—— 1992b. Oportunidades, limitações e estratégias para a economia extrativa vegetal na Amazônia. In *SIMDAMAZÔNIA: Seminário internacional sobre meio ambiente, pobreza e desenvolvimento da Amazônia, Belém, 16 a 19 de fevereiro de 1992*. Belém, Brazil: Secretaria de Estado de Ciência, Tecnologia e Meio Ambiente, pp. 252–256.

Homma, Alfredo K. O., A. R. Teixeira Filho, and E. P. Magalhães. 1991. Análise do preço da terra como recurso natural durável: O caso da Amazônia. *Revista Econ. Sociol. Rural* (Brasília) 29(2): 103–116.

Homma, Alfredo K. O., R. Carvalho, A. Conto, and A. C. Rocha. 1992a. Transamazônica: Sucesso ou insucesso? *O Liberal* (Belém), 29 July: 6.

Homma, Alfredo K. O., A. Contro, A. Carlos, and R. Carvalho. 1992b. A pecuária na Transamazônica. *O Liberal* (Belém), 30 July: 6.

Hoppe, A. 1992. Mining in the Amazonian rainforests. *Nature* 355: 593–594.

Hornick, J. R., J. I. Zerbe, and J. L. Whitmore. 1984. Jari's successes. *Journal of Forestry* 82: 663–667.

Howarth, R. B. and R. B. Norgaard. 1990. Intergenerational resource rights, efficiency, and social optimality. *Land Economics* 66(1): 1–11.

Huber, J. 1910. Mattas e madeiras amazonicas. *Boletim do Museu Goeldi de Historia Natural e Ethnographia* 6: 91–225.

Huber, P. 1992. Biodiversity vs. bioengineering? *Forbes* 150(10): 266.

Hurrell, A. 1990. The politics of Amazonian deforestation. *Journal of Latin American Studies* 23: 197–215.

IBDF. 1982. *Plano do sistema de unidades de conservação do Brasil: II etapa.* Brasília: Instituto Brasileiro de Desenvolvimento Florestal/Fundação Brasileira para a Conservação da Natureza.

IBGE. 1989. *Anuário estatístico do Brasil.* Rio de Janeiro, Brazil: Instituto Brasileiro de Geografia e Estatística.

INPE. 1990. *Avaliação da alteração da cobertura florestal na Amazônia utilizando sensoriamento remoto orbital.* São Paulo, Brazil: Instituto Nacional de Pesquisas Espaciais.

Irion, G. 1989. Quaternary geological history of the Amazon lowlands. In L. B. Holm-Nielsen, I. C. Nielsen, and H. Balslev (eds.), *Tropical forests: Botanical dynamics, speciation and diversity.* London: Academic Press, pp. 23–34.

Ives, Jack D. and Bruno Messerli. 1989. *The Himalayan dilemma: Reconciling development and conservation.* London: Routledge.

Janzen, D. H. 1970. Herbivores and the number of tree species in tropical forests. *American Naturalist* 104: 501–528.

JARI. 1989. *Solos do Jari.* Rio de Janeiro, Brazil: Companhia Florestal Monte Dourado.

Jarvis, P. G. 1989. Atmospheric carbon dioxide and forests. *Philosophical Transactions of the Royal Society of London. B. Biological Sciences* 324: 369–392.

Junk, W. J. and J. A. S. Nunes de Mello. 1987. Impactos ecológicos das represas hidrelétricas na Bacia Amazônica Brasileira. *Tubinger Geographische Studien* 95: 367–385.

Junk, W. J., B. A. Robertson, A. J. Darwich, and I. Vieira. 1981. Investigações limnológicas e ictiológicas em Curuá-Una, a primeira represa hidrelétrica na Amazônia central. *Acta Amazonica* 11(4): 689–716.

Juo, A. S. R. 1989. New farming systems development in the wetter tropics. *Experimental Agriculture* 25: 145–163.

Kahl, J. D., D. J. Charlevoix, N. A. Zaitseva, R. C. Schnell, and M. C. Serreze. 1993. Absence of evidence for greenhouse warming over the Arctic Ocean in the past 40 years. *Nature* 361: 335–337.

Kasperson, Roger E., Jeanne X. Kasperson, B. L. Turner II, Kirstin Dow, and William B. Meyer. 1995. Critical environmental regions: Concepts, distinctions, and issues. In Jeanne Kasperson, Roger Kasperson, and B. L. Turner II (eds.),

References

Regions at risk: Comparisons of threatened environments. Tokyo: United Nations University Press.

Keller, M., E. Veldkamp, A. M. Weitz, and W. A. Reiners. 1993. Effect of pasture age on soil trace-gas emissions from a deforested area of Costa Rica. *Nature* 365: 244–246.

Kelly, Brian and Mark London. 1983. *Amazon.* San Diego: Harcourt Brace Jovanovich.

Kerr, R. A. 1989. Volcanoes can muddle the greenhouse. *Science* 245: 127–128.

Kerr, W. E. 1986. Agricultura e seleções genéticas de plantas. In *Suma etnológica Brasileira, Parte 1, Etnobiologia.* Petrópolis, Brazil: Vozes, pp. 159–171.

Killian, L. 1991. Dead effort. *Forbes*, 24 June: 96.

Kinkead, G. 1981. Trouble in D. K. Ludwig's jungle. *Fortune* 103(8): 102–115.

Kirmse, Robert D., Luis F. Constantino, and George M. Guess. 1993. *Prospects for improved management of natural forests in Latin America.* LATEN Dissemination Note 9, Environment Division, Latin America Technical Department, World Bank, Washington, D.C.

Kishor, Nalin M. and Luis F. Constantino. 1993. *Forest management and competing land uses: An economic analysis for Costa Rica.* LATEN Dissemination Note 7, Environment Division, Latin America Technical Department, World Bank, Washington, D.C.

Landim, Leilah. 1988. *Sem fins lucrativos: As organizações não-governamentais no Brasil.* Rio de Janeiro, Brazil: Instituto de Estudos da Religião.

Langereis, C. G., A. A. M. Van Hoof, and P. Rochette. 1992. Variability in sea-ice thickness over the North Pole from 1977 to 1990. *Nature* 358: 224–226.

Lathrap, Donald W. 1968. Aboriginal occupation and changes in river channel on the central Ucayali, Peru. *American Antiquity* 33(1): 62–79.

——— 1970. *The upper Amazon.* London: Thames & Hudson.

Lavelle, P. 1987. Biological processes and productivity of soils in the humid tropics. In Robert E. Dickinson (ed.), *The geophysiology of Amazonia: Vegetation and climate interactions.* New York: Wiley, pp. 175–214.

Leal, C. 1990. No Marajó, a beleza que se confunde com velhos problemas. *O Liberal* (Belém), 29 May: 18.

Le Cointe, Paul. 1918. *A industria pastoril na Amazonia.* Belém, Brazil: Imprensa Official do Estado.

Ledec, George and Robert Goodland. 1988. *Wildlands: Their protection and management in economic development.* Washington, D.C.: World Bank.

Leonard, H. J. 1989. Environment and the poor: Development strategies for a common agenda. In H. Jeffrey Leonard, Montague Yudelman, J. Dirck Stryker, John O. Browder, A. John De Boer, Tim Campbell, and Alison Jolly (eds.), *Environment and the poor: Development strategies for a common agenda.* U.S.–Third World Policy Perspectives No. 11. Brunswick, NJ: Overseas Development Council, pp. 3–45.

Leopoldo, P. R., W. Franken, and E. Matsui. 1985. Hydrological aspects of the tropical rainforest in the central Amazon. In John Hemming (ed.), *Change in the Amazon basin, Vol. I: Man's impact on forests and rivers.* Manchester: Manchester University Press, pp. 90–107.

Lima, R. R. 1958. Os efeitos das queimadas sôbre a vegetação dos solos arenosos da região da estrada de ferro de Bragança. *Boletim da Inspetoría Regional de Fomento Agrícola no Pará* 8: 23–25.

Liu, K. and P. A. Colinvaux. 1985. Forest changes in the Amazon basin during the last glacial maximum. *Nature* 318: 556–557.

Livernash, R. 1992. The growing influence of NGOs in the developing world. *Environment* 34(5): 12–20, 41–43.

McAlister, Lyle N. 1984. *Spain and Portugal in the New World: 1492–1700*. Minneapolis, MN: University of Minnesota Press.

McDonald, L. and I. M. Fernandes. 1984. AMCEL: An Amazon pine plantation may be the largest of its kind. *Journal of Forestry* 82: 668–670.

Machado, P. F. 1992. O pólo siderúrgico de Carajás: Impactos e alternativas possíveis. In José Marcelino Monteiro da Costa (ed.), *Amazônia: Desenvolvimento ou retrocesso*. Belém, Brazil: Edições CEJUP, pp. 284–327.

Maddox, J. 1990. Two gales do not make a greenhouse. *Nature* 343: 407.

Magalhães, Basílio de. 1980. *O café na história, no folclore e nas belas-artes*. São Paulo, Brazil: Companhia Editora Nacional.

Magee, P. 1989. Peasant political identity and the Tucurui Dam: A case study of the island dwellers of Pará, Brazil. *Latinamericanist* (University of Florida) 24(1): 6–10.

Mahadevan, P. 1974. The buffaloes of Latin America. In W. Cockrill (ed.), *The husbandry and health of the domestic buffalo*. Rome: Food and Agriculture Organization, pp. 676–704.

Mahar, Dennis J. 1989. *Government policies and deforestation in Brazil's Amazon region*. Washington, D.C.: World Bank.

Malingreau, J. and C. J. Tucker. 1988. Large-scale deforestation in the southeastern Amazon basin of Brazil. *Ambio* 17: 49–55.

Mallas, J. and N. Benedicto. 1986. Mercury and goldmining in the Brazilian Amazon. *Ambio* 15(4): 248–249.

Malm, O., W. C. Pfeiffer, C. M. M. Souza, and R. Reuther. 1990. Mercury pollution due to gold mining in the Madeira River basin, Brazil. *Ambio* 19(1): 11–15.

Mares, M. A. 1992. Neotropical mammals and the myth of Amazonian biodiversity. *Science* 255: 976–979.

Marques, A. C. 1992. Saúde e doenças tropicais. In *SIMDAMAZÔNIA: Seminário internacional sobre meio ambiente, pobreza e desenvolvimento da Amazônia, Belém, 16 a 19 de fevereiro de 1992*. Belém, Brazil: Processamento de Dados do Estado do Pará (PRODEPA), pp. 1–5.

Martinelli, L. A., J. R. Ferreira, B. R. Forsberg, and R. L. Victoria. 1988. Mercury contamination in the Amazon: A gold rush consequence. *Ambio* 17(4): 252–254.

Mason, Anita. 1991. *The racket*. New York: Dutton.

Mattos, A. M. 1992. O interesse nacional e os interesses internacionais na Amazônia brasileira. In José Marcelino Monteiro da Costa (ed.), *Amazônia: Desenvolvimento ou retrocesso*. Belém, Brazil: Edições CEJUP, pp. 116–139.

Mattos, M. M., C. Uhl, and D. O. Gonçalves. In press. Economic and ecological perspectives of ranching in the eastern Amazon in the 1990s. *World Development*.

Medina, José T. 1988. *The discovery of the Amazon*. New York: Dover.

Mee, Margaret. 1988. *In search of flowers of the Amazon forests*. Woodbridge, Suffolk: Nonesuch Expeditions.

References

Meggers, Betty J. 1971. *Amazonia: Man and culture in a counterfeit paradise*. Chicago: Aldine/Atherton.

Merona, B., J. L. de Carvalho, and M. M. Bittencourt. 1987. Les effets immédiats de la fermeture du barrage de Tucurui (Brésil) sur l'ichtyofaune en aval. *Revue de Hydrobiologie Tropicale* 20(1): 73–84.

Miller, A. 1991. Economic models and policy on global warming. *Environment* 33(6): 3–5, 43–44.

Miller, Christopher. 1990. Natural history, economic botany, and germplasm conservation of the Brazil nut tree (*Bertholletia excelsa*, Humb & Bonpl.). Unpublished M.S. thesis, Department of Geography, University of Florida, Gainesville, FL.

Milton, K. 1984. Protein and carbohydrate resources of the Maku Indians of northwestern Amazonia. *American Ethnologist* 86: 7–27.

Mitchell, J. F. B., C. A. Senior, and W. J. Ingram. 1989. CO_2 and climate: A missing feedback? *Nature* 341: 132–134.

Modenar, T. 1972. On the road. *Saturday Review*, 30 September: 65–67.

Molion, Luiz C. 1975. A climatonomic study of the energy and moisture fluxes of the Amazon basin with considerations of deforestation effects. Ph.D. dissertation, University of Wisconsin, Madison, WI.

———— 1987. Micrometeorology of an Amazonian rain forest. In Robert E. Dickinson (ed.), *The geophysiology of Amazonia: Vegetation and climate interactions*. New York: Wiley, pp. 255–270.

Monastersky, R. 1993. The deforestation debate: Estimates vary widely over the extent of forest loss. *Science News* 144: 26–27.

Montecinos, C. and M. A. Altieri. 1991. *Status and trends in grass-roots crop genetic conservation efforts in Latin America*. Berkeley, CA: Consorcio Latino Americano sobre Agroecologia y Desarrollo.

Montoro Filho, A. F., A. E. Comune, and F. H. de Melo. 1989. *A Amazônia e a economia Brasileira: A integração econômica, os desafios e as oportunidades de crescimento*. São Paulo, Brazil: Associação dos Empresários da Amazônia.

Moran, Emilio F. 1981. *Developing the Amazon*. Bloomington, IN: Indiana University Press.

———— 1988a. Following the Amazon highways. In Julie S. Denslow and Christine Padoch (eds.), *People of the tropical rain forest*. Berkeley, CA: University of California Press, pp. 155–162.

———— 1988b. Amazonian development: Who benefits? *SPEA Review* (School of Public and Environmental Affairs, Indiana University) 10(1): 8–11.

———— 1990. *A ecologia humana das populações da Amazônia*. Petrópolis, Brazil: Vozes.

———— 1993a. Deforestation and land use in the Brazilian Amazon. *Human Ecology* 21(1): 1–21.

———— 1993b. *Through Amazonian eyes*. Iowa City, IA: University of Iowa Press.

Mori, S. 1992. The Brazil nut industry – Past, present, and future. In Mark Plotkin and Lisa Famolare (eds.), *Sustainable harvest and marketing of rain forest products*. Washington, D.C.: Island Press, pp. 241–251.

Moura, Ignácio Baptista de. 1989. *De Belém a S. João do Araguaia: Vale do Rio Tocantins*. Belém, Brazil: Fundação Cultural do Pará Tancredo Neves/Secretaria de Estado da Cultura.

242

Muller, K. D. 1988a. The impact of agricultural mechanization on population and migration in South Brazil: The example of West Paraná. *Latin American Studies* (University of Tsukuba) 9: 59–86.

—— 1988b. The impact of agricultural mechanization on land tenancy and farm size in South Brazil – The example of West Paraná. *Latin American Studies* (University of Tsukuba) 10: 181–210.

Myers, Norman. 1980a. The present and future prospects of tropical moist forests. *Environmental Conservation* 7(2): 101–114.

—— 1980b. The cost of a "Big Mac"? Latin America's forests. *World Environment Report* 6(18): 1–2.

—— 1984. *The primary source: Tropical forests and our future.* New York: W. W. Norton.

—— 1988. Tropical deforestation and climatic change. *Environmental Conservation* 15: 293–298.

—— 1990. *Natural resource-based export initiatives in Central America and the Caribbean.* Working Papers No. 15. Washington, D.C.: Commission for the Study of International Migration and Cooperative Economic Development.

—— 1991. Tropical deforestation: The latest situation. *Biotropica* 41(5): 282.

—— 1993. Biodiversity and the precautionary principle. *Ambio* 22(2–3): 74–79.

Myers, Norman and J. Goreau. 1991. Tropical forests and the greenhouse effect: A management response. *Climate Change* 19: 215–225.

Myers, Norman and R. Tucker. 1987. Deforestation in Central America: Spanish legacy and North American consumers. *Environmental Review* 11(1): 55–71.

Nair, P. K. 1991. State-of-the-art of agroforestry systems. *Forest Ecology and Management* 45: 5–29.

Nair, P. K. and J. C. Dagar. 1991. An approach to developing methodologies for evaluating agroforestry systems in India. *Agroforestry Systems* 16: 15–81.

Nations, J. D. and D. I. Komer. 1983. Central America's tropical rainforests: Positive steps for survival. *Ambio* 12(5): 232–238.

—— 1987. Rainforests and the hamburger society. *Ecologist* 17(4/5): 161–167.

Nelson, B. W., C. A. C. Ferreira, M. F. da Silva, and M. L. Kawasaki. 1990. Endemism centres, refugia and botanical collection density in Brazilian Amazonia. *Nature* 345: 714–716.

Nelson, Michael. 1973. *The development of tropical lands: Policy issues in Latin America.* Baltimore, MD: Johns Hopkins University Press.

Nepstad, D. C., C. Uhl, and E. A. S. Serrão. 1990. Surmounting barriers to forest regeneration in abandoned, highly degraded pastures: A case study from Paragominas, Pará, Brazil. In Anthony B. Anderson (ed.), *Alternatives to deforestation: Steps toward sustainable use of the Amazon rain forest.* New York: Columbia University Press, pp. 215–229.

—— 1991. Recuperation of a degraded Amazonian landscape: Forest recovery and agricultural restoration. *Ambio* 20(6): 248–255.

Newson, M. D. and I. R. Calder. 1989. Forests and water resources: Problems of prediction on a regional scale. *Philosophical Transactions of the Royal Society of London. B. Biological Sciences* 234: 283–295.

Nigh, R. B. and J. D. Nations. 1980. Tropical rainforests. *Bulletin of the Atomic Scientists* 36(3): 12–19.

References

Nisbet, E. G. 1988. The business of planet management. *Nature* 333: 617.
Nobre, C. A., P. J. Sellers, and J. Shukla. 1991. Amazonian deforestation and regional climate change. *Journal of Climate* 4: 957–988.
Norgaard, Richard B. 1991. *Sustainability as intergenerational equity: The challenge to economic thought and practice.* Internal Discussion Paper, Asia Regional Studies, Report No. IDP 97, World Bank, Washington, D.C.
Norman, Colin. 1981. *The god that limps: Science and technology in the eighties.* New York: W. W. Norton.
NRC. 1981. *The water buffalo: New prospects for an underutilized animal.* Washington, D.C.: National Research Council, National Academy Press.
———— 1991. *Managing global genetic resources: Forest trees.* Washington, D.C.: National Research Council, National Academy Press.
———— 1993. *Sustainable agriculture and environment in the humid tropics.* Washington, D.C.: National Research Council, National Academy Press.
Nriagu, J. O., W. C. Pfeiffer, O. Malm, C. M. M. Souza, and G. Mierle. 1992. Mercury pollution in Brazil. *Nature* 356: 389.

Odinetz-Collart, O. 1987. La pêche crevettière de *Macrobrachium amazonicum* (Palaemonidae) dans le Bas-Tocantins, après la fermeture du barrage de Tucurui (Brésil). *Revue de Hydrobiologie Tropicale* 20(2): 131–144.
Ojasti, J. 1991. Human exploitation of capybara. In John G. Robinson and Kent H. Redford (eds.), *Neotropical wildlife use and conservation.* Chicago: University of Chicago Press, pp. 236–252.
Oldeman, R. A. A. 1989. Dynamics in tropical rain forests. In L. B. Holm-Nielsen, I. C. Nielsen, and H. Balslev (eds.), *Tropical forests: Botanical dynamics, speciation and diversity.* London: Academic Press, pp. 3–21.
OTA. 1992. *Combined summaries: Technologies to sustain tropical forest resources and biological diversity.* Washington, D.C.: Office of Technology Assessment, Congress of the United States.

Padoch, C. 1988. Aguaje (*Mauritia flexuosa* L. f.) in the economy of Iquitos, Peru. *Advances in Economic Botany* 6: 214–224.
Padoch, C. and de Jong, 1991. The house gardens of Santa Rosa: Diversity and variability in an Amazonian agricultural system. *Economic Botany* 45(2): 166–175.
Padoch, C., J. Chota Inuma, W. de Jong, and J. Unruh. 1985. Amazonian agroforestry: A market-oriented system in Peru. *Agroforestry Systems* 3: 47–58.
Paegle, J. 1987. Interactions between convective and large-scale motions over Amazonia. In Robert E. Dickinson (ed.), *The geophysiology of Amazonia: Vegetation and climate interactions.* New York: Wiley, pp. 347–387.
Palmer, J. R. 1986. Jari: Lessons for land managers in the tropics. *Revue Bois et Forêts des Tropiques* 212(2): 16–27.
Parfit, M. 1989. Whose hands will shape the future of the Amazon's green mansions? *Smithsonian*, November: 58–74.
Parikh, J. K. 1992. IPCC strategies unfair to the South. *Nature* 360: 507–508.
Parker, E., D. Posey, J. Frechione, and L. F. da Silva. 1983. Resource exploitation in Amazonia: Ethnoecological examples from four populations. *Annals of the Carnegie Museum* 52: 163–203.

Parsons, J. J. 1955. Gold mining in the Nicaraguan rain forest. *Yearbook of the Association of Pacific Coast Geographers* 17: 49–56.

—— 1989. Forest to pasture: Development or destruction. In William M. Denevan (ed.), *Hispanic lands and peoples: Selected writings of James J. Parsons*. Dellplain Latin American Studies 23. Boulder, CO: Westview Press, pp. 275–295.

Paula, R. D. 1972. A rodovia Belém–Brasilia e os fazedores de desertos – e a Transamazônica?, e as outras? *A Amazônia Brasileira em Foco* 6: 78–95.

Pearce, F. 1990. Brazil, where the ice comes from. *New Scientist* 127(1724): 45–48.

Pendelton, L. H. 1992. Trouble in paradise: Practical obstacles to nontimber forestry in Latin America. In Mark Plotkin and Lisa Famolare (eds.), *Sustainable harvest and marketing of rain forest products*. Washington, D.C.: Island Press, pp. 252–262.

Penny, Norman D. and Jorge R. Arias. 1982. *Insects of an Amazon forest*. New York: Columbia University Press.

Penteado, Antonio R. 1968. *Problemas de colonização e do uso da terra na região Bragantina do estado do Pará*. Lisbon: Centro de Estudos Vasco da Gama, Sociedade de Geografia de Lisboa.

—— 1974. O homem e o equilíbrio ecológico regional na Amazonia brasileira. *Anais do Museu Paulista* 25: 5–21.

Perl, M. A., M. J. Kiernam, D. McCaffrey, R. J. Buschbacher, and G. J. Batmanian. 1991. *Views from the forest: Natural forest management initiatives in Latin America*. Washington, D.C.: World Wildlife Fund.

Perlin, John A. 1989. *A forest journey: The role of wood in the development of civilization*. New York: W. W. Norton.

Peters, C. M., A. H. Gentry, and R. O. Mendelsohn. 1989. Valuation of an Amazonian rainforest. *Nature* 399: 655–656.

Peters, William J. and Leon F. Neuenschwander. 1988. *Slash and burn farming in the third world forest*. Moscow, ID: University of Idaho Press.

Pfeiffer, W. C. and L. D. de Lacerda. 1988. Mercury inputs into the Amazon region, Brazil. *Environmental Technological Letters* 9: 325–330.

Pfeiffer, W. C., L. D. de Lacerda, O. Malm, C. M. M. Souza, E. G. da Silveira, and W. R. Bastos. 1989. Mercury concentrations in inland waters of gold-mining areas in Rondônia, Brazil. *The Science of the Total Environment* 87/88: 233–240.

Pickles, A. 1942. Cassava in the Amazon Valley. *Proceedings of the Agricultural Society of Trinidad and Tobago* 42: 141–149.

Pimentel, D., W. Dazhong, S. Eigenbrode, H. Lang, D. Emerson, and M. Karasik. 1986. Deforestation: Interdependency of fuelwood and agriculture. *Oikos* 46: 404–412.

Pimm, S. L. 1984. The complexity and stability of ecosystems. *Nature* 307(5949): 321–326.

Pimm, S. L. and J. L. Gittleman. 1992. Biological diversity: Where is it? *Science* 255: 940.

Pinedo-Vasquez, M., D. Zarin, and P. Jipp. 1990. Land use in the Amazon. *Nature* 348: 397.

Pires, J. M. and G. T. Prance. 1985. The vegetation types of the Brazilian Amazon. In Ghillean T. Prance and Thomas E. Lovejoy (eds.), *Key environments: Amazonia*. Oxford: Pergamon Press, pp. 109–145.

Pires-O'Brien, M. J. 1992. Report on a remote swampy rock savanna, at the mid-Jari river basin, lower Amazon. *Botanical Journal of the Linnean Society* 108: 21–33.

References

Plotkin, Mark J. 1993. *Tales of a shaman's apprentice: An ethnobotanist searches for new medicines in the Amazon rain forest*. New York: Viking.

Plucknett, Donald L. and N. J. H. Smith. 1986. Sustaining agricultural yields: As productivity rises, maintenance research is needed to uphold the gains. *Bioscience* 36: 40–45.

Plucknett, Donald L., Nigel J. H. Smith, and Selçuk O. Ozgediz. 1990. *Networking in international agricultural research*. Ithaca, NY: Cornell University Press.

Podesta, D. 1993. Slain Brazilian ecologist's legacy: Disarray in Amazon. *Washington Post*, 25 September: A47, A54.

Post, W. M., T. Peng, W. R. Emanuel, A. W. King, V. H. Dale, and D. L. DeAngelis. 1990. The global carbon cycle. *American Scientist* 78: 310–326.

Prance, G. T. (ed.) 1986. *Tropical forests and the world atmosphere*. Boulder, CO: Westview Press.

———— 1989. Economic prospects from tropical rainforest ethnobotany. In John O. Browder (ed.), *Fragile lands of Latin America: Strategies for sustainable development*. Boulder, CO: Westview Press, pp. 61–74.

———— 1990. Consensus for conservation. *Nature* 345: 384.

Pulgar, J. 1987. *Geografía del Perú*. Lima, Peru: Peisa.

Radulovich, R. 1990. A view on tropical deforestation. *Nature* 346: 214.

Raval, A. and V. Ramanathan. 1989. Observational determination of the greenhouse effect. *Nature* 342: 758–761.

Raven, P. H. 1990. The politics of preserving biodiversity. *Bioscience* 40: 769–774.

Ray, Dixy L. 1993. *Environmental overkill: Whatever happened to common sense?* Washington, D.C.: Regnery Gateway.

Redford, K. H. 1992. The empty forest. *Bioscience* 42: 412–422.

Redford, K. H. and S. E. Sanderson. 1992. The brief, barren marriage of biodiversity and sustainability? *Bulletin of the Ecological Society of America* 73(1): 36–39.

Reichel-Dolmatoff, Gerardo. 1974. *Amazonian cosmos: The sexual and religious symbolism of the Tukano Indians*. Chicago: University of Chicago Press.

Reier, S. 1990. Enchanted forest: How Daniel Ludwig's disastrous pulp project in the Amazon became increasingly profitable. *Financial World* 159(4): 54–55.

Reis, Arthur C. F. 1960. *A Amazonia e a cobiça internacional*. São Paulo, Brazil: Editôra Nacional.

———— 1972. *O impacto Amazônico na civilização Brasileira: A Transamazônica e o desafio dos trópicos*. Rio de Janeiro, Brazil: Editôra Paralelo/Ministério de Educação e Cultura.

Renner, S. S., H. Balslev, and L. B. Holm-Nielsen. 1990. *Flowering plants of Ecuador: A checklist*. AAU Reports 24, Botanical Institute, University of Aarhus, Aarhus, Denmark.

Revkin, Andrew. 1990. *The burning season: The murder of Chico Mendes and the fight for the Amazon rain forest*. Boston: Houghton Mifflin.

Richards, P. W. 1977. Tropical forests and woodlands: An overview. *Agro-Ecosystems* 3: 225–238.

Richardson, J. H. 1982. Some implications of tropical forest replacement in Jamaica. *Zeitschrift für Geomorphologie*, Supplementband 44: 107–118.

Richey, J. E., C. Nobre, and C. Deser. 1989. Amazon River discharge and climate variability. *Science* 246: 101–103.

Riebsame, W. E. 1990. Anthropogenic climate change and a new paradigm of natural resource planning. *Professional Geography* 42: 1–12.

Rios, M., M. J. Dourojeanni, and A. Trovar. 1973. La fauna y su aprovechamento en Jenaro Herrera (Requena-Perú). *Revista Florestal del Perú* 5(1–2): 73–92.

Rivière, Peter. 1972. *The forgotten frontier: Ranchers of northern Brazil.* New York: Holt, Rinehart & Winston.

Robinson, E. 1991. Stone age crumbling: Modern world threatens Brazil's Indians. *Washington Post*, 24 June: A1, A16.

Roddick, Anita. 1991. *Body and soul.* New York: Crown.

Rodrigues, Ecio. 1991. *Mapeamento das relações sócio-econômicas das reservas extrativistas do Cachoeira e São Luis do Remanso.* Rio Branco, Acre, Brazil: Fundação de Tecnologia do Estado do Acre.

Romeiro, A. R. 1987. Alternative developments in Brazil. In Bernhard Glaeser (ed.), *The green revolution revisited.* London: Allen & Unwin, pp. 79–110.

Roosevelt, A. 1989. Resource management in Amazonia before the conquest: Beyond ethnographic projection. *Advances in Economic Botany* 7: 30–62.

——— 1991. *Moundbuilders of the Amazon: Geophysical archaeology on Marajo Island, Brazil.* San Diego: Academic Press.

Roosevelt, A., R. A. Housley, M. Imazio da Silveira, S. Maranca, and R. Johnson. 1991. Eighth millennium pottery from a prehistoric midden in the Brazilian Amazon. *Science* 254: 1621–1624.

Rosengarten, Frederic. 1991. *Wilson Popenoe: Agricultural explorer, educator, and friend of Latin America.* Lawai, Kauai, Hawaii: National Tropical Botanical Garden.

Rudel, T. K. 1983. Roads, speculators, and colonization in the Ecuadorian Amazon. *Human Ecology* 11(4): 385–403.

——— 1989. Population, development, and tropical deforestation: A cross-national study. *Rural Sociology* 54(3): 327–338.

Ruttan, V. W. 1991. Review of *Climate change and world agriculture*, by Martin L. Parry. *Environment* 33(6): 25–29.

Ryan, John C. 1992. *Life support: Conserving biological diversity.* Worldwatch Institute, Paper 108, Washington, D.C.

St. John, T. V. 1985. Mycorrhizae. In Ghillean T. Prance and Thomas E. Lovejoy (eds.), *Key environments: Amazonia.* Oxford: Pergamon Press, pp. 277–283.

Salati, E. 1987. The forest and the hydrological cycle. In R. E. Dickinson (ed.), *The geophysiology of Amazonia.* New York: Wiley, pp. 273–296.

——— 1992. Possible climatic impacts. In Theodore E. Downing, Susanna B. Hecht, Henry A. Pearson, and Carmen Garcia-Downing (eds.), *Development or destruction: The conversion of tropical forest to pasture in Latin America.* Boulder, CO: Westview Press, pp. 173–189.

Salati, E. and P. B. Vose. 1984. Amazon basin: A system in equilibrium. *Science* 225: 129–138.

Salati, E., J. Marques, and L. Molion. 1978. Origem e distribuição das chuvas na Amazônia. *Interciencia* 3(4): 200–205.

Sanderson, Steven E. 1992. *The politics of trade in Latin American development.* Stanford, CA: Stanford University Press.

Santos, Breno Augusto dos. 1981. *Amazônia: Potencial mineral e perspectivas de desenvolvimento.* São Paulo, Brazil: Editora da Universidade de São Paulo.

Santos, R. H. S. and I. M. Cardoso. 1992. Opinion: Alternative agriculture in the Third World. *American Journal of Alternative Agriculture* 7(3): 98.

Sauer, J. D. 1979. Living fences in Costa Rican agriculture. *Turrialba* 29(4): 255–261.

Sawyer, D. R. 1990. Possibilidades e limites de formas alternativas de exploração econômica da Amazônia brasileira. *Nova Economia* 1(1): 91–108.

Schmidt, R. 1987. Tropical rain forest management. *Unasylva* 39(2): 2–17.

Schmink, Marianne. 1985. Social change in the *garimpo*. In John Hemming (ed.), *Change in the Amazon basin, Vol. 2: The frontier after a decade of colonisation.* Manchester: Manchester University Press, pp. 185–199.

——— 1988a. A case study of the closing frontier in Brazil. In Donald W. Attwood and Thomas C. Bruneau (eds.), *Power and poverty: Development and development projects in the third world.* Boulder, CO: Westview Press, pp. 135–153.

——— 1988b. Big business in the Amazon. In Julie S. Denslow and Christine Padoch (eds.), *People of the tropical rain forest.* Berkeley, CA: University of California Press. pp. 163–174.

Schmink, Marianne and Charles H. Wood (eds.). 1984. *Frontier expansion in Amazonia.* Gainesville, FL: University of Florida Press.

Schmink, Marianne and Charles H. Wood. 1987. The "political ecology" of Amazonia. In Peter D. Little and Michael M. Horowitz (eds.), *Lands at risk in the third world: Local level perspectives.* Boulder, CO: Westview Press. pp. 38–57.

——— 1992. *Contested frontiers in Amazonia.* New York: Columbia University Press.

Schneider, Robert. 1993. *Land abandonment, property rights, and agricultural sustainability in the Amazon.* LATEN Dissemination Note 3, World Bank, Washington, D.C.

Schneider, S. H. 1989. The greenhouse effect: Science and policy. *Science* 243: 771–780.

Schultes, Richard E. 1988. *Where the gods reign: Plants and people of the Colombian Amazon.* Oracle, AZ: Synergetic Press.

Schultes, Richard E. and Robert F. Raffauf. 1990. *The healing forest: Medicinal and toxic plants of the northwest Amazonia.* Portland, OR: Dioscorides Press.

——— 1992. *Vine of the soul: Medicine men, their plants and rituals in the Colombian Amazonia.* Oracle, AZ: Synergetic Press.

Schwartzman, S. 1989. Extractive reserves: The rubber tappers' strategy for sustainable use of the Amazon rainforest. In John O. Browder (ed.), *Fragile lands of Latin America: Strategies for sustainable development.* Boulder, CO: Westview Press, pp. 150–163.

Seré, C. and L. S. Jarvis. 1992. Livestock economy and forest destruction. In Theodore E. Downing, Susanna B. Hecht, Henry A. Pearson, and Carmen Garcia-Downing (eds.), *Development or destruction: The conversion of tropical forest to pasture in Latin America.* Boulder, CO: Westview Press, pp. 95–113.

Serra, M. T. F. 1992. Economic growth, hydropower development, and population resettlement in Brazilian Amazonia. Paper presented at the 41st Annual Conference of the Center for Latin American Studies on Involuntary Migration and Resettlement in Latin America, University of Florida, Gainesville, FL, 1–4 April.

Serrão, Emanuel A. S. 1986a. Pastagem em área de floresta no trópico úmido brasileiro: Conhecimentos atuais. In *Anais do primeiro simpósio do trópico umido, Belém, Pará, 12 a 17 de novembro de 1984.* Brasília: Empresa Brasileira de Pesquisa Agropecuária, vol. 5, pp. 147–174.

—— 1986b. Pastagens nativas do trópico úmido brasileiro: Conhecimentos atuais. In *Anais do primeiro simpósio do trópico umido, 12 a 17 de novembro de 1984.* Brasília: Empresa Brasileira de Pesquisa Agropecuária, vol. 5, pp. 183–205.

—— 1989. Pecuária na Amazônia: A evolução da sustentabilidade das pastagens substituindo florestas. *Pará Desenvolvimento* 25: 117–127.

—— 1990. Pasture development and carbon emission/accumulation in the Amazon. Paper presented at the Intergovernmental Panel on Climate Change (IPPC) Meeting on Gas Emission from Conversion of Tropical Forests, Universidade de São Paulo, São Paulo.

Serrão, Emanuel A. S. and Alfredo K. O. Homma. 1989. A questão da sustentabilidade da pecuária substituindo florestas na Amazônia: A influência de variáveis agronômicas, ecológicas, econômicas, e sociais. Unpublished manuscript.

—— 1993. Brazil. In *Sustainable agriculture and the environment in the humid tropics.* Washington, D.C.: National Research Council, National Academy Press, pp. 256–351.

Serrão, Emanuel A. S. and J. M. Toledo. 1988. Sustaining pasture-based production systems for the humid tropics. Paper presented at the Man and the Biosphere (MAB) Conference on Conversion of Tropical Forests to Pasture in Latin America, Oaxaca, Mexico, 4–7 October.

—— 1992. Sustainable pasture-based production system in the humid tropics. In Theodore E. Downing, Susanna B. Hecht, Henry A. Pearson, and Carmen Garcia-Downing (eds.), *Development or destruction: The conversion of tropical forest to pasture in Latin America.* Boulder, CO: Westview Press, pp. 257–280.

Serrão, Emanuel A. S., I. C. Falesi, J. B. Veiga, and I. F. Teixeira Neto. 1979. Productivity of cultivated pastures on low fertility soil in the Amazon of Brazil. In Pedro A. Sanchez and L. E. Tergas (eds.), *Pasture production in acid soils of the tropics.* Cali, Colombia: Centro Internacional de Agricultura Tropical, pp. 195–225.

Shaeff, Gary W. 1990. Igloos of fire: Charcoal production for Brazil's Programa Grande Carajás. M.A. thesis, University of Florida, Gainesville, FL.

Shane, Douglas R. 1986. *Hoofprints on the forest: Cattle ranching and the destruction of Latin America's tropical forests.* Philadelphia, PA: Institute for the Study of Human Values.

Shilling, J. D. 1992. Reflections on debt and the environment. *Finance & Development* 29(2): 28–30.

Shrimpton, R. and R. Giugliano. 1979. Consumo de alimentos e alguns nutrientes em Manaus, Amazonas, 1973–4. *Acta Amazonica* 9(1): 117–141.

Silva, J. N. M. and C. Uhl. 1992. Atividades madeireiras como uma alternativa viável para utilização sustentada dos recursos florestais na Amazônia brasileira. In *SIMDAMAZÔNIA: Seminário internacional sobre meio ambiente, pobreza e desenvolvimento da Amazônia, Belém, 16 a 19 de fevereiro de 1992.* Belém, Brazil: Secretaria de Estado de Ciência, Tecnologia e Meio Ambiente, pp. 257–261.

Simões, M. F. 1981. Coletores-pescadores ceramistas do litoral do Salgado (Pará). *Boletim do Museu Paraense Emilio Goeldi, Nova Série, Antropologia* 7: 1–26.

Simons, M. 1989. Brazil accuses scholar of aiding Indian protest. *New York Times*, 14 August: A14.

Sioli, H. 1986. Tropical continental aquatic habitats. In Michael E. Soulé (ed.), *Conservation biology: The science of scarcity and diversity.* Sunderland, MA: Sinauer Associates, pp. 383–393.

—— 1987. The effects of deforestation in Amazonia. *Ecologist* 17(4/5): 134–138.

Skole, D. and C. Tucker. 1993. Tropical deforestation and habitat fragmentation in the Amazon: Satellite data from 1978 to 1988. *Science* 260: 1905–1910.

Slingo, T. 1989. Wetter clouds dampen global greenhouse warming. *Nature* 341: 104.

Smith, Nigel J. H. 1974a. Agouti and babassu. *Oryx* 12(5): 581–582.

—— 1974b. Destructive exploitation of the South American river turtle. *Yearbook of the Pacific Coast Geographers* 36: 85–102.

—— 1976. Utilization of game along Brazil's Transamazon Highway. *Acta Amazonica* 6: 455–466.

—— 1979. Aquatic turtles of Amazonia: An endangered resource. *Biological Conservation* 16(3): 165–176.

—— 1980. Anthrosols and human carrying capacity in Amazonia. *Annals of the Association of American Geographers* 70: 553–566.

—— 1981a. *Man, fishes, and the Amazon.* New York: Columbia University Press.

—— 1981b. *Wood: An ancient fuel with a new future.* Paper 42. Washington, D.C.: Worldwatch Institute.

—— 1981c. Fuel forests: A spreading energy resource in developing countries. *Interciencia* 6(5): 336–343.

—— 1981d. Colonization lessons from a tropical forest. *Science* 214: 755–761.

—— 1982. *Rainforest corridors.* Berkeley, CA: University of California Press.

—— 1990. Strategies for sustainable agriculture in the humid tropics. *Ecological Economics* 2: 311–323.

—— in press. Human-induced landscape changes in Amazonia and implications for development. In B. L. Turner and F. Gonzalez-Bernaldez (eds.), *Principles, patterns, and processes: Some legacies of the Columbian encounter.* Madrid: Consejo Superior de Investigaciones Científicas.

—— in prep. Home gardens as a springboard for agroforestry development in Amazonia.

Smith, Nigel J. H. and H. Popenoe. 1992. Tropical Eden: History and future of Florida's tropical fruit industry. *Diversity* 8(1): 30–31.

Smith, Nigel J. H. and R. E. Schultes. 1990. Deforestation and shrinking crop gene-pools in Amazonia. *Environmental Conservation* 17(3): 227–234.

Smith, Nigel J. H., P. Alvim, A. Homma, I. Falesi, and A. Serrão. 1991a. Environmental impacts of resource exploitation in Amazonia. *Global Environmental Change* 1(4): 313–320.

Smith, Nigel J. H., J. T. Williams, and D. L. Plucknett. 1991b. Conserving the tropical cornucopia. *Environment* 33(6): 6–9, 30–32.

Smith, Nigel J. H., J. Trevor Williams, Donald L. Plucknett, and Jennifer P. Talbot. 1992. *Tropical forests and their crops.* Ithaca, NY: Cornell University Press.

Smitinand, T. 1989. Thailand. In David G. Campbell and H. David Hammond (eds.), *Floristic inventory of tropical countries.* New York: New York Botanical Garden, pp. 63–82.

Smythe, N. 1991. Steps towards domesticating paca (*Agouti = Cuniculus paca*), and prospects for the future. In John G. Robinson and Kent H. Redford (eds.), *Neotropical wildlife use and conservation.* Chicago: University of Chicago Press, pp. 202–216.

Solow, A. R. and J. M. Broadus. 1989. On the detection of greenhouse warming. *Climatic Change* 15: 449–453.

Sousa, Gabriel Soares de. 1971. *Tratado descritivo do Brasil em 1587*. São Paulo, Brazil: Companhia Editôra Nacional/Editôra da Universidade de São Paulo.

Southworth, F., V. H. Dale, and R. V. O'Neill. 1991. Contrasting patterns of land use in Rondonia, Brazil: Simulating the effects of carbon release. *Global Environmental Change* 43(4): 681–698.

Souza, Márcio. 1990. *O empate contra Chico Mendes*. São Paulo, Brazil: Marco Zero.

Spencer, R. W. and J. R. Christy. 1990. Precise monitoring of global temperature trends from satellites. *Science* 247: 1558–1562.

Spitler, A. 1987. Exchanging debt for conservation. *Bioscience* 37: 781.

Sponsel, L. E. 1986. Amazon ecology and adaptation. *Annual Review of Anthropology* 15: 67–97.

Staniford, Philip. 1973. *Pioneers of the tropics: The political organization of Japanese in an immigrant community in Brazil*. London: Athlone Press.

Stearman, A. M. 1978. The highland migrant in lowland Bolivia: Multiple resource migration and the horizontal archipelago. *Human Organization* 37(2): 180–185.

Steer, A. 1992. The environment for development. *Finance & Development* 29(2): 18–23.

Stein, Stanley J. 1985. *Vassouras, a Brazilian coffee county, 1850–1900: The roles of planter and slave in a plantation society*. Princeton, NJ: Princeton University Press.

Sternberg, Hilgard O'R. 1953. *A agua e o homem na várzea do Careiro*. Rio de Janeiro, Brazil: Universidade do Brasil.

——— 1973. Development and conservation. *Erdkunde* 27(4): 253–265.

——— 1975. The Amazon River of Brazil. *Erdkundliches Wissen* 40: 1–74.

——— 1982. Refugial theory and Amazonian environment. In V. J. A. Novak and J. Milkovsky (eds.), *Evolution and environment, Proceedings of the international symposium, Brno, Czechoslovakia*. Trha: Czechoslovak Academy of Sciences, p. 997.

——— 1987a. "Manifest destiny" and the Brazilian Amazon: A backdrop to contemporary development and security issues. *Yearbook of the Conference of Latin Americanist Geographers* 13: 25–35.

——— 1987b. Aggravation of floods in the Amazon River as a consequence of deforestation? *Geografiska Annaler* (Series A, Physical Geography) 69A(1): 201–219.

Stone, T. A. 1992. South America's vanishing natural vegetation. *Cultural Survival Quarterly* 16(3): 67–70.

Stone, T. A. and P. A. Schlesinger. 1992. Using 1 km resolution satellite data to classify the vegetation of South America. In H. Gyde Lund, Risto Paivinen, and Songkram Thammincha (eds.), *Remote sensing and permanent plot techniques for world forest monitoring: Proceedings of the IUFRO S4.02.05 Wacharakitti international workshop, 13–17 January, Pattaya, Thailand*, pp. 85–93.

SUDAM. 1990. *Ação governmental na Amazônia: Subsídios ao zoneamento ecológico-econômico e ao plano de desenvolvimento da Amazônia*. Belém, Brazil: Superintendência de Desenvolvimento da Amazônia.

Swinbanks, D. and A. Anderson. 1989. Amazon forests: Japan and Brazil team up. *Nature* 338: 103.

Szulc, T. 1986. Brazil's Amazon frontier. In A. Maguire and J. W. Brown (eds.), *Bordering on trouble: Resources and politics in Latin America*. Bethesda, MD: Adler & Adler, pp. 191–234.

References

TAC. 1988. Sustainable agricultural production: Implications for international agricultural research. Technical Advisory Committee, Consultative Group on International Agricultural Research, Rome.

Thigpen, M. E., P. Marongiu, and S. R. Lasker. 1987. *World demand prospects for jute*. World Bank Staff Commodity Working Papers, Number 16, Washington, D.C.

Thornton, I., D. Cleary, S. Worthington, and N. Brown. 1991. *Mercury contamination in the Brazilian Amazon: A report for the Commission of the European Communities (Directorate General 1-K-2, Environment).* Brussels.

Treece, D. 1989. The militarization and industrialization of Amazonia: The Calha Norte and Grande Carajás Programmes. *Ecologist* 19(6): 225–228.

Trenbath, B. R., G. R. Conway, and I. A. Craig. 1990. Threats to sustainability in intensified agricultural systems: Analysis and implications for management. In S. R. Gliessman (ed.), *Agroecology: Researching the ecological basis for sustainable agriculture*. New York: Springer Verlag, pp. 337–365.

Turner II, B. L and K. W. Butzer. 1992. The Columbian encounter and land-use change. *Environment* 34(8): 16–20, 37–44.

Turner II, B. L., R. E. Kasperson, W. B. Meyer, K. M. Dow, D. Golding, J. X. Kasperson, R. C. Mitchell, and S. J. Ratick. 1990a. Two types of global environmental change: Definitional and spatial-scale issues in their human dimensions. *Global Environmental Change* 1(1): 14–22.

Turner II, B. L., William C. Clark, Robert W. Kates, John F. Richards, Jessica T. Mathews, and William B. Meyer (eds.). 1990b. *The earth as transformed by human action: Global and regional changes in the biosphere over the past 300 years*. Cambridge: Cambridge University Press.

Turner II, B. L., Jeanne X. Kasperson, Roger E. Kasperson, Kirstin Dow, and William B. Meyer. 1995. Comparisons and conclusions. In Jeanne Kasperson, Roger Kasperson, and B. L. Turner II (eds.), *Regions at risk: Comparisons of threatened environments*. Tokyo: United Nations University Press.

Uhl, C. and I. C. G. Vieira. 1989. Ecological impacts of selective logging in the Brazilian Amazon: A case study from the Paragominas region of the state of Pará. *Biotropica* 21(2): 98–106.

Uhl, C. H., R. Buschbacher, and E. A. S. Serrão. 1988. Abandoned pasture in eastern Amazonia. I. Patterns of plant succession. *Journal of Ecology* 76: 663–681.

Uhl, C. H., C. F. Jordan, and R. Herrera. 1982. Amazon forest management for wood production: An assessment of limitations and potentials based on field studies at San Carlos de Rio Negro, Venezuela. In E. G. Hallsworth (ed.), *Socioeconomic effects and constraints in tropical forest management*. Chichester, Sussex: Wiley, pp. 143–157.

Veiga, J. B. 1986. Associação de culturas de subsistencia com forrageiras na renovação de pastagens degradadas em areas de floresta. In *Anais do primeiro simpósio do trópico umido, Belém, Pará, 12 a 17 de novembro de 1984*. Brasília: Empresa Brasileira de Pesquisa Agropecuária, vol. 5, pp. 175–181.

Veiga, J. B. and E. A. S. Serrão. 1990. Sistemas silvopastoris e produção animal nos trópicos úmidos: A experiência da Amazônia brasileira. In *Pastagens*. Piracicaba, Brazil: Sociedade Brasileira de Zootecnica, pp. 37–68.

Vera, F. and E. Alves. 1985. Desafio à produtividade agrícola. *Conjuntura Econômica* 39(3): 159–167.

Vincent, J. R. 1992. The tropical timber trade and sustainable development. *Science* 256: 1651–1655.

Von der Pahlen, A., W. E. Kerr, H. Noda, and W. O. Paiva. 1979. Melhoramento de hortaliças na Amazônia. *Ciência e Cultura* 31(1): 17–24.

Vosti, S. A. 1991. Successful agricultural policies: Lessons from case studies applicable to Latin America. Paper presented at the CIP-sponsored Symposium on Food for the Future: A New Chapter in Peruvian Agriculture, Lima, Peru, 22–23 April.

——— 1993. Some reasons to be wary about Jari. *Christian Science Monitor* (Boston), 27 May.

Weischet, Wolfgang and Cesar N. Caviedes. 1993. *The persisting ecological constraints of tropical agriculture.* Harlow, Essex: Longman Scientific and Technical.

Wesche, Rolf. 1974. Planned rainforest family farming on Brazil's Transamazonic Highway. *Revista Geografica* 81: 105–114.

Wesche, Rolf and Thomas Bruneau. 1990. *Integration and change in Brazil's middle Amazon.* Ottawa: University of Ottawa Press.

West, Robert C. 1952. *Colonial placer mining in Colombia.* Baton Rouge, LA: Louisiana State University Press.

Westoby, Jack. 1989. *Introduction to world forestry.* Oxford: Basil Blackwell.

Whitmore, Timothy C. 1990. *An introduction to tropical rain forests.* Oxford: Clarendon Press.

Whitten, Anthony J., Sengli J. Damanik, Jazanul Anwar, and Nazaruddin Hisyam. 1987. *The ecology of Sumatra.* Yogyakarta, Java: Gadjah Mada University Press.

Whitten, Anthony J., Muslimin Mustafa, and Gregory S. Henderson. 1987. *The ecology of Sulawesi.* Yogyakarta, Java: Gadjah Mada University Press.

Wilson, Edward O. 1992. *The diversity of life.* New York: W. W. Norton.

Wilson, Edward O. and Frances M. Peter (eds.). 1988. *Biodiversity.* Washington, D.C.: National Academy Press.

Wood, Charles H. and José A. M. Carvalho. 1988. *The demography of inequality in Brazil.* Cambridge: Cambridge University Press.

Wood, Charles H. and M. Schmink. 1978. Blaming the victim: Small farmer production in an Amazon colonization project. *Studies in Third World Societies* 7: 77–93.

Wood, W. B. 1990. Tropical deforestation: Balancing regional development demands and global environmental concerns. *Global Environmental Change* 1(1): 23–41.

World Bank. 1992. *Environment and development in Latin America and the Caribbean: The role of the World Bank.* Latin America and Caribbean Region, World Bank, Washington, D.C.

WRI. 1985a. *Tropical forests: A call for action. Part 1, The plan.* Washington, D.C.: World Resources Institute.

——— 1985b. *A call for action, Part II: Case studies.* Washington, D.C.: World Resources Institute.

Yared, J. A. G. and S. Brienza. 1989. A atividade florestal e o desenvolvimento da Amazônia. *Pará Desenvolvimento* 25: 60–64.

York, E. T. 1988. Improving sustainability with agricultural research. *Environment* 30(9): 18–20, 36–40.

Zobel, Bruce J., Gerrit Van Wyk, and Per Stahl. 1987. *Growing exotic forests.* New York: Wiley.